THE TRAVELS OF
Lord Charlemont
in Greece & Turkey
1749

Lord Charlemont in 1785, painted by Richard Liversay

THE TRAVELS OF
Lord Charlemont in Greece & Turkey
1749

Edited by

W.B. STANFORD

and

E.J. FINOPOULOS

Drawings by Richard Dalton

TRIGRAPH - LONDON
for the
A.G. LEVENTIS FOUNDATION

First published 1984
for the A.G. Leventis Foundation by
Trigraph Limited,
West Africa House,
Hanger Lane,
London W5 3QR

British Library Cataloguing in Publication Data

Lord Charlemont's Travels in Greece and Turkey, 1749.
  1. Greece — Description and Travel —
  1453-1820 2. Turkey — Description and Travel
  I. Stanford, W.B.
  914.95´ 045 DF721

ISBN 0 9508026 5 4

Limited edition of 200 numbered copies (leather)
ISBN 0 9508026 6 2

Printed and bound in Great Britain by
Biddles Ltd., Guildford and King's Lynn

CONTENTS

To Troy &

E U B O E A

Parnassos ▲

Lake Hylica
Lake Copais

Chalcis
Eretria

Aulis

Livadia ●
Thebes ●
Helicon ▲
BOEOTIA

Oenoe ●
Delium
Vathi

The Euripos

Plataea
R. Asopos
● *Eleutherae* ▲Parnes
CITHAERON

ACHAIA

Sicyon ●

Eleusis
▲*Pentelicos*

Megara
Athens

SALAMIS
Corinth
The Isthmus
Piraeus
▲Hymettos

SARONIC GULF

PELOPONNESE

△
AEGINA
PATROCLOS

MAKRONISI

C. Sunium
KEOS

TINOS

Nauplion ●

◄ ARCADIA

SYROS

CYTHNOS

DE

RHENEIA

PAROS

● *Sparta*

LACONIA

ANTIPAROS

MANI

0   20   40   60   80   100 Kilometres

ned by Charlemont.

N

nople

ESBOS

IOS

ANATOLIA

SAMOS

IKARIA

PATMOS

LEROS

Bodrum (Halicarnassos)

CALYMNOS

KOS

CERAMIC GULF

CARIA

COS

AMORGOS

C.Crio

Cnidos

NISIROS

TILOS

CALCHIS

RHODES

To Crete

To Carpathos

LIST OF ILLUSTRATIONS

ACKNOWLEDGEMENTS

In editing these far-ranging manuscripts with their references extending from prehistoric archaeology and early Greek literature to eighteenth-century Greek and Turkish history we have had the benefit of advice and guidance from many helpers, especially the following: the late Miss Iphigeneia Anastasiadou, Miss Sonia Anderson, Mrs Helen Philip Argenti, Miss Edith Clay, Mr. B.F. Cook, Dr. M.J. Craig, Monsieur Jean Favier, Professor J.N.R. Granger, Mr. D. Gürakan, Sir David and Lady Hunt, Professor G.L. Huxley, Dr. J. de Courcy Ireland, The Most Reverend Metropolitan of Mytilene, Iakovos G. Kleomvritos, Dr. E.J. McParland, the Earl of Mount Charles, Miss Leonora Navari, Mrs. Cynthia O' Connor, and Dr. B.J. Slot. We regret that owing to considerations of space it has not been possible to use all of the supplementary material which they kindly provided. It is hoped that this will be incorporated in a further publication. We are grateful to Dorothy and Philip Stanford for their help with the proof-reading. For photographs of the Dalton drawings and other material and for permission to reproduce we would like to thank the Trustees of the British Museum, the Ministère de la Culture, Paris, the Koràis Library and the Philip Argenti Museum of Chian Folklore, Chios, the National Gallery of Ireland, the Royal Library, Windsor Castle, the Library of Trinity College, Dublin, and the Royal Irish Academy. We are greatly indebted to the A.G. Leventis Foundation for making this publication possible.

W.B. STANFORD
E.J. FINOPOULOS

INTRODUCTION

The manuscript records of Lord Charlemont's travels in Greece and Turkey deserved a better fate than to lie unpublished, apart from a few excerpts, for over two centuries. They offer much of interest to many kinds of readers. Historians and sociologists are likely to welcome their detailed descriptions of people and places in the Ottoman Empire during a period when western observers were still scarce. Archaeologists can study in them accounts of monuments and sites not previously surveyed in post-classical times. Philhellenes may respond to Charlemont's warm, but not uncritical, sympathy for the Greeks under Turkish rule. Turcophiles — that rare breed in the West — will value his repudiation of many prejudices against what he calls that 'much injured race.' And general readers can hardly fail to enjoy these fresh and frank observations and impressions of a lively and intelligent young aristocrat full of *joie de vivre* and curiosity.

James Caulfeild, fourth Viscount Charlemont,[1] set out on his Grand Tour of the Continent in 1746. Rich, handsome, well-bred, amorous, impressionable and in his eighteenth year, he had begun to show an ominous interest in the dissolute society of some of his aristocratic contemporaries in Dublin. This alarmed his mother — his father had died twelve years earlier — as well as his devoted tutor Edward Murphy who later wrote to his pupil ' I quickly saw that, having quitted your studies, you must soon inevitably be snatched up by the young profligates of your country at their plays and assemblies and so get a seasoning in taverns, stews and gaming sets; whereby all your modesty, fine parts, fine character and worth of various kinds must soon end in the nauseous dregs of riots, revels, idleness, stupidity and nonsense.' As it proved, Charlemont did not entirely escape riots, revels, and stews, on his travels. But these foreign escapades were incidental, and the more serious side of his mind was given full

---

[1]   For fuller biographical information see Hardy, Craig and Stanford, as cited in Bibliography.

scope for development in lands so full of strange customs and characters as Turkey and Greece.

Though in the present book we are concerned more with Greece and Turkey than with young Charlemont himself, yet we may be grateful for the fact that we shall be seeing these countries through the eyes of a young man full of zest and eagerness for knowledge and adventure, who also had a remarkable gift for winning friendship and admiration wherever he went. Essentially he was a dilettante in the better sense of that word, studying the arts and society for pleasure rather than for profit or for professional reasons. But he was neither a hedonist nor an ignoramus. His tutor was a better-than-average scholar, and he probably made sure that his pupil should read all the main sources of information, both classical and modern, about the classical sites which they visited.

Charlemont reached the Hague in the autumn of 1746. There he met the wicked Earl of Sandwich who had visited Greek lands eight years earlier. Sandwich advised him to hasten on to Turin where there was a polite and friendly court and a cultivated society. Charlemont however, being naturally disinclined to hurry, took his time on the journey through southern Germany, spending three days in finding the source of the Danube and observing the deplorable state of the country as he passed through. At Turin he attended meetings of the Royal Academy and saw a good deal of the Scottish philosopher David Hume, then internationally celebrated. Hume took a liking to the young Irish nobleman and tried unsuccessfully to convert him to his sceptical philosophy. Charlemont, too young and light-hearted for such a doctrine, rewarded Hume by writing a vivid description of his ugliness and of a farcical amorous *affaire* between him and an Italian countess which Charlemont witnessed, like a character in the contemporary theatre, from behind a curtain. He tartly commented: 'Silenus on his knees to one of the Graces, or a Bear making love to an Italian Greyhound would be Objects rediculous *(sic)* enough — But neither Silenus nor the Bear are Philosophers.'

Charlemont left Turin in October 1748 and spent the next six months in Rome and Naples. No account of this period survives. In April, 1749 he prepared to visit Greece, an enterprise still fairly adventurous for Western Europeans, with pirates on the seas, Turks on the land, and an ubiquitous risk of catching the plague. Being rich, he chartered a French frigate captured by the British, and had it equipped for a lengthy voyage. Named *L'Aimable Vainqueur* — aptly enough for the adventures of her new owner — she was a ship of over two hundred tons carrying a professional crew and armed with cannon for defence. Charlemont and Murphy were now accompanied by a pair of fellow-countrymen, Francis Pierpoint Burton (afterwards Baron Conyngham), a Falstaffian figure who played Sancho Panza to

2

Charlemont's Don Quixote, and Burton's friend, Alexander Scott. Before leaving Italy, they encountered another Irishman whose books won him early fame, Robert Wood, who was also on his way to the Levant. He and Charlemont may have considered joining forces. Perhaps it was better that they did not. Wood was chiefly interested in the past. Charlemont was more like what we now call a sociologist. The title-pages of his Greek and Turkish journals, which we are now publishing, make this clear. The Greek volume is presented as *'A Traveller's Essays / Containing an Account of Manners rather than of Things / The Proper Business of Mankind is Man / Written for my own Amusement / And for that of my Friends / only ... / Treating of Matters, hitherto, as I believe, unobserved in the Grecian Islands, and in Part of the Continent of Greece.'* The Turkish volume is presented as *'An Essay towards a New Method of Travel writing / being a succinct Relation / of several / Miscellanious* (sic) *occurrences / during my travels / principally relative to the Character of the / several Nations with whom I have had Intercourse / with some Observations/ Homo sum, humani nihil a me alienum puto / The Proper Study of Mankind is Man / Haec olim meminisse juvabit.* In other words while Wood was mainly a historian and archaeologist, Charlemont was a man of the moment. Whether his general claim to offer 'a new method of travel-writing' is justifiable must be left to the judgment of readers skilled in the writings of all his predecessors from Pausanias to Pococke. But undeniably there is much that is original in what he records so well in his elegant Augustan style.

The 'travellers for curiosity,' in Charlemont's phrase, sailed from Livorno in April, 1749. As they traversed the Straits of Messina Charlemont duly recalled memories of Scylla and Charybdis (though Homer in fact did not specifically locate them there). At Messina far worse horrors met them — the aftermath of an appalling outbreak of the plague. With typical courage the travellers went ashore and surveyed what was virtually a city of the dead.[1] Charlemont assiduously collected all the information that he could about the origin, symptoms and effects of the epidemic and recorded them fully, with apt comparisons from Thucydides' account of the plague in Athens. Next they reached Catania where they encountered two Englishmen who were sailing round Sicily in a smaller vessel accompanied by an artist named Richard Dalton. The two parties joined forces as far as Malta. There Dalton was persuaded to go with the Irishmen as their draughtsman, an accessory then considered as necessary for serious observers as a photographer today. This alliance was historically

---

[1]   Charlemont's accounts of his visit to Messina on his outward voyage and of his visit to Malta on his return are in a separate manuscript volume. For uncertainties on the voyage between Sicily and Constantinople see Stanford p. 71 n.1.

fortunate but personally unfortunate. Dalton's drawings of the sculptural reliefs in the Castle at Halicarnassus, of the chief monuments in Athens, of the Dancing Dervishes in Constantinople, and of people, places, and events, in Egypt as well as in Turkey and Greece, are valuable as being among the first of their kind, though from an artistic and archaeological point of view they are not of the highest quality. Regrettably, however, Dalton and Charlemont seem to have quarrelled before the end of the voyage. (Charlemont subsequently had a similar quarrel with Piranesi in Rome.) Consequently when Dalton published his pictures in editions between 1752 and 1791 it was apparently without any sanction or support from Charlemont.[1]

All this, however, was still in the future when *L'Aimable Vainqueur* sailed from Malta to Constantinople in June 1749. Its amiable passengers went ashore at Sigeion in the Troad according to Dalton who in the introduction to his *Antiquities* describes two pieces of sculpture seen there — one of a young Greek holding a scroll in his hand and the other (on a sarcophagus) of women holding newborn children in their arms and giving thanks to the goddess of childbirth. The travellers may also have landed at Tenedos and other islands on their way to the Hellespont, and presumably after landing at Sigeion they went inland to look for Troy (then, of course, unidentified and unexcavated). Unfortunately Charlemont left no record of his voyage before reaching the Turkish capital. Perhaps he was too busy doing his homework for that momentous occasion, for apparently he had provided that his ship should be amply stocked with relevant histories and books of reference, as well as with scientific instruments for measuring buildings and artefacts. Wisely too, as experience proved, he brought suitable presents for smoothing his way through Turkish officialdom. These included watches, pistols, silverware and English cloth.

Here before we take up the narrative of Charlemont's travels in Turkey and Greece it may be well to describe the nature of his surviving records. They consist of two folio volumes of manuscript bound by his grandson in handsome mid-nineteenth-century morocco leather and embossed with the earl's coronet and monogram. The Turkish volume contains one hundred and thirty-three leaves, the Greek two hundred and forty-one. Many pages have entries on the reverse side of the leaves, these being mostly footnotes or afterthoughts, though the continuous narrative on the recto side sometimes overflows onto the verso of the previous page. The hand-writing is entirely Charlemont's apart from a few minor interpolations and editorial notes. It is fairly homogeneous in the main narratives — a clear, round, youthful hand. But some alterations appear to have been made in a more mature

---

[1] On Charlemont's trouble with Dalton and on Dalton's publication of drawings made on the voyage see Stanford pp. 81-4 and the Appendix to the present work.

4

script, and the writing on the verso side is generally thicker, darker, more compact and more angular, with a few additions in a spidery senile script.[1]

An intriguing feature of both manuscripts is the occurrence of obliterations which vary in length from a single line to half a page. Some passages have been so heavily blacked out as to be totally illegible to the naked eye. A few of these are opposite passages describing subjects of sexual interest such as the courtesan Phryne, the poetess Sappho, the chastity of Turkish women, and the castration of youths. But other deletions seem to have no such correlation. In the lighter deletions in which it is possible to read what was written underneath Charlemont generally seems to have been simply withdrawing some expression of opinion which he presumably decided, on reconsideration, to be untenable or irrelevant. Perhaps some or all of the heavy deletions were made by successors over-careful of his reputation; but they are more likely to have been made by Charlemont himself.

It is clear from several additions as well as from the variation in handwriting that Charlemont kept on supplementing and revising these manuscripts long after his return from the East. For example, in the Turkish manuscript, he remarks in a footnote to his praise of British freedom, 'N.B. This was written in the reign of George the Second when England was a free country' (i.e. in or before 1760). Other evidence for late additions comes in references to authors like Guys, Porter and Tott, whose works were published several years after Charlemont's travels had ended. His spelling, too, which is distinctly eccentric in the main narrative, becomes more regular in the supplementary material. In the Greek manuscript he quotes at times directly from what he calls his 'journals' (which are now, it seems, lost). He may not have kept a journal regularly during his visit to Constantinople where, he says, his time was 'necessarily, tho' foolishly, taken up with ceremonious visits to ambassadors etc.' On his Greek cruise he had much more leisure to record his experiences and observations, and he was freer to choose where he went and whom he met. In Constantinople he stayed with the British Ambassador, James (afterwards Sir James) Porter, a Dublin-born man of genial and benevolent character who helped Charlemont generously with hospitality and with introductions and letters of recommendation for his subsequent travels.[2] Porter obviously liked Charlemont, describing him later as 'the worthiest youth I ever knew, as full of good sense as of

[1] For fuller descriptions of the manuscripts and the proposed illustrations see Stanford pp. 69-78 and 80, and *cf.* pp. 13-14 below and Appendix.

[2] See the *Dictionary of National Biography* (subsequently referred to as *DNB*), and Larpent in the Bibliography.

virtue, abounding with amicable qualities.' (In return Charlemont rather ungratefully referred to Porter's *Observations on the Religion, Law, Government and Manners of the Turks* (1768) as the 'very imperfect Essay' of 'my excellent and well-meaning friend'.) Porter's careful surveillance could not entirely restrain his young guest's adventurousness. Some of the escapades described are as picaresque as any in the Greek narrative.

A good deal of Charlemont's Turkish manuscript consists of two introductions and several separate essays on Turkish history. They were composed some time after his tour in 1749. As our purpose in the present book is to publish Charlemont's account of his travels and not his later opinions, these parts are omitted here. His final conclusion is that 'in nations as well as among individuals *perfect depravity* is as seldom to be found as perfect virtue.' When, for instance, we deplore Turkish destruction of ancient monuments and artefacts, what about Morosini's shell that blew up half the Parthenon in 1687, and the devastations of Cromwell's soldiers in English churches? If we consider Turkish social life uncivilised, what about the kind of conduct to be seen in Ireland and Britain at gaming houses, cockpits, boxing rings, horse-races, and the liquorous dinners of foxhunting squires? If we deplore eunuchs — a subject that he discusses elaborately, — what about the *castrati* of Italy? The Moslem religion has its superstitious and bizarre cults, he admits, but Italy has its Flagellants and its liquefaction of the blood of Saint Januarius (both of which Charlemont himself had witnessed, as he records, with distaste).

At times Charlemont rises to rather vaporous heights of eighteenth-century rhetoric, as when, like Edmund Burke, he denounces 'the unpunished rapine of our Christian Nabobs in the East Indies' and deplores the British Government's treatment of the colonists of North America. Occasionally he turns to Swiftian irony. (Swift had died in Dublin in 1745.) He tells us, for example, that when scrupulously abstemious Moslems were told that punch was the English equivalent of sherbet they 'got drunk in the most Christian manner.' And he exclaims after a description of how the satires of Archilochus caused their victims to hang themselves for shame, 'how useful would they be to society in the present times!'

He treats other topics with relish — wine, women, dress, ornaments, furniture, religious toleration, marital and amorous relations, policemen, bribery and much else. He visits a brothel, or as he more delicately expresses it, 'one of those modern temples of Venus, which are found in every metropolis whatever be the religion of the country,' and a Turkish bath, after which he corrects Lady Mary Wortley Montagu's 'beautiful and voluptuous description of Turkish bathing'[1]

---

[1] See Bibliography and *DNB*.

6

and he watches displays of howling and dancing dervishes. Thanks to the indiscreet conduct of his friend Burton, he and his party come close to serious trouble, but, with typical good fortune, they emerge safely. He enquires in vain whether there were any manuscripts of lost works by classical authors in the Sultan's libraries. He copies out Turkish love-songs and interrogates a communicative Turk on his religious beliefs. He expresses admiration towards the Sultan, and his detestation of the 'Kisler Aga' (i.e. the Kizlaragasi 'Master of the Girls') chief of the black eunuchs in the Seraglio. And much more. The narrative ends with an excursus describing a few events witnessed on Charlemont's visit to Egypt. He apparently intended at one time to record his experiences there in a separate set of essays. But nothing has survived except a few passing references in his Greek essay, and Dalton's commentary on the prints in his *Antiquities.*

The Greek essay shows much greater enterprise and mastery of its materials. Charlemont begins with an enthusiastic but rather conventional eulogy of Greece and its sunny climate. Soon he is in Mytilene (Lesbos), describing its antiquities, modern buildings, inscriptions and a strange matriarchal custom among the women, which he afterwards discussed in a paper read to the Royal Irish Academy in 1789. He dilates, too, on the ancient history of the island and on the local wines (with a note on *retsina*). The memory of Sappho clearly intrigued him, but he later deleted — very thoroughly — half a page of his remarks on her. He found the contemporary ladies of the island 'haughty' but 'piquant.' Next Chios, where he visited a Turkish official, a rural convent, 'the School of Homer' (recently described by his compatriot Richard Pococke), the famous monastery of Néa Moné and a Turkish warship, where he conversed with Italian, Spanish, French and English slaves among the crew. At Myconos he and his party had a 'whimsical' adventure — 'whimsical' is a favourite word of his in the sense of 'amusing,' 'comical' — of an amatory kind and investigated a curious pre-marital custom. Regrettably for archaeologists, he declined to describe the antiquities of Delos because 'an unhabited *(sic)* land can never be brought within the compass of my plan.' But he and his companions spent three days there, sleeping on seaweed, and had a jolly time watching the crew of his Greek felucca dancing on the shore. On Naxos his principal adventure was a memorable reception by a benevolent French baron, formerly a page to Louis XIV and now a voluntary and happy exile. On Tinos he observed its comparative freedom from Turkish interference and, as often elsewhere, the dress and figures of the women. Syros and Paros followed, and then Antiparos with its famous cave which Dalton drew in dramatic style. Hospitality at the residence of the Vaivode on Paros included a meeting with the local Archbishop, as well as 'incomparable' wine and fulsome eulogies by a local bard.

Next the ship sailed to Alexandria. As already noticed, nothing of the journal kept by Charlemont there has survived apart from incidental references in the other journals. They left Alexandria on 22nd October 1749, hoping to visit Cyprus, island of Aphrodite, next. They were disappointed owing to contrary winds and perhaps, Charlemont suggests, because they had omitted to offer 'Sacrifices to Venus' during their visit to Egypt. Rhodes with its memories of the Colossus and the Crusaders fascinated him for a while with its scenic beauty and ancient monuments. There he also — with characteristic serendipity — discovered a brother of the Persian Emperor imprisoned in the former palace of the Grand Master of the Knights Hospitallers.

After this sophisticated interlude the voyagers sailed along the Caramanian coast of Southern Asia Minor. They landed at what they guessed, correctly, to be Cnidos, drawn there principally perhaps by the fame of its temple of Aphrodite and the celebrated statue by Praxiteles. Charlemont offers a good description of the topography and ruins, especially the theatre and temple. He was the first to do so in modern times.

In Cos Charlemont saw 'the plane tree of Hippocrates' and heard about the superbly sited Asklepieion. He also showed some personal interest in the transparent material of the dresses of Coan women in antiquity. Just across the straits lay the site for which Charlemont deserves most credit as an antiquarian — 'Bodroumi,' the ancient Halicarnassus. Thévenot had been there before but had failed to identify either the site of the Mausoleum or the remains of its sculptures (which Dalton drew, for the first time in modern history). He offered quite plausible suggestions about the architecture of the Mausoleum, and copied a previously unnoticed inscription of major historical importance from a private house in the town.

The time had now come to make for the culmination of the whole tour, Athens. *En route* they passed Calymnos, Leros, Patmos, Icaria, Samos, and other islands, landing on Cythnos (whose inhabitants were 'poor, but civilised and extremely obliging'). Having weathered a severe three-day storm (a 'Fortuna'), Charlemont reached Piraeus on 23 November. There he surveyed the Themistoclean wall and collected evidence for some intelligent observations on its construction. Then traversing the plain of Athens 'rich in corn and thickly planted with olive trees' he at last came to Athens. At this point, as if Charlemont was rather overawed by the reputation of the place, he turns for a while from continuous narrative to separate essays on aspects of the city and on mainland Greece in general. But during his visit he did not fail to interview representative members of Athenian society both Turkish and Greek. He dutifully examined the well-known monuments, and Dalton sketched them. (This, it should be remembered was before the visit by Stuart and Revett.) After difficulty in persuad-

8

ing the governor of the Acropolis, they were finally allowed to use their measuring instruments for recording the proportions of the Parthenon (on which Charlemont discourses with considerable erudition). Charlemont visited the monastery at Kaisariani and heard the abbot recite Homer ecstatically. They tasted Hymettan honey and observed, at a regretted distance, Athenian women. As one might have expected, from time to time Charlemont indulges in some rhetorical flourishes on his hopes for the liberation of Greece and on his regrets for the decline of Britain since the death of Chatham.

Next the party set out on a journey to Eleusis, Megara, Corinth, Thebes, and Euboea, accompanied by two Albanian guards and a janissary, as brigands were prevalent. At Corinth they found eleven columns of the temple of Apollo still standing (only seven survive now), climbed Acrocorinthus with its magnificent view, visited the stadium, and surveyed the remains of the Isthmian Wall (which Charlemont discusses at some length). Then, after visits to Sicyon and Megara, they crossed Cithaeron, where their Albanian guards fired a *feu de joie* and sang a song of triumph in honour of a victory over Turkish troops. Charlemont's descriptions of the 'beautifully romantic' mountain scenery and of a historic site, probably Eleutherai, are particularly vivid. Having been cordially and hospitably received at Thebes, they traversed the Boeotian plain with 'a most noble and poetic view of Parnassus and Helicon cover'd with snow,' and crossed the Euripus to the city of Negripont (Chalcis) where the French Consul had arranged 'a sort of Triumphal Entry' for the visiting nobleman. (One must continually admire the care that Charlemont and his influential friends had taken to ensure respectful attention at the chief places on their route.) A long and memorable description of Euboea and its history resulted from this pleasant visit, including a discussion of the notorious vagaries of the currents of the Euripus. After 'sumptuous and elegant' hospitality from the French Consul at Chalcis, on 13 December they sailed down the Euripus to Vathy where next day they left on horseback for Athens, having satisfied their minds with ample meditation on the legends associated with neighbouring Aulis. Twelve hours later they reached Athens, to be congratulated by all their Athenian friends on having escaped 'the perils of a road, which, from the frequency of Robberies, is here accounted highly dangerous.'

Then the narrative abruptly breaks off. The remaining pages contain supplementary classical translations and references relevant to the places visited besides discussions of some historical and antiquarian topics. Most of these have been omitted in our transcript as their information is available in reference books.

Elsewhere Charlemont recorded episodes in their prolonged journey homewards.[1] *L' Aimable Vainqueur* ran into a severe storm on

---

[1] In Royal Irish Academy MS 12. R7. pp. 535-51.

the way to Malta, but survived. At Malta they observed the decadence of the Knights of Saint John and surveyed the 'one vast brothel' of the city. In Italy Charlemont — in no hurry, it seems, to return to Dublin — spent the next three years among the fashionable and cultivated societies of Rome, Florence, Venice, Lucca and Siena. At Rome in 1752 he was painted, playing a flute, among other *dilettanti* by Sir Joshua Reynolds in his caricature of Raphael's *School of Athens*. In 1754 he stayed for a while in France where he conversed with Montesquieu and duly recorded the conversation.

At last in 1755 he was back in Dublin to take his hereditary seat in the Irish House of Lords. He brought with him some souvenirs of his tour — several pictures by Dalton, a fourth-century Attic stele,[1] coins, vases (but these perhaps from Italy), a bas-relief of Minerva and a head of a girl from Alexandria, besides several Roman and Italian works of art. Among these last was a symbol of his less antiquarian adventures — a good copy of the Medicean Venus (modelled on Praxiteles' Cnidian Aphrodite). Other statues acquired in Italy can also be taken as having symbolical associations with incidents described in his essays — Bacchus, Silenus, Diogenes the Cynic, Antinous and Homer. A fine renaissance Mercury, god of travellers, dominated the main corridor of his house in Dublin.

Meanwhile he had begun to collect a large library containing many classical and modern sources of information about Greece and Turkey from which he continued to supplement his manuscripts. There is no doubt that for an amateur he was a very competent scholar. In the Greek essay he lists forty-nine editions of classical Greek and Roman authors in his text, as well as fifty medieval and modern authorities. The Turkish essay refers to sixteen ancient texts and fifteen others. The sale catalogue of the Charlemont library in 1865 contains some eight hundred classical books alone, including fifteen editions and translations of Homer, six of Herodotus, and five of Dionysius of Halicarnassus, besides a large collection of medieval and modern books on Greece and Turkey. (Some of these could have been added by his son, the second Earl, but that is unlikely.) The same catalogue also mentions over three thousand four hundred coins and 'medals.' Charlemont was by no means uncritical in using his sources. He disagrees with several modern authorities, and is usually right in doing so. It must be remembered, however, that in the early stages of his essays he was probably helped substantially by his tutor Edward Murphy, and that he kept on revising and supplementing both essays until the end of his life, that is, for fifty years after his visit to Greece,

---

[1] Recently discovered in the grounds of Charlemont's residence near Dublin by Mrs Cynthia O'Connor: see Cynthia O'Connor and B.F. Cook in *The Antiquaries Journal* 61 (1981) pp. 27-34.

perhaps with the assistance of other classical scholars.

Shortly after his return to Dublin, Charlemont was elected a member of the Society of Dilettanti. Soon he served on committees to petition the King for land to build a house for the Society and to organise the Ionian expedition by Chandler, Revett and Pars. (But when Chandler wrote to him in 1774 asking, for a second time, about inscriptions copied by Charlemont in Ionia he seems to have received no reply.) In 1773, he became a member of Samuel Johnson's Literary Club. Apparently he declined to talk there about his youthful travels, for Johnson in discoursing on the effects of travel on one's conversational range remarked apropos of Charlemont 'I never but once heard him talk of what he had seen, and that was of a large serpent in one of the pyramids of Egypt.'[1] At home in Dublin he was an active patron of several works of classical scholarship — Thomas Moore's *Odes of Anacreon,* Thomas Leland's *Speeches of Demosthenes,* Thomas Cooke's *Plautus* and Robert Jephson's *Roman Portraits.* (But he had nothing to do with Richard Dalton's successive publications of his drawings from Greece, Turkey and Egypt, presumably because of a quarrel.) For his own personal satisfaction he made a series of translations from Greek and Latin poets — Hesiod, the Homeric Hymn to Apollo, the Greek Anthology, Catullus, Horace, Martial, and others — besides a long *Essay towards the History of Italian Poetry.* These fill some fifteen hundred pages of his unpublished manuscripts.

Charlemont's most important contribution to the promotion of scholarship and science in Ireland resulted from his successful efforts to found the Royal Irish Academy. Elected its first President in 1785, he read two papers on classical subjects at its meetings: *An account of a singular Custom at Metelin with some Conjectures on the Antiquity of its Origin* in December 1789, and *Some Considerations of a Controverted Passage of Herodotus* in July, 1790. Both were based on parts of his Greek essay.

But most of Charlemont's time and energy after his return home was devoted to patriotic service of his own country, Ireland, and to family affairs.[2] As an active member of the Irish House of Lords, and as a nobleman of considerable wealth and influence, he was bound to be drawn into the controversy between the Irish Parliament and the English Government over the right of disposal of surplus Irish revenue. This controversy was a symptom of the growing demand for greater independence for the Irish Parliament in general (which then, owing to penal legislation against Catholics, was confined to Protestants). Charlemont joined the patriotic party and did much to bring about

---

[1] In James Boswell's *Life of Samuel Johnson* chap. 48 (on May, 1778).

[2] For fuller biographical information see Hardy, Craig and Stanford, as cited in the Bibliography.

their success in winning an increased measure of independence in 1782, both in parliament and as leader of the Irish Volunteers, a para-military force whose demonstrations helped to convince the British Government of the necessity to yield to the Irish demands. As it happened, the duration of the independent Irish Parliament, under the leadership of Charlemont's friend Henry Grattan, was short, lasting for only eight years. But, happily for himself, so far as politics was concerned, Charlemont died in the year before the Irish Parliament was entirely abolished by the Act of Union in 1800.

Meanwhile he had received many honours. He was awarded an honorary Doctorate in Laws in Dublin University in 1755. In 1763 his hereditary viscountcy was raised to an earldom. He became a Fellow of the Royal Society and as we have seen, first President of the Royal Irish Academy in 1785. As leader of the Volunteers he was enthusiastically cheered by the populace in many parts of Ireland.

In 1760 he married Mary Hickman who was connected with the once royal Irish family of O'Brien of Thomond. Soon afterwards he began to make plans for magnificent new residences in Dublin and the suburbs, as well as for the elegant little 'Casino' which stands as a memorial of his classical good taste in architecture. He had five children, including three sons.

Charlemont died in 1799, aged almost seventy-one. Despite the exigencies of his political, social and domestic activities, he constantly reverted to his two essays (especially the Greek one), supplementing and correcting them until his handwriting became so senile and shaky as to be barely legible. Not without good cause had he quoted from Virgil's *Aeneid* on the title page of his Turkish manuscript, *Haec olim meminisse juvabit*, 'It will be pleasant to remember these things in the times to come.' In the present volume readers can fully share this intellectual pleasure for the first time.

NOTES ON THE EDITING
OF THE MANUSCRIPTS

The manuscripts of Charlemont's Greek and Turkish travels present a complicated and at times an incoherent, collection of material. Besides their main narratives they include later corrections and additions inserted on the verso sides of the pages or on supplementary leaves. In the adaptation of the text that is offered here these alterations and additions have been integrated, as far as possible, into the narrative to make continuous reading — as presumably Charlemont himself would have done if he had decided to publish his work. This has occasionally required some slight adjustments in the original phrasing. The special problem of the Turkish manuscript is considered in the introductory note to that section.

Much of the additional matter — especially in the Greek manuscript — consists of quotations from ancient writers about the customs and places he observed. Since this information is now readily accessible in works of reference and guide-books, most of it has been either omitted or abbreviated. Repetitive matter in the narrative has also been omitted or abridged, and only a few of the classical texts, quoted by Charlemont more for ornament and display than for usefulness, have been retained. Such omissions are indicated by three or (at the end of a sentence) four full stops, thus .... It is only fair to Charlemont to record that for an amateur he shows a remarkably high level of classical scholarship in his use of Greek and Roman sources. (As has been described in Stanford, 1980, pp. 87-90.)

Another difficulty is Charlemont's spelling. It is often erratic and inconsistent, varying both for personal reasons and, in the case of proper names and titles, according to the latest authority he has consulted. It also differs from the usage of our time by conforming to the orthography of the educated classes in Ireland and Britain in the middle of the eighteenth century. Where these variations are obvious errors, and where they would be likely to puzzle present-day readers, they have been regularized and modernized. Similar adjustments have also been made when needed in punctuation and grammar. We have inserted headings to mark changes of scene or subject.

Regrettably some of the flavour of Charlemont's style is bound to be lost by these changes, and scholars would doubtless have preferred an exact reproduction of the original text. But Charlemont's expressed intention was to write for general readers, not for specialists, and the personal qualities of his style are too pervasive to be seriously weakened by such editing.

Chronologically the visit to Constantinople preceded Charlemont's travels in Greek territories and in Egypt. The Greek Essay is, however, presented here in the first place as it shows considerably greater spontaneity and originality than its counterpart and is likely to be of greater interest to the average reader Certainly it seems to have been Charlemont's own favourite, to judge from the constant additions that he made to it.

For bibliographical details of works cited only by authors' names the Bibliography should be consulted. *DNB* refers to the *Dictionary of National Biography* (London and Oxford, 1885-1901).

The Index should be consulted for modern spellings of names and titles.

THE GREEK ESSAY

Remarkable Circumstances and Transactions in some of the Greek Islands

If I cou'd be content to live, as I trust I never shall be, forgetting and forgotten, Oblitus meorum, obliviscendus et illis, there is no Country I have ever seen, no Climate I have ever experienced, to which I shou'd not prefer the Islands of the greek Archipelago, and more especially those on the Asiatick or Eastern Side — These fortunate and favour'd Spots, exclusive of the Veneration They derive from Antiquity, are possess'd of Advantages, conducing both to Health and to Pleasure, which perhaps no other Parts of the Globe can boast. Tho' in many of them Cultivation and artificial Beauty are, even in their present State of Degradation, by no means wanting, Those among them which owe least to Art, are in possession of such Benefits of Nature as Art cou'd never produce or imitate. Their Soil is dry, fruitful, and easy to be cultivated; and, even in the most mountainous Parts, produces naturally a Profusion of aromatick Herbs, of a Fragrance not to be des:cribed, and scarcely to be conceived, which render every Step, every Tread of the Foot a Source of Odours. The respective Neibourhood of their Situation produces an easy Intercourse of People with People, which renders Society delightful by widening the Bounds of that social Communication, which, if restricted within the Limits of each of them, might, by those who wish for an extensive Circle of Acquaintance, be accoun:ted too confined. Every Hill exhibits a View of many nei:bouring Nations, and produces a Prospect which no human Industry can ever hope to emulate. The Climate is at all Seasons, at all Times, fitted for Health and for Delight — Never too cold in Winter — Never too Hot in Summer — Subject to no parching Blast. Liable to no noxious Dews — In the Island of Delos, that Waste of venerable Ruins, uninhabited, uncul:tivated, We slept upon a Bed of dry Seaweed, cover'd only by an Awning made of the Sails of our Felucca, and never suffer'd from Cold, or from it's destructive Effects. The Day is clear and temperate — the Night is dry and warm — The Air is at all Seasons healthful and pleasant, and Spring is ex:tended thro' the whole Year —

Hic Ver assiduum, atque alienis Mensibus Æstas!

But, if they are now what I have described them, and no Des:cription, even of Poetry, can equal their Charms, what must

The first page of Charlemont's manuscript

REMARKABLE
CIRCUMSTANCES AND TRANSACTIONS
IN SOME OF THE GREEK ISLANDS
(Charlemont's heading)

If I could be content to live, as I trust I never shall be, forgetting and
forgotten, ... there is no country I have ever seen, no climate I have
ever experienced, to which I should not prefer the islands of the
Greek Archipelago, and more especially those on the Asiatic or
Eastern side. These fortunate and favoured spots, exclusive of the
veneration they derive from antiquity, are possessed of advantages,
conducing both to health and to pleasure, which perhaps no other
parts of the globe can boast. Though in many of them cultivation and
artificial beauty are, even in their present state of degradation, by no
means wanting, those among them which owe least to art, are in possession of such benefits of nature as art could never produce or imitate. Their soil is dry, fruitful, and easy to be cultivated; and, even in
the most mountainous parts, produces naturally a profusion of aromatic herbs, of a fragrance not to be described, and scarcely to be conceived, which render every step, every tread of the foot, a source of
odours. The respective neighbourhood of their situation produces an
easy intercourse of people with people, which renders society delightful by widening the bounds of that social communication, which
if restricted within the limits of each of them, might, by those who
wish for an extensive circle of acquaintance, be accounted too confined. Every hill exhibits a view of many neighbouring nations, and
produces a prospect which no human industry can ever hope to
emulate. The climate is at all seasons, at all times, fitted for health
and for delight. Never too cold in winter, never too hot in the summer. Subject to no parching blast, liable to no noxious dew. In the
island of Delos, that waste of venerable ruins, uninhabited, unculti-
vated, we slept upon a bed of dry seaweed, covered only by an awning
made of the sails of our felucca, and never suffered from cold, or from
its destructive effects. The day is clear and temperate, the night is dry
and warm. The air is at all seasons healthful and pleasant, and spring is

17

extended through the whole year.... But, if they are now what I have described them, and no description, even of poetry, can equal their charms, what must they have been, when every decoration of art, every magnificence which wealth and taste could produce, was added to the beauties of nature, when, the chosen seats of philosophy and of the Muses, they were inhabited by the first of people, and when, from any one of them, a hundred populous, opulent and enlightened nations might, in the compass of a few days, in the navigation of a few leagues, be visited with facility and with pleasure! But, to stop these general observations, these efforts of retrospective imagination, I will now proceed to give some short account of whatever occurrence worth notice happened to us in these celebrated islands, and of whatever circumstances respecting them have not, to my knowledge, been remarked by other travellers.

LESBOS

Though it be difficult to make a choice among perfect beauties, if I were desired to declare a preference in respect to any one of the Grecian islands, I should probably fix upon Metelin, the ancient Lesbos. This enchanting island, proud of the birth of Alcaeus and of Sappho, still retains those charms which gave rise to their poetry, and inspired their numbers; and, though its groves no more resound with their sacred strains, the cause that inspired them still seems to exist, and love still lingers in his favourite retreat! ... Nature here reigns triumphant, and by showing what she can perform alone and unassisted, teaches us to despise the weak efforts of her inadequate mimic. The mountains whose rugged tops exhibit a pleasing interspersion of rocks and pine-groves, have their sides, for many miles along the coast, covered with olives, whose less agreeable verdure is corrected, embellished, and brightened by a lovely mixture of bays and of laurels aspiring to the height of forest trees, of mulberries growing wild, and laden with fruit, and of every other tree of noblest kind for sight, smell, taste! While the luxuriant vine, climbing wild and unrestrained even to their topmost branches, adorns and enriches them with its vivid green, and with its clustering fruit. Winter is here unknown. The climate forbids it, and the verdure is perpetual. The parching heat of summer is never felt. The thick shade of trees, and thousands of crystal springs, which everywhere arise, and form themselves into numberless rivulets, joined to the refreshing sea-breeze, qualify the burning air, and render the year a never-ending May....

No wonder then if the inhabitants, the better to enjoy these various beauties, should construct their houses in the following peculiar manner. Each house is a square tower, neatly built of hewn stone, so high as to overtop the trees. The lower stories are store-houses and granaries, and the habitable apartments are all at the top, to which you ascend by a stone stair, built, for the most part, at the outside, and surrounding the tower, so that from the apartment the trees are overlooked, and the whole country is seen, while the habitations themselves, which are very numerous, peering above the

19

groves add life and variety to the enchanting prospect, and give an air of human population to these woodlands, which might otherwise be supposed the region of dryads, of naiads, and of satyrs. But the charms of this delightful spot have so far transported my imagination that I have almost forgotten the subject which I meant to treat, and which is no other than a remarkable and singular custom[1] of this island, peculiar, I believe, to itself, and, as far as I know, unnoticed by any former traveller.

The women here seem to have arrogated to themselves the department and privileges of the men! Contrary to the usage of all other countries the eldest daughter here inherits, and the sons, like daughters everywhere else, are portioned off with small dowers, or, which is still worse, frequently turned out, penniless, to seek their fortune. If a man has two daughters, the eldest, at her marriage, is entitled to all her mother's possessions, which are by far the greater part of the family estate, as the mother, keeping up her prerogative, never parts with the power over any portion of what she has brought into the family, until she is forced to it by the marriage of her daughter, and the father also is compelled to ruin himself by adding whatever little money he may have scraped together by his industry. The second daughter inherits nothing, and is condemned to perpetual celibacy. She is styled a *Calogria*, which signifies properly a religious woman or nun, and is in effect menial servant to her sister, being employed by her in any office she may think fit to impose, frequently serving her as waiting maid, as cook, and often in employments still more degrading. She wears a habit peculiar to her situation, which she can never change, a sort of monastic dress, coarse, and of dark brown. One advantage however she enjoys over her sister, that, whereas the elder, before marriage, is never allowed to go abroad, or see any man, her nearest relations only excepted, the Calogria, except when employed in domestic toil, is in this respect at perfect liberty. But, when the sister is married, the situation of the poor Calogria is rendered still more humiliating by the comparison between their conditions. The married sister enjoys every sort of liberty. The whole family fortune is hers, and she spends it as she pleases. Her husband is her first domestic. Her father and mother are dependent upon her. She dresses in the most magnificent manner, covered over, according to the fashion of the island, with pearls, and with pieces of gold, which are commonly sequins, while the wretched Calogria follows her as a servant, arrayed in simple homespun brown, and without the most distant hope of ever changing her condition. But the misfortunes of the family are not yet at an end. The father and mother, with what little is left them, contrive by their industry to accumulate a second little

---

[1] See Charlemont's paper on this subject as listed in Bibliography.

20

fortune, and this, if they should have a third daughter, they are obliged to give to her upon her marriage, and the fourth, if there should be one, becomes the Calogria, and so on through all the daughters alternately.

Whenever the daughter is marriageable, she can, by custom, compel the father to procure her a husband, and the mother, such is the power of habit, is foolish enough to join in teasing him into an immediate compliance, though its consequences must be equally fatal and ruinous to both of them. From hence it happens that nothing is more common than to see the old father and mother reduced to the utmost indigence, and even begging about the streets, while their unnatural daughters are in affluence; and we ourselves have frequently been shown the eldest daughter parading it through the town in the greatest splendour, while her mother and second sister followed her as servants, and made a melancholy part of her train of attendants. The sons, as soon as they are of an age to gain a livelihood, are turned out of the family, sometimes with a small present or portion, but more frequently without anything to support them. They either endeavour to live by their labour, or, which is more usual, go on board some vessel as sailors, or as servants, remaining abroad till they have got together some competency, and then they return home to marry and to be henpecked. Some few there are who, taking advantage of the Turkish law, break through this whimsical custom who marry their Calogrias, and retain to themselves a competent provision; but these are accounted men in singular cast, and are hated and despised as conformists to Turkish manners, and deserters of their native custom; so that we may suppose that they are but few indeed, who have the boldness to depart from the manners of their country, and to brave the contempt, the derision, and the hatred of their neighbours and fellow-citizens.

Of all these extraordinary particulars I was informed by the French Consul, a man of sense and veracity, who had resided in this island for several years, and who solemnly assured me that every circumstance was true. But indeed our own observation left us without the least room for doubt, and the singular appearance of the ladies fully evinced the truth of our friend's relation. In walking through the town it is easy to perceive, from the whimsical manners of the female passengers, that the women, according to the vulgar phrase, *wear the breeches*. They frequently stopped us in the streets, examined our dress, interrogated us with a bold manly air, laughed at our foreign garb and appearance, and showed so little attention to that decent modesty, which is, or ought to be, the true characteristic of the sex, that there is every reason to suppose that they could, in spite of their haughtiness, be the kindest ladies upon earth, if they were not strictly watched by the Turks, who are here very numerous, and would be ready to punish any transgression of their ungallant laws with arbitrary fines.

In all their customs they seem to have changed sexes with the men. The lady rides astride. The man sits sideways upon the horse. Nay, I have been assured that the husband's distinguishing name is his wife's patronymic. The women have town and country houses, in the property and management of which the husband never dares interfere. Their gardens, their servants, are all their own, and the husband from every circumstance of his behaviour, plainly appears to be no other than his wife's first domestic, perpetually bound to her service and slave to her caprice. Hence it is that a tradition obtains in the country that this island was formerly inhabited by Amazons, a tradition however founded upon no ancient history that I know of. Sappho indeed, the most renowned female which this island has ever produced, is said to have had manly inclinations, in which, as Lucian informs us, she did but conform with the whimsical manners of her countrywomen, but I do not find that the mode in which she chose to show these inclinations is imitated by the present female inhabitants, who seem perfectly content with the dear prerogative of absolute sway, without endeavouring in any other particular to change the course of nature. Yet will this circumstance serve to show that the women of Lesbos had always something peculiar, and even peculiarly manly, in their manners and propensities. But be this as it may, it is certain that no country whatsoever can afford a more perfect idea of an Amazonian commonwealth than this island of Metelin.

These lordly ladies are for the most part very handsome in spite of their dress, which is singular and disadvantageous. Down almost to the waist they wear nothing but a shift of thin and transparent gauze, red, green, or brown, through which everything is visible, except their breasts, which they cover with a sort of handkerchief; and this, as we are informed, the Turks have obliged them to wear, while they look upon it as an incumbrance, and as no inconsiderable portion of Turkish tyranny. Their principal ornaments are chains of pearl, to which they hang small pieces of gold coin. Their complexions are naturally fine, but they spoil them by paint, of which they make great use; and they disfigure their pretty faces by shaving the arched part of the eyebrow and replacing it with a straight line of hair, neatly applied with some sort of gum, the brow being thus continued in a straight and narrow line till it joins the hair on each side of their face. They are well made, of the middle size, and for the most part plump, but they are distinguished by nothing so much as by a haughty, disdainful, and supercilious air, with which they seem to look down upon all mankind, as creatures of an inferior nature, born for their service, and doomed to be their slaves. Neither does this peculiarity take away from their natural beauty, but rather adds to it

22

Greek woman in island dress, probably Lesbos

that sort of bewitching attraction, which the French call piquant. But, as it is difficult to describe a peculiarity of countenance or of dress, so as to be perfectly intelligible, I shall refer my reader to a very exact portrait of one of the handsomest of these ladies, upon whom, with much difficulty, and by piquing her pride, we prevailed to sit for her picture, having met with her at a festival celebrated in a small village about four miles from the city, where we had a lucky opportunity of seeing all the principal women of the island assembled in their best and finest dresses....

[Here Charlemont has a long note on parallels to 'the peculiar custom' of Lesbos to be found in ancient Greek sources. See bibliography for the paper he published later on this. He also quotes 'the venerable and truly amiable Froissart' for a reference to lavish hospitality from a 'Lady of Metelin' in the Frankish period and for parallels to the customs of Lesbos].

Since my writing the text I have found this singular custom respecting the women of Metelin, mentioned, but by no means detailed in its circumstances or consequences, in the letters concerning Greece, written from Constantinople by Monsieur de Guys. 'He had,' as he tells us, 'been informed that, according to an ancient institution at Metelin, all estates, both real and personal, descend to the eldest daughter, whereby the males, and the younger children of the female sex, are disinherited. I was assured,' continues he, 'by one of the inhabitants of that part where I landed, that my information was literally true, that the custom was of very ancient date, and that the males had consented to it, out of love to their sisters, and to procure better establishments for them. The men, said my informer, would have no difficulty in getting their right of inheritance, if they chose to claim the benefit of the Turkish law, which admits the children of both sexes to an equal share in the parents' fortune; but the man, who should attempt to promote his interest by an appeal to a foreign power, would appear infamous in the eyes of his countrymen' (*Sentimental Journey Through Greece* vol. 2 p. 205).

We may perceive, from the manner in which this institution is mentioned, that Monsieur de Guys' information was partial, and by no means sufficiently circumstantial, a defect which was occasioned, as I suppose, from his having as he himself tells us, made no stay in the island. I cannot however avoid feeling much pleasure to have found some authority for the existence of an usage of a nature so very extraordinary as not to be easily believed upon the credit of a single testimony. Neither can I help expressing my surprise that a matter so singular in the history of mankind should have been deficient in point of evidence, and should have escaped the notice of such travellers as have spent much time in these islands.

24

Monsieur de Guys next proceeds to account for the rise of this custom, which he supposes to have been very ancient in the island. And this he does, in a manner that appears to me rather unsatisfactory, by a detail, extracted for the most part from Diodorus Siculus, [12, 55], of the bloody quarrels between the Lesbians and the Athenians, and of the many revolutions to which the island had been subject, during the course of which, as there must have been a great slaughter of the men, he supposes that the women would naturally have made their own terms with the few who remained alive in the island, and with those who returned from exile; and this usage, he concludes, was probably the result of such negotiation.

I cannot entirely agree with Monsieur de Guys that a scarcity of men affords to the women the best opportunity of making their own terms — *tout au contraire.* I fear however that I have misunderstood my author, who, upon a second perusal, appears to suppose that the Lesbian ladies, having lost the greater part of their own men, and consequently of the heirs male in the island, made these extraordinary terms with the conquering Athenians. But this seems still more improbable, as terms are seldom made by the women with successful invaders, who are but too apt to take their wicked will.

But unfortunately there are few countries in Greece, or indeed I fear in the world, where the women might not have had, at some time or other, the same opportunity for encroachment. Neither can we allow the probability of their hazarding so strange a proposition, unless indeed we should suppose some pre-existing peculiarity in their manners, and in the ancient customs of their country, which might induce them to propose such extraordinary terms, and encourage them with some hope of their being accepted. And this supposition will bring us back to the early establishment of the Lycian usage, as mentioned in the text, which, having possibly grown into disuse in a long course of ages, may have been renewed upon this occasion when the ladies found themselves strong enough to reassume that ancient superiority, which, though for a time they might have been compelled to yield, it is highly probable they never would forget.

Monsieur de Guys, upon the faith of a travelled friend, in the same letter tells us another story of the Metelinean ladies.'About three days' journey from the capital,' says he, 'is a small town, where every stranger upon his arrival is compelled to marry, and, after cohabiting with his wife, leaves her as soon as he pleases, she, and her parents being thoroughly contented if the obstacle, which is, it seems, in that country, not only ignominious but disgusting, be completely removed. This requisite being performed, which must be done by a stranger, the people of the province thinking, as it should seem, the operation troublesome and undignified, the lady is at liberty, after a year has passed, to marry with whoever offers, and seldom fails of a good husband.' This wonderful fact I confess I never heard, neither do I thoroughly believe it, as in my discourses upon this topic with the French Consul, he would have undoubtedly mentioned a custom so very singular, and of which we cannot well suppose him to have been ignorant. Indeed his good breeding would have prevented him omitting so interesting a narration, if it were but to have procured his young friends the pleasure of a journey into that delightful part of the island. One thing indeed renders the story wholly inadmissible in one of its circumstances, that in an island nearly round, of 150 miles circuit at the most, there can be no town three days journey from the capital.

The town, and the whole country round it, is full of broken basso relievos, mutilated inscriptions, marble columns, and capitals of different orders, wrought in the best taste. Some of these columns are regularly fluted, while others are worked spirally, in the manner of those which still exist in the small temple on the banks of the Clitumnus. In the court of the Bishop's palace, no contemptuous building, is a curious piece of antiquity. A most beautiful chair or throne of marble, enriched with basso relievos of excellent style and workmanship, with an inscription showing it to have been the throne of Potamon, son of Lesbonax:

ΠΟΤΑΜΩΝΟΣ
ΤΩΛΕΣΒΩΝΑΚΤΟΣ
ΠΡΟΕΔΡΙΑ[1]

This Potamon may probably be the same as the person of that name mentioned by Strabo in his catalogue of the eminent men produced by Lesbos. He lived in his time, that is to say, in the age of Augustus and Tiberius. But the principal antiquity of the island, and indeed one of the best remains now extant of ancient elegance, is an aqueduct of marble an hour and a half distant from the town. The height of the stone work is 67 feet, over which is the channel for the water built of fine brick, 15 feet high. The middle arch is twenty three feet and a half wide, and the whole building, between the hills which it is meant to connect, 110 yards in length. Traces however of its ruins are still discernible for nine hours journey into the island. It is built of the purest white marble, and the blocks of which it is composed, are of a great size, some of them measuring six feet and a half in length by three and a half deep and two feet and a half in thickness, all jointed in the most exact, elegant, and truly ancient manner. I have the rather mentioned this building, as I believe it to be yet undescribed by any traveller. The capital, now called Castro, is large, well built and well peopled, and it is said that the island contains

[1] The front seat by right belonging to Potamon (a rhetorician and politician of Lesbos), son of Lesbonax (a philosopher).

not less than 120 villages, no inconsiderable population since its whole circuit is not more than 140 miles. I forgot to mention that the peninsula on which the Castle stands is by some supposed to have been formerly an island, which notion they ground on the lowness of the neck of land, and on some pillars yet to be seen on the land side, which have the appearance of having been intended as moorings for ships. This island abounds with hot baths, said to be of the most salutary nature. Many of these we visited, and found them everywhere decorated with ancient ruins. One in particular, very hot and salt, and peculiarly remarkable for its effects in various diseases, is a vast cistern, finely vaulted, and supported in the middle by a noble antique fluted column, which whether it originally was a part of the bath, or has been taken from some temple, I cannot take upon me to decide, as the antiquity of the cistern is by no means certain. But every part of the island as far as we travelled, and our curiosity led us over a great portion of it, was replete with ancient remains; and fragments of antiquity are so frequent that the inhabitants complain that the cultivation of their grounds is perpetually interrupted, and rendered inconvenient by them. Inscriptions also are found in such numbers that it would be the work of several months to copy them. Of these we took down as many as our time would permit. Almost all these inscriptions are in the Doric dialect, which appears somewhat singular, as this island was always accounted a part of Aeolia.

The principal trade of this island is in oil, with which it abounds, producing, as we were assured, a quantity sufficient to freight forty vessels annually; but we are to observe that the vessels employed upon this commerce are small, and are never to be rated at more than the burden of an hundred tons. The inhabitants trade also in sponges, which are found in great abundance upon their coasts, and in diving for which they are remarkably expert. They make great quantities of wine, which, though it did not entirely come up to our idea of the old Lesbian, is very good, though too strong and heady, and might, I am convinced, be much better if they knew how to manufacture it, in which skill they are very deficient.

The manner of propagating vines practised at Metelin, is, I believe, singular. When they prune their vineyards, they lay aside all the good slips. These they tie up in little parcels, and bury them in a dung-hill, till they have pushed roots and leaves. These faggots they then take up, separate them carefully, and plant out. The leaves, which they had pushed, presently wither and fall off, and new leaves are quickly produced in their place.

It would be tedious to trouble my reader with the many ancient authorities which might be produced in favour of the Lesbian wine, which seems to have been held in the highest esteem. The wines throughout the islands are still naturally good, and their muscatel or sweet wine, is excellent, being carefully made, and generally un-adulterated ; but the dry wines of the continent — and sometimes, to the best of my recollection, of the islands also — are often rendered very unpalatable by a mixture of resin, which they suppose, makes them keep better. This custom prevailed also among the ancients as we find by a line in the seventy-seventh epigram of the third book of Martial, where, speaking of one singular in his taste, who, rejecting good things, chose what is bad, he says :

Resinata bibis vina, Falerna fugis[1]

This was, I suppose, their method to make wines of an inferior qua-lity keep as long as those which were stronger and more generous. Nothing ever showed more clearly the influence of custom over taste, than our liking these resinated wines after we had been for a little while used to them.

The fruits of Metelin are excellent, but its figs are incomparable, and esteemed the best of any produced by the Greek islands which seem to be peculiarly adapted by soil and by climate for the pro-duction of this fruit in its highest perfection.

Yet, notwithstanding these beneficial commodities the island is by no means rich, as we may judge from the assessment of the Captain Pasha, who left the port a few days before our arrival, and had carried away with him no more than six purses.

[1] 'You drink resinated wines; you avoid the Falernian kind' (Martial, *Epigrams* 3, 77, 8).

CHIOS

Having mentioned the Captain Pasha's annual visitation as a criterion whereby to judge of the respective poverty of the islands, I think it necessary to mention what has come to my knowledge respecting this famous depredation, which is, not without reason, accounted one of the worst plagues to which these islands are subjected, and for this enquiry the following article will afford a proper opportunity. As we approached the town of Scio, capital of the island so called by the modern Greeks, and which was the ancient Chios, we observed in the bay, at the outside of the harbour, two very large men-of-war, and turning into the port, we perceived there a number of Turkish galleys, which, being ornamented with many flags, pennants and colours of every sort, made a most beautiful appearance. This we found to be a fleet, commanded by the Captain Pasha,[1] or Turkish High Admiral, who annually at this season makes a tour of the Archipelago, in order, as it is pretended, to keep that sea clear of corsairs, by whom it is much infested, and to do justice in the several islands by hearing and redressing their grievances, for which purpose he is instructed with an ample commission from the Porte.

This progress however, far from being attended by those salutary consequences for which it was originally instituted, is, as it is now managed, in a high degree oppressive and ruinous to the Greeks, who are obliged to pay to the Admiral, for his protection, and under colour of defraying the expense of the equipment, whatever sum he chooses to extort, and we may easily judge that his demands are not always of the most reasonable kind, since, as we have been assured from good authority, he pays at the Porte, for the profits of his cruise, no less than one hundred and eighty purses each purse containing five hundred piastres. Neither is the inconvenience, which the islands suffer by this annual visit, confined merely to the sums which are extorted from them. The Captain Pasha, while the fleet is in port, always lives on shore, and the island is obliged to defray all his expenses, as well as those of his numerous attendants, and besides

---

[1] Spasouvarzade Mustafa was the Captain Pasha 1746-50.

all this, suffers exceedingly from the riotous disposition of the *levantis,* or Turkish sailors, who, like all other seamen, are apt, when on shore to be troublesome, expensive, and dangerous to their entertainers.

The manner however in which the contributions, for supplying money to answer these exorbitant demands, are raised, is as little oppressive as possible. The Captain Pasha upon his first arrival informs the magistracy of the extent of his intended exaction, and the Vaivode and other chiefs of the island meet together in council to consider the best and easiest method of raising the money, and such as may be most conveniently borne, so that the islanders are at least allowed to tax themselves, and to fix upon the least oppressive mode of taxation.

[Charlemont adds a note that the ancient Athenians taxed the Chians and other Greek islanders in payment for protection by the Athenian navy from piracy and harassment. He suggests that the Romans and Byzantines did the same and that the Turks followed this precedent.]

The Sciotes informed us that this year they had been much better treated than usual, the demand being no more than twenty purses, an inconsiderable sum considering the wealth of this island, which is accounted the richest in the Archipelago. Last year however they paid one hundred purses, and they suppose that, upon an average, their annual contribution is not less than sixty. The method of taxation agreed on for this year was that every man should pay a piastre for each purse of which he is possessed, an equitable tax by which the poor can be little affected ; and from this assessment we may judge that the wealth of the island cannot amount to less than ten thousand purses. These annual contributions are however extremely distressful to the islands, as they are paid exclusively of the stated tribute and all other taxes. The tribute, or capitation tax in Scio is eleven piastres for each man, and the father pays six piastres for his son till he is married, but the women are free from every sort of taxation. This, together with the duties upon imports and exports, produces to the Grand Signor from this island alone a sum of four hundred purses annually, besides the yearly robbery above mentioned, and yet, as the people appear happy and wealthy, many individuals in the island being possessed of sums from sixty to a hundred and fifty purses, we cannot suppose that the country is greatly oppressed, but must conclude that, as our information has been received from the people of the island only, who can hardly be supposed free from prejudice, their complaints of oppression are not altogether well founded.

If Scio, the subject of the present essay, were the only island aggrieved and oppressed by their depredations, we should be apt to look upon its slavish depression without any great degree of pity, and

Greek woman from Chios

to consider its present abject state as a just and providential retribution. For the Chians first among the Greeks began and practised the inhuman and infernal custom of purchasing slaves to be forcibly employed in their more laborious and servile works, thereby brutalising the state of man, and degrading his nature to the lot of beasts, impiously counteracting the bounteous dispensations of providence, which has given reason that we might be free, and vitiating the nature not only of the wretched objects of their tyranny, but of themselves also; for the tyrant master is perhaps deeper depressed from the rank of humanity even than his miserable slave!

Many Turks, allured by the wealth of the island, and by its commodiousness for trade, have made this their place of residence, and seem to live with the inhabitants upon a footing tolerably equal and friendly. In their mode of inheritance the Sciotes follow the Turkish law. Whatever a man dies possessed of is divided into a certain number of equal parts, two of which each son inherits, and each daughter one, the married daughters refunding their portions into the common stock, and getting their respective shares. One custom however they have peculiar to themselves. If a wife should die without children, her father has a right to demand from the widower one sixth of her portion for her *virginity,* and the mother another sixth in consideration of the *suck which she has given her.*

Our curiosity now prompted us to pay a visit to the Captain Pasha, but we were deterred from prosecuting this intention by the representations of some Greeks who came on board, and informed us that the Admiral was a severe, avaricious and proud man, and was not likely to receive us politely, nor according to our quality, hinting also that a present of considerable value would be necessary to render our visit in any degree acceptable. This last circumstance, the truth of which seemed probable, especially as he was then upon a money-making, not to say a plundering plan, appeared to us an argument of much weight, and with great unwillingness we relinquished our scheme, and changed our purpose of visiting this formidable personage to that of paying another visit much more agreeable, and fully as worthy of our curiosity.

We had some reason to believe that we were not misinformed with regard to the character of the Captain Pasha, who seemed, as we were assured, to have a strong inclination to order the bastinado to be inflicted upon our consul's dragoman because he had omitted to lay our *firman,* or Grand Signor's passport, before him immediately upon our arrival. This however may be an omission of a serious nature, since in all countries it is thought necessary that passports should immediately be shown to those in command; and perhaps also he was angry that we were not made known to him officially, and that he was by that failure prevented from showing a proper respect to the *firman* by a polite treatment of us. The subsequent behaviour of his second-in-command renders this supposition more than probable.

We walked to a palace belonging to Mustapha Pasha, a Pasha of Rhodes, whom we had seen and known at Malta, and of whom hereafter particular mention will be made, at which place was then lodged the brother of the present Cham of Tartary. This Prince, whose names and titles are Sain Girai Meimet Calgan Sultan, Calgan in the Tartarian language signifying Vizir, and indicating that he had been Grand Vizir to his brother, and Sultan being the common appellation of all princes of the blood royal, upon some affront had rebelled against the reigning Cham, and, being powerful, and much beloved, had raised a great army, with the assistance of which and of his own bravery and conduct, he had been victorious in two battles. At length however, having been vanquished, and overpowered by numbers, he fled into Poland, where he was protected, and resided for some years, till tired of that country, and of a dependence absolutely foreign, he betook himself to Constantinople, and took refuge at the Porte, claiming the protection of his kinsman the Grand Signor, by whom he was well received, and kept for some time, with all the respect due to his dignity and merit, in the Seraglio.

At length the Emperor not deeming it prudent to suffer at his court the presence of so great, so brave, and so popular a prince, who was so very nearly allied to him, the Tartarian family being a branch of the Ottoman, and next in succession to the present line, thought fit to send him, in a sort of honourable exile, to the island of Scio, where he has dwelt these two years past, and where he is extremely well treated, having a palace and harem allowed him, with fifty women for his use, and with liberty also of going abroad when he pleases, provided he does not go out of the island, being always attended by guards of his own, and by such of his officers and servants as followed him out of his own country. A rare instance of clemency and moderation, when we consider what we are taught to believe concerning the bloody executions of the Seraglio against the kindred of the reigning prince, and more especially, when we reflect that the present Grand Signor has no children of his own.

Arriving at the palace we sent up word that some English gentlemen, travellers from curiosity, were desirous of the honour of paying their respects to him and wished greatly for a favourable audience, in answer to which message, without being detained a moment, we were immediately shown up to his apartment, and received in the most polite manner imaginable. His chamber, according to the usual custom of an eastern great man, was crowded with his attendants, dressed in the Tartarian fashion with calpacks, i.e. furred caps, and green gowns. He received us sitting on his sofa, gave us coffee and sherbet, and scented us with perfumes after the manner heretofore mentioned. He asked us many pertinent questions concerning our travels, and particularly relative to England, and enquired with a peculiar eagerness into the circumstances of the war with France, and of the late peace, expressing himself extremely obliged to us for our visit, and wishing us all happiness and success in our future travels. He is a very handsome man, tall, well made, and of the most dignified appearance. His manner is remarkably graceful, and his whole behaviour was a mixture of good sense, polite condescension, and princely dignity. He seems to bear his misfortunes with the most philosophical ease and complacency and is accounted a man of the greatest personal bravery, and a most accomplished general.

We now spent some days in traversing this beautiful island, and particularly in visiting the mastic villages, for a full and exact account of which *vide* Tournefort. In one of these villages is a convent of nuns, the jolliest girls of the kind I ever yet met with. They make a vow of chastity, which they are supposed to keep as oaths against nature usually are kept, yet have they a better chance of adhering to their profession, as they are not confined but are at liberty to go where they please. They are dressed in black, and wear head-dresses of the same colour, which are by no means unbecoming. With these ladies we passed an hour or two very agreeably, and for the small reward of a sequin, they chanted for us their whole service most angelically. Their church is small, but very pretty.

The country is beautiful beyond expression, thronged with people, and cultivated with the utmost industry. The principal cultivation is in orange and lemon groves, olives and mulberries, vineyards, cotton, and corn, though of this last necessary article a great quantity is imported, the island, as we were assured, not producing more than one fourth part of its consumption, which we may suppose to proceed from its surprising population, and from all its central parts consisting of high, barren, and rocky mountains, scarcely habitable by goats. The contrast however between these bare rocks and the wonderful cultivation and amenity of the coast forms one of its most striking beauties. But any further account of this sort is inconsistent with the nature of my present plan, and I have mentioned these excursions principally with the view of remarking that, notwithstanding the formidable reports we had received concerning the *levantis,* in all our rambles we never met with the smallest insult, though the island was at that time full of them neither did we ever once hear of any riot committed by them during the whole time of our residence. We were indeed told that the fear of the Captain Pasha prevented us from seeing the women on festival days in their best apparel, lest by appearing too rich they might be accordingly plundered; and we were also given to understand that our amusements were injured by the *levantis,* as, through fear of them the ladies were more reserved than they otherwise would have been. Yet did not this prevent us, on the eve of our departure, from getting together a parcel of pretty country girls, with whom we danced Greek dances on the shore for a couple of hours, and this, too, close to a spot not a little dignified by its appellation, the school of Homer, which is no other than a circular seat, a small amphitheatre, cut out of the solid rock, with a square seat of the same rock in the centre, which has the appearance of a kind of pulpit from which lectures might be read to the surrounding disciples. On each side of the pulpit are lions carved out of the same material, but they are nearly defaced by time, and by the corrosive quality of the sea air. The mountains, which in this place approach the shore, are styled Homer's rocks, and this I mention to show that a tradition still prevails in the country that this island had given birth to that immortal bard, for the honour of whose nativity it formerly disputed with six contending cities.

Chios ... was not backward in asserting her pretensions, and ... coined medals to his honour, on one of which he is represented at full length, sitting on a chair, with a roll of written papers in his hand. The reverse is a sphinx, symbol of the island. From this medal of the Chians, which is supposed to be of great antiquity, it is evident that Homer was not thought by them to have been born blind, as he is represented with a book in which he is apparently reading. This indeed is sufficiently evinced by his works, which could never have been composed by a person who laboured originally under that defect; and we may I think with much certainty suppose that his fate and that of our great epic [poet] were in this particular perfectly similar, both of them having lost their sight when so far advanced in years as to have afforded them all the time to have enriched their minds with every species of knowledge. To a mind thus previously stored the loss of sight may rather be serviceable than otherwise in the composition of a great work, by concentrating the ideas already formed and arranged, and by shutting out such extraneous objects as might divert the attention.

The women of Scio are remarkably handsome, and obtain a preference even among the beauties of the Archipelago. They are plump, and well made, with lovely complexions, and unite an inexpressible sprightliness of countenance to the large eyes of Juno, and to the true Grecian nose. Their head-dress is perfectly picturesque, but the rest of their garb, like that of all the islands, Tinos only excepted, is unbecoming and ugly. Their waist is placed immediately under their breasts, and their petticoats are so short as to show a great part of the leg, a circumstance of which we certainly should not complain, if they did not render it disadvantageous by a whimsical predilection for thick legs which they esteem a beauty, and to procure which they wear several pairs of stockings. This is a fashion in almost all the islands, and perhaps it may have originated from a principle of modesty. In some islands particularly Micone, Paros, and Naxia, they show the leg up to the knee, and may think that the concealing its shape may obviate the indecency of such an exhibition.

The Latins, who are numerous on this island, have five churches and monasteries here. The Turks have six mosques, and the Greeks convents and churches without number, most of which are neatly built of hewn stone the product of this island, which was always famous for its quarries, and in a good style of architecture, the Genoese and Venetians having left behind them many obvious traces of their taste.

On the fifth evening after our arrival we returned to our ship, designing to sail with the first favourable change of the wind, which was now contrary. We slept on board, and early the next morning were pleasingly surprised by the sight of a barge alongside of us, of four and twenty oars. Upon enquiry we found that the second-in-command to the Captain Pasha, Commander of the ships of war, had sent this his best barge, with his own Captain on board, to pay us his compliments, to enquire after our health, and to inform us that the Commodore, by which title we translate that given by the Turks to the second-in-command, supposing that we should be pleased with the sight of a Turkish man-of-war, would be glad of our company on board his ship. Delighted with the peculiar propriety of this politeness, we returned him answer that we were greatly obliged, and would immediately wait on him, and dressing ourselves in our best clothes, which we always kept in readiness for such occasions, we repaired to the man-of-war, where we were received with the greatest civility and distinction.

The son of the Commodore received us upon the quarter deck, and told us that his father would himself have met us there, but that he was confined by a fit of the gout to his cabin, where, if we would take the trouble of visiting him, he would be greatly obliged. We were now conducted by the young man to his father, whom we found sitting on a sofa in his cabin, surrounded by his attendants, and particularly by a number of handsome boys, whose destination, as we were afterward informed, was not of the most honourable kind. The Commodore received us with the utmost politeness, excusing himself for not rising at our entrance, questioned us concerning our travels, and having treated us with coffee, sherbet, and perfumes, asked us if we did not choose to visit the ship, and, excusing himself for not waiting on us in person on account of his disorder, told us that his son would take upon him that office, and could show every part of the vessel. It is, I believe, needless that I should warn my reader that all this conversation was carried on by means of our interpreter, who constantly attended us in all our visits. Handkerchiefs were now distributed

36

Greek woman in island dress probably Chios or Myconos

among us, which, with the Turks, is the usual mark of kindness and respect. The handkerchief is commonly of a sort of thick gauze or muslin, and is for the most part edged with a border of gold or silver. It is used principally to wipe the face, and is sometimes worn about the neck. With many compliments we now left the Commodore, and followed our obliging guide, who conducted us through every part of the ship from the hold upwards. This man-of-war mounted seventy-four guns, but was full as large as any of our ninety-gun ships, which seems to be the case of all the Turkish ships of war as far as my observation can reach, all, which I have seen, being much larger than those of the same rate in our fleet. She was called the *Capitano;* but this I take to be a name given to all commanding ships. Thus at Constantinople the monstrous vessel, which lies in the port, and is shown to all strangers, and which is the Admiral of the Turkish fleet, is called by this name. Her building was clumsy, and all her accommodations ill understood, and worse executed. Her rigging in particular was heavy, confused, and badly put together. Her breadth was enormous in proportion to her length, and her stern was raised so high by several ranges of decks, for the sake of accommodating the officers, that I should suppose she must be very ungainly at sea, and could with difficulty weather a strong gale of wind. Her guns were monstrous, and we were assured by our conductor that those of her lower deck tier carried a stone ball of no less than a *cantar,* 110 pounds, weight. But this appears so very extraordinary that I cannot help suspecting that we were misinformed, and that our young guide was willing to make the most of the strength of his father's ship. To us, who had been used to English sailors, the seamen appeared extremely awkward, and to perform their functions in a sluggish and ungainly manner, to which also their long dress not a little contributed.

Among the crew we observed four persons, who eyeing us wistfully, seemed desirous to accost us, and upon our enquiring who they were, we were told that they were Christian slaves, who did duty on board the ship. We immediately accosted them and found that they were of four several nations, an Italian, a Spaniard, a Frenchman, and an Englishman. With these we presently entered into an entertaining conversation, and never surely were the different characters of their respective countries more clearly distinguished and exemplified than in the appearance, behaviour, and converse of these persons. The Italian seemed activated by a lively resentment against his fate for having reduced him to a condition, which he endured with peevishness and impatience. The Spaniard was grave and sullen, and seemed to dwell more upon the humiliating part of his situation than upon any other disagreeable circumstance which might attend it. The Frenchman was gay, lively, and talkative, laughed at his masters the Turks as ungainly and lubbardly seamen, paid us a thousand compliments, exulted in the pleasure of meeting us, was *charmé de nous voir,* and appeared as full of spirits as he could have been in his native country, and in the most prosperous situation.

But the Englishman was a perfect philosopher. He seemed glad to meet his countrymen, but without any show of exultation. He told us that he had long since made up his mind with regard to his present condition, which however he assured us was by no means a bad one: that the Turks treated their slaves with the utmost lenity; that he and his companions fared as well, and were obliged to do no more work than the rest of their shipmates ; that he had been a soldier among the Spaniards, and together with his comrades, he had been made prisoner at Oran, but that he found himself much better treated as slave by the Turks, than by the Spaniards as a soldier ; that, as it was the peculiar property of every Englishman to love Liberty, he had taken the pains to write to our ambassador at the Porte to procure him his freedom, but that he was not very anxious concerning the success of his application, since he found himself as little unhappy where he now was, as he probably should be elsewhere.

As a proof of the lenity, goodness, and toleration of the Turks he told us that at their first coming on board, they had been asked of what religion they were, and upon their declaring themselves Catholic Christians, some mild endeavours had been used to persuade them to renounce their faith, and to become Mohametans ; but upon their steady denial, they were told that, since they refused to embrace the true faith, they must, as the next best chance for salvation, serve God assiduously in their own way ; and immediately a small cabin was alloted them, which they were desired to fit up as a chapel, and in which they were compelled to pray daily and regularly. Neither had the Turks ever threatened to treat them ill except when they appeared remiss in this duty.

Amazed at this wonderful goodness, this genuine spirit of toleration so little to be expected among Turkish sailors, and scarcely crediting the fact, I desired to see their chapel, and was presently conducted to a small cabin near the hold, where something like an altar was erected, upon which were placed small images of baked clay, and prints of the Crucifixion, and of the Virgin and Child were pasted up as a kind of altarpiece. This matter being thus proved to a demonstration I could not help admiring and cordially loving the astonishing goodness of this people, by us so wantonly termed barbarous, who, notwithstanding their hate of Christianity, and more particularly their detestation of image and picture worship, had thus, on board a ship, where religion is not, by us at least, supposed to be in its most advantageous situation, and where every foot of space is precious, allotted to their *slaves* a place of worship, and then suffered them to display those representations, which they look upon as abominations ; and this from the wise, just, and noble consideration that it is far better the Almighty should be worshipped even erroneously than not at all. Ye Christian pretenders to religion, who, blest with the purest doctrine and precept, in your practice come so far short of this transcendent, this angelic beneficence, blush at the truth of this fact, and strive to imitate it!

Having now seen everything on board, and taken leave of our kind Commodore, we prepared to leave the ship, distributing some money among the crew, and gratifying our four Christian brethren with a particular bounty. As soon as we got into our barge, which still waited on us, we were saluted with three guns, the utmost compliment ever paid by the Turks, and, according to orders which we had left for that purpose, the compliment was returned from our ship with a royal salute. Our Christian friends hung upon the shrouds to pay us their last duties, and by their hearty cheers intimated their gratitude and good wishes. But the behaviour of the Frenchman was too characteristic not to be here recorded. As we were leaving the ship's side, he called out to me — *Milord, oserois je vous demander si vous avez été en France? — Oui, j'y été. — Avez vous vû Fontainebleau? — Non, je n'ai pas vû. — Ah Milord, si jamais vous retournez en France pour l'amour de Dieu voyez Fontainebleau. C'est bien le plus bel endroit du monde!* We now returned to our ship, where our first care was, as well in compliance with the Turkish custom as to testify our gratitude for the civilities received, to gratify our benefactors with a proper present, sending to the Commodore a silver etuye[1] made at Birmingham and to the Captain a snuff box of the same metal....

[Here Charlemont gives other examples of good treatment of slaves by the Turks and of their toleration towards other religions.]

In Constantinople, and in all the other great towns of Europe and Asia, the Greeks have numberless churches stored with all the foppery of their religion. The priests officiate in their vestments without any degree of concealment, and appear abroad in their religious habits. The islands are also stocked with churches ; nor is there any ceremony disallowed excepting only the ringing of bells, which is held in detestation by the Mahometans on account, as we were informed, of the people who drove the Prophet out of Mecca, having been called together by the tolling of a bell. Yet even this distinction is allowed to some privileged churches, for example to the church of the convent of Néa Moné in this very island of Scio. Monasteries they have without number, and many of them richly endowed, of which the convent just mentioned is a remarkable instance.

---

[1] A small box for light articles of personal use (French *étui*).

With regard to this monastery I shall give the following extract from my journal, as it is, I believe the principal foundation of this kind throughout the Archipelago:

Saturday, August 2nd

— We set out on mules for a Greek monastery the principal in the island, called Néa Moné, i.e. 'new retreat.' In about two hours we travelled little more than three miles through mountains of solid rock, of which the central parts of this island are entirely composed. The road was execrable. Here one may observe with pleasure the indefatigable industry of this people, for wherever there is half a foot deep of soil over the rock, which in these parts seldom happens, it is cultivated to the utmost. At length we arrived at the monastery, which is a large, but ugly, building resembling an old castle, such as with us are frequently seen. The church is pretty enough for the age in which it was built. Its plafond, [ceiling], which, according to the fashion of architecture during the Greek Empire, consists of several small circular domes, is covered with tolerable mosaics. The monks informed us that it was built in the year 1045, and showed us an old painting of the Emperor and Empress who founded and endowed it. Over the head of the former is written in letters such as I have copied:

ΚΩΝΣΤΑΝΤΙΝΟΣ Ο ΜΟΝΟΜΑΧΟΣ Κ.ΚΤΙΤΩΡ,[1]

and over the head of the Empress,

Η ΖΩΗ

The body of the church is made out of pieces of most precious marbles, collected from more ancient buildings, but these fragments are ill put together, and wretchedly jointed. The monastery consists of two hundred members, fifty of which are Fathers, and of them eight are Principals of the order. The remaining 150 are lay brethren and servitors.

They are possessed of very considerable revenues — not as Tournefort asserts, one eighth of the island, but certainly about one twentieth. They have had a great deal of ready money in their treasury, but the Captain Pashas have found means to rid them of it. They enjoy the privilege of having bells in their church, which they ring on festival days. On common days they make use of sticks and pieces of iron. They showed us many relics, dirty and ill preserved — among others an old piece of board, with scarce an atom of colouring upon it, which they call a portrait of the Virgin by St. Luke. Nothing can be more ridiculous than the paintings in the porch of the church. The Virgin is represented on the top of Jacob's ladder — in the burning bush of Moses, and in the little stone which broke Nebuchadnezzar's image.

[1] 'Constantine Monomachos and Zoë, the founders.'

They have a sort of library with many manuscripts lying in dust and rubbish. We spent an hour in looking them over, hoping to have discovered some ancient treasure, but found nothing but some manuscripts of the Greek Fathers. There are also many printed books, and, among others, a St. Chrysostom printed at Eton, 1612. The Fathers rang their bells for us, and were rewarded with some sequins to be distributed in charity. The founder of the Monastery, Constantine IX, surnamed Monomachus, obtained the Empire in the year 1042, and was last husband to the unfortunate and wicked Zoë, who, having poisoned her first husband Romanus II, married Michael the Paphlagonian, and having afterwards raised to the Empire another Michael Calaphates, by whom she was dispossessed, again reassumed the purple which she shared with her last husband the aforesaid Constantine. The history of this imperial dame makes Messalina appear a prude. But such are too often the founders of monasteries.

The monks wear the habits of their respective orders, and are liable to no species of insult. There is a Patriarch at Constantinople, and another at Cairo. The archbishops and bishops are numerous, and decently provided for, and the church enjoys its whole hierarchy, if not in splendour, at least in competence and in security. One thing however must be allowed that all these dignitaries pay pretty smartly at the Porte for their preferements, for which expense they re-imburse themselves by selling the livings in their gift; so that simony is at present universal throughout the Greek Church; and the Greeks complain bitterly that all their high ecclesiastical offices should be filled by the appointment of a government, whose religion they hold in detestation. But how far they have reason for these complaints, let politicians and statesmen decide.

The Latins also, for so they call the professors of the Romish religion, are everywhere tolerated. They likewise have their churches and their monasteries, and appear publicly in the habits of their respective orders. With the usual Catholic zeal for making proselytes they sometimes endeavour to convert the Mahometans and this practice, as in all well regulated governments it ought to be, is prohibited under the severest penalties. Yet do we very rarely hear of any priest or monk being punished even upon this score; and indeed the success of their pious endeavours is but inconsiderable....

[Here Charlemont gives further examples of religious toleration in the Ottoman Empire.]

This populous and wealthy island possesses many commodities fitted for exportation, but her principal and most lucrative trade is in silk, of which not less than thirty thousand pounds weight is annually produced, and by far the greater part of it manufactured into velvets, damasks, and other rich stuffs, sometimes mixed with gold and silver, which find an easy and beneficial vent through every part of the Turkish empire, being sent from Scio to the seaport towns of Asia, Egypt, and Barbary. Oil, wool, wax, cheeses, lemons, oranges, and figs are also exported advantageously.

For these last the island is particularly famous, producing them in great abundance, and of the most exquisite flavour. It is needless to speak of the fame of the Chian wine among the ancients, in favour of which numberless quotations might be adduced as well from the naturalists as from the poets. At present however it seems to have degenerated, I suppose from some defect in the manner of making it. At least I had not the good fortune of tasting any which appeared to me very palatable. It is extremely strong, and very rough and harsh. Oenepion,[1] the son of Bacchus, who first taught the Chians to cultivate the vine, seems now to have withdrawn his patronage. And besides the articles abovementioned, this island enjoys one branch of commerce peculiar to itself from its numerous mastic groves. For, though the Lentiscus grows in many of the other islands, and even in the more southern parts of France and of Spain, I do not find that the gum is anywhere produced in quantities sufficient for sale, except in Scio. Yet is this trade rendered of little avail by the rapacity of the Porte, twenty-one thousand oches of mastic, (each oche three pounds two ounces), being annually sent as a tribute to the Grand Signor, though, according to the best information I could procure, the island at a medium does not produce in the year much above double that quantity.

Either the quantity of mastic produced in this island is much lessened since the time of Tournefort, or that usually accurate traveller is greatly mistaken. He tells us that the Grand Signor receives annually one hundred thousand and twenty five oches, and according to the best information I could procure the whole quantity gathered in Scio does not arrive to near that amount.

In consequence of this tribute the inhabitants of the mastic villages, which are twenty in number, enjoy the following privileges. They pay but half of the capitation tax. They are perfectly independent of the Mazulheim[2] at Scio, and all their causes are tried by magistrates of their own town. They have a right to wear white turbans, a colour which, with this exception only, the Turks reserve to themselves, as a mark of distinction and pre-eminence. And they are allowed to have bells in their churches. The Turks set a great value upon this gum. They put it into their bread to give it a flavour, and burn it as a perfume. The women in the Seraglio are continually chew-

[1]   Oinopion, legendary King of Chios.
[2]   The Deputy of the Captain Pasha.

ing it from a supposition that it is highly beneficial to the teeth, and to the breath. The Lentiscus is a beautiful evergreen, something in appearance like our Tree Box, and grows to the height of thirteen or fourteen feet. The turpentine also of this island is of a peculiar quality accounted the best in the world; and the Terebinthus, or Pistachia Tree, grows here in great abundance. The port of Scio, which is naturally a good one, though the Turks, with their usual carelessness, suffer it to be half choked with sand, and with sludge, is always full of ships, this being the usual waiting place for all vessels on their way to and from Constantinople....

The town of Scio is defended by a garrison of one hundred and twenty five janissaries, augmented in time of war. This town is larger than that of Castro, well built and thickly peopled. The streets are narrow, and ill paved, but houses are high, and built of stone. Of stone however quarried for the purpose, as there are but few remains of antiquity to be met with here, the Venetians,[1] who were so long masters of the island having probably carried away all that was curious or valuable. It is commanded by an Aga. The politeness of this officer procured me his acquaintance, and I had the pleasure of his company on board our ship, where, though his religion forbade him to taste wine, he was greatly delighted with what he called our *English sherbet, viz.* arrack punch. He was one of the handsomest and best made young men I ever saw, and at our parting he took from his girdle, or belt, a very handsome sword, which is still in my possession, and presenting it to me, told me that it had already killed two men, and that he was well assured it would not be idle in my service. The sabre has however been perfectly at rest ever since, but in return I gave him a pair of English pistols.

In this island we met with another remarkable instance of Turkish civility. Walking one morning through the streets of Scio, a Turkish gentleman espied us from his window, and immediately sent his servant to desire our company to drink coffee. He received us with the greatest and most unaffected politeness, telling us that, having observed that we were strangers of condition, he had taken the liberty of desiring our company upon a supposition that it would not be unpleasant to us to get acquainted with the gentry of those countries to which our curiosity led us, and when, after half an hour's conversation, we took our leave, he desired to see us often during our residence in the island, and offered us, with great cordiality, every service that lay in his power.

However it may be foreign to my plan I cannot quit this island without indulging myself with a few words respecting its incomparable beauty. The centre of it is wholly occupied by a very high

[1] The Genoese controlled Chios for a longer period.

mountain, the roots of which are partly cultivated with corn, cotton, mulberries, and vineyards, and partly covered with wood, above which the summits rise in the most romantic terms, consisting of nothing but bare rock, and mixing their massy tops with the incumbent clouds. From its foot to the seashore is an inclined plain, which at the widest is not more than three miles in breadth, of the most fertile soil, thick planted with the most luxuriant orange, lemon, and citron groves, interspersed with numberless country houses, built of hewn stone, neat, elegant, and designed with taste. Each house has its well paved court, in the centre of which rises a fountain of the most transparent water, and its garden, trim and well dressed. Many churches also, which, though small, are all of them built in an excellent style of architecture, contribute to decorate the scene, and add to our idea of the polish and population of the country. Industry reigns through the whole region, accompanied by its constant dependents, neatness and affluence. The people, who are handsome, healthy, and well-clad, throng everywhere, and add life to the delightful landscape, but more especially the women, whose natural beauty, and sprightly air is rather heightened than impaired by the singularity of their dress. Nothing indeed could be more enchanting than our prospect at leaving this island. The sun shone bright. The mountain was illuminated. The orange groves and villas, for the space of thirteen miles on either side of the city, appeared as one continued village interspread with the most beautiful gardens, contrasting the wood and the rocky mountain which rise behind them, and form the most inimitable background. The port was full of galleys, and innumerable other vessels decorated in their gayest trim, and displaying to the breeze their many-coloured flags and pennants. The men-of-war lay outside the harbour, and by their enormous bulk and stateliness added dignity and splendour to the scene, and completed the picture with the most noble foreground imaginable. As we passed them we saluted with nine guns, and our salute was returned from the Commodore's ship by three, a particular and great compliment, as the imperial pride of the Turk seldom answers any salute with more than one gun.

AN AMOROUS ADVENTURE
IN MYCONOS

The mention, which in the last article I have had occasion to make of the *levantis*, or Turkish sailors, reminds me of a whimsical adventure we encountered at Micone, an island, which, as it possesses nothing very singular, and as it has been already fully described by other travellers, I should otherwise have passed over in silence, having heard much of the peculiar charms, and irresistible attractions of the ladies of this island, as well as their unequalled kindness and condescension, particularly from the report of a late traveller Dr. Askew,[1] who boasted that, during a short abode in this land of love, he had entered no less than fifteen times into the holy bonds of matrimony, and declared that no women upon earth were in any degree comparable to the fair and all-accomplished Miconites, we could not avoid, in quality of accurate travellers, to use our endeavours towards verifying this curious fact, in order to the advancement of natural knowledge.

Frank Burton therefore, who in matters of this nature was usually the agitator, and was indeed in such researches the keenest of all naturalists, set himself to work, and soon discovered a skilful and friendly coadjutor who promised that our laudable curiosity should be amply gratified, but warned us that, as the town was now full of *levantis*, one of the Captain Pasha's squadron lying at that time in the harbour, it would be neither prudent nor safe to attempt our interview, or to perform our experiments in the city, but that, if at night we would walk with him a little way into the country, he would take care to fix us in a proper and secure station, where we might remain in perfect safety till he should conduct to us such a damsel as would surprise and please us, and fully verify whatever wonderful reports we might have heard.

With the utmost alacrity we accepted the proposition and accordingly, as soon as the old folk, who, fond of and bigoted to the knowledge of their own day, are naturally averse from new experiment, were gone to bed, we sallied forth with our obliging Mercury,

---

[1] Dr. Anthony Askew, medical doctor and classical scholar, had visited Turkey and Greece in 1747-48. See Turkish Essay p. 179.

46

who led us at least two miles out of town, and stopped at a sort of ruined old castle, into which he bade us enter, and there await his return, which he assured us should be speedy. In this wretched uninhabited mansion there was but one room, if such it may be called, which had any covering, and that too by no means sufficient to keep out the rain. It was perfectly unfurnished, the walls cracked in various parts, and apparently ready to fall into ruin. Here we waited with some degree of patience for above an hour, when at length we began to be weary of our situation, and not a little alarmed at the probable consequences of our adventure. To attempt a return would have been madness. We were totally ignorant of the road. The night was dark and dismal. We doubted not but that these formidable *levantis,* of whom we had heard such terrible reports, were straying about the country, and we had been foolish enough to bring no arms, concluding that, for our purpose, those we usually *carried about with us were fully sufficient.* [Charlemont's italics to emphasize the innuendo.]

Calling therefore a council of war, after due deliberation we concluded that it would be most prudent to keep garrison where we were, and to wait the approach of the morning, which we doubted not would find us here, in the meantime fortifying our castle as well as we could, and for this purpose strongly barricading our door, which had no fastening, and was by no means foolproof, with beams, boards and great stones, which we collected from among the ruins. Having thus in some measure secured ourselves from any sudden attack we sat down on the ground in pitiful plight, cursing at once the Doctor, whose information had seduced us, our Mercurial friend, who had conducted us, our unlucky gallantry, and our unknown mistress.

In this disagreeable situation we had not remained above half an hour when we were additionally alarmed by a most violent thumping on the door, and upon our calling out to know who it was that knocked so furiously, we were answered by our Mercury, who, in the greatest seeming agitation, begged for heaven's sake, and as we valued our lives, that we should forthwith come out, and betake ourselves to fight as our only resource. He informed us, with a voice interrupted by fear, that, in returning to us with the nymph, he had been overtaken by a desperate crew of *levantis,* who had beaten him cruelly and taken from him the unhappy maiden, who was at this instant probably ravished by a dozen at least. That he had with difficulty escaped out of their hands, and had evaded their pursuit by the darkness of the night, and his superior knowledge of the country — but that they were even now at his heels, and that if they found us, we were dead men!

Without requiring a second bidding, we instantly evacuated the garrison, and followed our guide, who ran at full speed, over hedge and ditch, through miry crossroads, and passages hardly passable by daylight. We however, for fear of being bewildered, were obliged to keep up with him, and nothing surely could be more truly ludicrous than the figure we made upon this occasion. Poor Frank especially, whose body, any more than his soul, was never formed for flight, exhibited the most exact and the most humorous representation of Sir John Falstaff's precipitate retreat from Gadshill. Out of breath with running, and scarcely able to keep up, he damned the *levantis,* the pimp, the whore, the Greeks, and the Turks! 'Is it not better to have one's throat cut than to burst one's wind? I cannot stir an inch farther. Let them come and be damned. Zounds, I'm in a ditch — up to the neck by Jove! What the devil brought me awhoring in this unchristian country? Stay for me. Let me recover breath. Zounds man, stay!'

In this manner after having run several miles, weary, wet, and splashed up to our eyes, we at length regained the wished-for town, and reached our habitation as perfectly free from all amorous inclinations as if we had returned from an interview with Doctor Askew's fifteen wives. A little rest however having repaired our courage, we began to be vexed at our disappointment, and in a day or two after we prevailed upon our friend, partly by promises, and partly by threats, to obtain for us an assignation with the lady, who had cost us so dear, insisting however that this interview should be in town. With great difficulty we prevailed, and how much soever it may grieve me, I am compelled by that truth, which shall ever be inseparable from my narration, to declare that this *teterrima causa*[1] was rather more fit for the arms of the *levantis,* than for our more refined and sentimental passion! I cannot quit this subject without informing my reader that, having enquired of our Mercury whether he had been acquainted with Doctor Askew, he answered in the affirmative, and assured us that he himself had been servant to the Doctor during the whole time of his residence at Micone. We then asked whether he was not a man of great gallantry? 'No,' replied our friend, 'far from it. He was a studious man, and spent his whole time in reading and in the search of curiosities, and I am thoroughly confident that he was not acquainted with more than one woman in this island, and she too of the commonest sort — very much inferior to the lady I had the honour of procuring for you!' Such was the Doctor's boasted harem, and such are the stories of travellers!

In many of the smaller islands, as well as in this of Micone, the following singular custom is commonly practised, upon which the gallant Doctor grounded his wonderful love-tale. If a stranger should wish to enjoy anyone of the young unmarried women, he addresses himself immediately to her parents, and demands the girl in marriage. The

---

[1] 'Foulest of causes' (Horace, *Satires* 1, 3, 107-8).

bargain is presently struck, and the couple are brought before a magistrate, where they swear mutual fidelity during the man's residence in the island, the bridegroom engaging himself to pay at his departure a great sum of money, as well as a present advance, and, in case the lady should prove with child, a still larger sum. This money is set apart in the girl's portion, and with this, upon the departure of her consort, she soon procures herself a real husband among her countrymen, who esteem her not a whit the less for this previous connexion, deeming her a widow to all intents and purposes. The parents warrant the damsel to be a maid, and the price is fixed according to her beauty and accomplishments, being seldom however less than one hundred sequins, about fifty pounds, a sum large enough to preclude travellers from profiting as much as they would wish of this convenient institution, as the short stay they usually make at each of the islands would by the frequency of its repetition, render this species of gallantry rather too expensive, especially as these islands, in which it is practised, are unluckily, in every other respect, the least worthy of a traveller's notice....

[Here Charlemont discusses ancient examples of similar practices, citing Herodotus 1, 93 and 2, 126 on its occurences in Lydia and Egypt.]

But to return from this digression, I shall only add that, though as an antiquarian I thought it right to produce this ancient ... authority, I am however rather inclined to believe that the usage in question has a later and much more modern origin. Wheler informs us that in his time the greater part of the inhabitants of Micone were pirates, and that this island was one great staple for their prey; that there they kept their wives, children, and mistresses, and he goes on to relate how the Captain of the ship, on board which he then was, purchased here a girl from her father as a provision for his voyage to Constantinople. Now it appears to me by no means improbable that these corsairs have left behind them some traces of their manners, and that the custom above mentioned may be derived from that system of life which they had established. Indeed this island, as well as many of the smaller islands in the Archipelago, is still much molested by pirates, who, as we may naturally suppose, being now what they ever have been, a set of dissolute wretches, carefully keep up a usage so well suited to their manners, and prevent any possibility of the people being reclaimed. It must however be allowed that the women of Micone are in general very handsome, in spite of their monstrous dress, which is, if possible, still uglier than any we have yet seen.... They are moreover, in comparison with their circumstances, very expensive in this article.

At Micone I obtained from one of the ladies an account of the several articles of their garb, with their respective prices:

	The head-dress	8 piastres
	the shift	6
For an explanation of	the under shift	2
these terms *vide* a baby[1]	the plastron	2
in my possession	back plastron	3
dressed in the garb	the apron	5
of Micone.	armour	5
	stockings	3
	slippers	3

which makes in all seven and thirty piastres, so that either Tournefort must be mistaken, or the expense in dressing must be considerable lessened since his time. He tells us that at Micone the habit, *même le plus commun*, costs at least two hundred crowns. Perhaps however he may take into his account the gold chains and strings of pearl which they wear about their necks, in which case his estimate is not exaggerated; but as these are in the nature of jewels, and last for ever, they ought not to be taken as part of their current expense in dressing.

They have their necks and breasts covered over with chains of gold and strings of pearl, in which magnificent trim they are not however ashamed impudently to beg, and that for so small a sum as a single *para* or penny, teasing passengers sometimes on their own account, but more commonly for objects, which they tell you they will receive with your bounty. Their idleness is extreme, and, except a few cotton stockings, and abundance of cuckolds, nothing is made in this island, for which latter manufacture they have the greatest convenience, as the men, who are for the most part sailors, are commonly from home, and nothing but women are to be seen in the town. So that we may form a tolerable judgment of the morals of these ladies from their being possessed of those very useful and accommodating accomplishments and qualities, beauty, love and dress, impudence, poverty idleness, and convenience. The island of Micone, apparently one of the poorest in the Archipelago, pays the Turk twenty-two purses, seventeen in taxes and tribute, and five upon an average to the Captain Pasha. We found this island in the utmost confusion upon account of the Vaivode, who, upon some trifling complaint, had been summoned to appear before the Captain Pasha, by whom it was supposed he would be plundered, every complaint being productive of an *avania*, or fine, which is always appropriated to the private use of that tremendous judge; and this, as the islanders informed us, was his method

[1] A doll.

of doing justice. In matters of this kind we must however be cautious of giving implicit credit, as our information proceeds from prejudiced parties. At least we may fairly conclude that all accounts of this nature are in some degree aggravated. The trade of Micone consists chiefly in wine of which they annually made twelve thousand barrels of the best for a fundaclee sequin,[1] about nine shillings.

Indeed this island was always favoured by Bacchus, and Wheler tells us that he purchased a medal there, which he supposed to be of Myconos, with a bunch of grapes for its reverse. But the chief method by which the Miconites make money is by carrying to and fro the commodities of the other islands, having several large caiques belonging to their town for which they find constant employment. I shall add but one circumstance more relative to this island, and that merely to show how wonderfully old traditions have been kept up among the inhabitants of Greece. Pliny[2] assures us that Inopus, a famous fountain of Delos, rises and falls with the Nile. The less credulous Strabo doubts the fact, but records the opinion. At Micone, which is only nine miles from Delos, I met with an old priest, Papa Limiotis, who assured me that, when young, he had heard that a certain fountain in that island increased and decreased at the same periods with a great river in Egypt, the name of which he had forgotten; and upon my mentioning the Nile he told [me] that was indeed the name.

[1] Fundakli (or foundoukli) sequin, a gold coin.

[2] *Natural History* 2, 106, 229; *cf.* Strabo, *Geography* 10, 5.

DELOS

My near vicinity to the sacred island would almost persuade me to break through the rules, which in writing these Essays I have prescribed to myself, by launching out into a description of Delos, but an uninhabited land can never be brought within the compass of my plan, and I am luckily prevented from transgression by finding that it has been already perfectly well described by Tournefort, who, though not always accurate in his measurements, is laboriously exact in his detail of the antiquities. I shall content myself therefore with saying that this renowned centre of the Cyclades, esteemed so sacred that it was reverenced even by the Persian invaders, who had denounced war against the gods and men of Greece, the childbed of Latona, the birthplace of Apollo and of Diana, the Loretto, the Mecca of the heathen world, enriched with gifts from the greatest monarchs, splendidly adorned by the most skilful architects, decorated with the works of the most exquisite sculptors, favoured theme for the immortal hymns of Pindar and of Callimachus, is now reduced to a heap of marble fragments, and is become a quarry for the neighbouring islanders, who find here stones ready hewn to be made use of even for their meanest purposes. Among other indignities offered to these sacred remains we could not avoid observing with indignation that it is the constant practice of the neighbouring islanders to carry from hence the finest capitals, which they hollow, and use for mortars, on which account few or no capitals are now to be found among the ruins. So perfectly is Delos deserted that not even a goat is seen upon it, nor any living thing but rats and rabbits, and those singular lizards, called *Koscordili*,[1] of one of which Tournefort has made an accurate drawing; so that, for our sustenance, we were obliged to send for a mutton and some milk to the neighbouring Rhenea, which were brought to us from thence by a half-starved shepherd, who might well have reproached his patron Apollo that his godship had now forgotten the time when he himself was of that vocation.

---

[1] *Lacerta stellio*, according to R. Walpole (ed.) *Travels in various countries of the East* (London 1820) p. 26. Tournefort who has an illustration at p. 373 of vol. 1 describes them as *lacerta muralis*.

Respecting this island [Rhenea] I shall give the following quotation from my Journal:

Friday, August 15

— Early this morning we rowed in our small boat to Rhenea, which the Greeks call the great Delos.... We passed the two Rematiari [Revmatiari], bare rocks. The largest of these was anciently called Insula Hecate, and consecrated to Diana under that name. Over this rock Tournefort supposes that Polycrates, Tyrant of Samos, passed the chain, by which according to Thucydides[1] ... he bound Rhenea to Delos, thus consecrating the former to Apollo. Having landed upon the island, our shepherd conducted us to a point of land called Glaropoda,[2] which seems to have been the extremity of a considerable town, as appears from the remains of some magnificent building, built with great blocks of marble, separately squared and well jointed. From hence all along the declivity of a hill, to the farthest point of the greater Rematiari the whole extent was covered with ruins, extremely ill treated by time. Pillars, some of very great size, altars without number but miserably decayed, and heaps of stones, which have served for building, cover the whole shore. Amongst these ruins we observed the colossal body of a lion, its head having been broken off. It measured in length 5 feet and a half, and seems well executed. We saw also in great numbers the tombs of which Tournefort speaks, which belonged to the Delians, who were prohibited from burying in their sacred island. Of all these two only were tolerably entire, and these correspond exactly with Tournefort's drawing. We went to the top of a high hill not far from the shore, where are the remains of some great edifice, probably a temple. This island is much larger and more fertile than Delos, and when we saw it, it was covered by flocks of sheep, which the Miconites send hither, as to excellent pasture ground. From hence we rowed back to Delos in nine minutes the passage appearing to us about an English mile, though Strabo fixes the distance within four stadia, that is to say rather less than five hundred yards.

I have given this long extract from my Journal principally because it tends to point out the only mistake I have ever yet met with in the usually accurate Strabo, who describes this island, covered as it is with the remains of ancient magnificence, as a small desert island remarkable for nothing but the tombs of the Delians.... A mistake like this in so accurate a writer seems very unaccountable, neither can we suppose, in excuse of Strabo, that in his time the island had fallen into decay. Even so late as in the reign of Alexander Severus its capital was dignified by the title metropolis....

Water also we had been compelled to bring with us [to Delos]

[1] *History* 3, 104, 2.
[2] Now called Glaropoula.

from Micone; for the famous fountain Inopus now yields little better than mud, with which its sacred waters are so tainted as to be scarcely drinkable. Here however we passed three pleasant days and nights sleeping upon the seashore, as the only place free from ruins, under an awning made of the sail of our boat. Our beds were of dry seaweed and our dreams were inspired by Phoebus in reward for the pains we had taken to investigate his sacred island. Returning late one evening from our toilsome researches we were agreeably surprised by a singularly pleasing night scene. Three musicians, two lyres and a guitar, passing from Tinos, had spied our boat, and in hopes of employment, had landed here. Our crew, who were all Greeks, had willingly received them, and were dancing their country gambols by the light of a parcel of dry sticks, (for we had no candles), burning in an iron pot. The view of Mount Cynthus, at the foot of which our homely tent was pitched. The contemplation of those venerable ruins, which raised in our minds the most awful and painfully pleasing ideas. The sprightly whimsical music, not a little improved and dignified to our fancy by the respected and consecrated name of *lyre,* and accompanied by the solemn buzz of the still sea, which served as a sullen base. The grotesque dancing, and the strange illumination, which looked as if prepared for enchantment. All these circumstances, joined to the genial goal[1] of this delightful climate, and a night beyond expression serene and beautiful, contributed to render as agreeable as it was picturesque and singular this unexpected scene. But I have detained my reader too long with this digression and must hasten to matters more consonant to the plan of these essays.

[1] This word is uncertain in the manuscript.

NAXOS

From what has been mentioned of the disagreeable effects of the Captain Pasha's visits, it may well be presumed that those islands, which from their want of proper harbours are inaccessible to his fleet, are thought by their inhabitants to enjoy a peculiar privilege, since, though they may be obliged to pay a proportion of the tribute, they are in a great measure delivered from his rapacity, and are wholly free from the expenses incurred by his entertainment, and from the riots, outrages, and exactions of the *levantis*. In this happy predicament is the island of Naxia, the ancient Naxos, and one of the most beautiful spots of the Archipelago. For though from being deprived of an extensive trade, an inconvenience which for the reasons above mentioned is joyfully suffered, this island be not so well cultivated as many others, nature has been so profusely lavish in her bounty that there are few regions upon earth which abound more in those inimitable beauties that immediately depend upon her. The country, as in almost all the islands, is very hilly, and the centre of the island is wholly occupied by great mountains finely wooded, from whence descend numberless torrents, which, forming themselves into rivulets, water the whole country, and encourage the luxuriant growth of orange, lemon, and citron trees, olives, pomegranates, mulberries, and figs, with which the declivities are covered, and the valleys, richly and beautifully interspersed and shaded. The veneration of antiquity conspires also to sanctify the region, and adds its awful charms, its reverential ideas to the romantic beauties of these enchanting scenes. Here was the infant Bacchus nourished under the care of the nymphs Coronis, Philia, and Cleis, and to corroborate this ancient tradition, a mountain still exists, which even now retains the name *Corono*. Here did Theseus abandon to the god of wine his mistress Ariadne, who received from the jolly deity that dear consolation, which is the best and surest comfort to deserted ladies....

Here also is a mountain, the highest of the island, which still preserves the appellation Zia, corrupted from Dia, the mountain of Jupiter.... To the top of this we climbed, and, though the walk was laborious, our toil was far overpaid by the romantic beauties of the way. About the middle of the ascent a vast rock of marble presents itself, on the face of which is deeply engraved in huge capitals, unimpaired and indelible:

ΟΡΟΣ ΔΙΟΣ ΜΗΛΩΣΙΟΥ[1]

— the mountain of Jupiter Guardian of Flocks.

Not far from hence a spacious and romantic cave or grotto opens itself, where, as tradition assures, the Bacchanals were wont to celebrate their orgies. Close to its ample mouth grows a most amazing vine, which, from its size and apparent age, imagination may suppose to have been planted by Bacchus himself. The dimensions of its trunk are astonishing, and it winds itself from tree to tree to an inconceivable extent, covering a whole region with its shade. From the summit of the mountain the prospect is beyond description. All the Cyclades seem immediately under you, and island rises upon island as far as the view can reach. The beauties of the country also are from hence at once discovered, and all that natural fertility which gave cause to the ancients to term this island Sicilia Minor.

I have dwelt the longer upon the beauties and advantages of this island, because it is principally upon their account, and more especially from its being inaccessible to the Turkish fleet, that this secluded spot is become an almost universal asylum to men of all countries, whom either disappointments, misfortunes, or weariness of the world have driven to seek a retreat, where they may dwell in peace forgetting and forgotten, and pass the remnant of their lives in calm tranquillity, enjoying in their full extent these real and never cloying blessings, the contemplation of natural beauty, and the benefit of a fine climate. Many such were here at our arrival, but at the head of them all was a remarkable personage, the amiable singularity of whose character and situation has given rise to this article. Baron Vigoureux de la Stike,[2] a French gentleman of a noble family in Gascogny, had in his childhood been page to Louis the Fourteenth, had served with the greatest credit in all the wars of that restless Prince, and had risen to the rank of Lieutenant General. Grown old in arms, and wearied with the laborious trifling of a court, vexed with disappointment, cloyed with dissipation, harassed with the vain pursuits of pleasure and ambition, and sick of the world, he at length retired hither with his wife, and a young son. With the remains of his paternal fortune, which had been diminished by the inevitable expenses of a life spent

---

[1] The inscription is engraved on the lower surface of a marble rock which juts out from the face of the mountain: this covered situation is one cause of its being perfectly preserved. (Charlemont's note.)

[2] François de Lastic de Vigouroux.

in the field and in the court, he purchased an estate, which yields eight hundred pounds annually, a revenue, which here is equal to twice as many thousands at Paris, and enables him to live as a prince in the island, and prince indeed he is, if the free choice of a people can give a right to sovereignty! His easy manners, his charitable disposition, his continual good offices, have gained him the hearts of all the islanders, and his knowledge of the world, his learning, and his abilities, made them look up to him as to one of a nature far superior to theirs — a privilege truly exclusive, and possessed by no other potentate upon earth!

At our first arrival we were visited by this admirable person, and were inconceivably struck by his good mien, his graceful deportment, and by a countenance the animated yet complacent beauties of which even fourscore years could scarcely impair. He was tall and well made, robust without clumsiness, fresh coloured, with an air of unaffected vivacity tempered by the calm of content, and possessed of that degree of unencumbering plumpness, which seems the effect of health and good humour, and serves to conceal the deformities of old age. Far from that cynic moroseness, which some miscall philosophy, this true philosopher had retreated from the world the better to enjoy life, and, as his object was happiness, he still loved and cultivated the sweets of society, of which we were soon made sensible by his frankly inviting us to his house, which with a sincere earnestness he besought us during our abode in the island to make our own. The invitation was too cordial and too pleasing to be refused, and we followed him to a large and handsome habitation, seated upon a beautiful hill just above the town, in the apartments and furniture of which all was simplicity, and that elegant convenience, which is so far superior to magnificence. His wife had for some time been dead, but we were cordially received and welcomed by his son and daughter-in-law, one of the principal women of the island, to whom he had, not long since, given his son in marriage. It was soon known by the people of the country that their patron had received into his house some favoured guests, and presently a concourse assembled from all parts, giving us the most hearty welcome, and assuring us that every good office in their power would be far too little for what they wished to show to those who were favoured by their friend and father. We now sat down to a plentiful repast, and after dinner a walk was proposed by our landlord, who led us through the town, while the inhabitants from all sides crowded about him with every sincere mark of respect and of love. Returning home we found a ball prepared, for which purpose the handsomest youths and the prettiest women of the country were collected together, who were all entertained at supper, and the night closed with Greek dances.

Thus did every day pass away. The son was sensible and good humoured. The daughter-in-law was handsome, affable, and lively. The other hermits of the island, who, though in every respect far inferior to our landlord, were however men of sense and of breeding, made always, one or other of them, a part of our society, and by the singular turn of their discourse, each of them having somehow or other quarrelled with the world, and consequently seen mankind in the most disadvantageous light, added spirit and novelty to the conversation, but our dear host was still the soul of every party. His good sense, his keen but inoffensive observation, his experience of life in its most entertaining and instructive walks, his truly polite and easy manners, his genuine good humour, and his constant flow of spirits, rendered him the most agreeable of companions, and made us easily conceive how impossible it was that a man so endowed, and possessed of a heart fitted for every social endearment, should not be idolized in a country which he had chosen for his dwelling, and where he wished to make himself beloved.

And idolized indeed he was. I remember one day when in the course of our walk, the heat of the weather, and the throng of those who pressed upon him, had so far overpowered his strength and spirits, that he was suddenly seized with a fainting fit, the symptoms of distress, which appeared among the people, were in the highest degree affecting, and expressive of love and of sorrow. The consternation was universal. The whole town was in tears. 'What will become of us? Was ever loss like ours? We are bereft of our friend, our protector, our father!' Such accents as these were everywhere re-echoed. At length he recovered. All was joy. The whole island rang with shouts of exultation. In the first transports of their delight the people crowded about him to assure themselves of his safety. They kissed his hands. They embraced his knees! — till their desire of seeing him giving way to their fears lest the throng should too much oppress him, they retired to a due distance, and made a lane for us through which we conducted him home.

Nor should this their anxious love for him excite our wonder. He was indeed their father! Since his arrival all litigation had ceased. Was there a difference between any two of the islanders? He was the arbitrator, and his judgment was definitive. No appeal was likely to be made from a sentence pronounced by the friend of both parties, the justice and wisdom of which were apparent, and where there was no reason to doubt the least shadow of partiality. Had any misfortune, unforeseen and unmerited, reduced an inhabitant to poverty? His house, his purse were open to him, his advice assisted him, his munificence supported him! Were the enjoyments of mutual love denied by the inequality of fortune. His generosity made up the difference, and the happy pair was united! He had made it his business to study medicine, and annually imported large quantities of the best drugs.

The sick were brought to him. He prescribed. He administered, and health was restored!

Under his patronage manufactures flourished. The diligent were encouraged by his rewards, and still more by his applause. The idle were awed into industry by his frown! The customs of the island had been changed by his salutary influence. Whatever was harsh or savage was softened by his goodness. Whatever was inconvenient was corrected by his judgment, and as his word was law, so all his laws were beneficial, equitable, and easy. Such was this excellent man! This friend to mankind! This honour to human nature! Happy in the merited love of a grateful people, happy in giving happiness to a whole country, spending the remnant of an honourable life in doing more real good than all the potentates of Europe can boast to have done in a century! Read this, ye proud philosophers. Read this, ye recluse and useless anachorites! Read this, ye austere pretenders to sanctity. Read this, ye kings, and blush! Or rather, for your pride's sake, and secret self-satisfaction, read this, and esteem the relation an incredible fable.

It may easily be conceived that we were not in haste to depart from this society; but time pressed, and we must be gone. Already had the entreaties of our host detained us a whole week, but at length his kindness and our wishes yielded to necessity, and we were compelled to depart, being conducted to our bark by all our friends, and by the good wishes of thousands expressed in acclamations. And here we discovered the last kind act of our dear landlord's hospitality. Our felucca was laden with every sort of provision – sheep, bread, wine, lemons oranges, and every kind of the best fruit.

Notwithstanding the want of proper ports the trade of this island is not inconsiderable. Its principal exportations are corn, wine, cattle, figs, salt, silk, and cotton, which last the inhabitants manufacture into stockings and some other articles of dress. Oil also is exported, which is here good, and exceedingly cheap. Bacchus still favours his beloved island, and the Naxian wine is excellent – that it has always been so we know from Diodorus Siculus [5, 3, 78]. The figs are incomparable, and the grapes most excellent, as are indeed all other kinds of fruit. Those [figs] of Marseilles, so greatly esteemed by us, are insipid when compared to them. There are of all sorts, large and small, purple and grey. When ripe the whole surface is covered with a clammy juice, which exudes from the cracks, and is in consistence like honey, though far more rich and fragrant in its flavour. The small grey fig is however, in my opinion, the best. The most excellent I have tasted are those of Mitilen, Scio, Naxia, Paros, and Micone. Fuel, which is scarce in most of the islands, is here in great plenty, on account of the woods with which the mountains are covered. There is also gathered a large quantity of the gum called ladanum. It is also called labdanum and is a medicinal aromatic gum, which exudes from the *Cistus Ledon* or

Ladanifera. The Greeks call it Ladanum and Ledanum. It is produced in great quantities, and in much perfection in the island of Crete or Candia. But as the manner of procuring it is by cutting off the hair of those animals who have rubbed against the shrub by which it is produced, it is usually dirty and unfit for general use.

There are a considerable number of Latins established in this island, being the posterity of those Venetians who settled here under Marco Sanudo, a native of Venice who possessed himself of this and many of the neighbouring islands, and obtained the splendid title of Duke of the Archipelago. This event happened soon after the seizing of Constantinople by the Latins, and the Duchy remained in the hands of Venetian noblemen during the space of three hundred years, till Jacomo Crispo the twenty first Duke, was finally dispossessed by the Turks under the Emperor Selim the Second.[1] The number of Catholic inhabitants is certainly one cause of the preference which the hermits have given to Naxos, where many families still remain descended from those Venetians who formerly possessed the island among which are many of considerable name and distinction, whose representatives are more likely to form a society adapted to the reception and amusement of strangers from our parts of Europe than any which the other islands could afford. Some of these had usually a share in those agreeable parties which have been mentioned in the text, and among them we met with some who bore the great name Giustiniani. Between the Latins and the Greeks there is, as usual, much aversion, and little intercourse. But we may readily conceive that our dear baron has kept totally clear of this foolish and wicked distinction. Indeed he has done his utmost to put an end to it. Greeks, Latins, and Turks — there are however very few Turkish inhabitants on this island — are all equally his friends, since he is equally the friend to all!

[Here Charlemont adds a long note on the ancient history of Naxos, ending 'but I have been betrayed, I know not how, into this display of antiquity, and shall now return to matters more consonant to my plan.']

[1] The son of Suleiman 'the Magnificent.'

TINOS

The island of Tino, anciently Tenos, ... possesses also the privilege of being free from the visits of the Captain Pasha, in common with that of Naxia, though for a different reason. This island remained under the dominion of Venice long after that republic had lost all the rest of her possessions in the Archipelago, and, when at length it surrendered itself to the Turk, the people were wise enough to stipulate that they should pay a stated tribute, forty purses, at Constantinople, and that the Captain Pasha should, upon no pretence whatsoever, come into their ports, a condition which the Turks have strictly observed, a fidelity to treaty, which, considering that it is at all times in their power to break through it, does them much honour. In consequence of this wise stipulation, the Tiniotes pay in silk, the principal commodity of their island, the value of forty purses to an officer at Constantinople, who is appointed by the Porte to receive it, and who keeps a deputy or agent at Tino, the only Turk residing here. This freedom from oppression is easily to be observed in the state of the country, which is beautiful and well cultivated, and in the appearance of the inhabitants, who are industrious, well clothed, happy, and lively. Not long ago they exhibited a striking instance that the spirit of liberty still exists among them. Their Vaivode, having been guilty of some tyrannic action, was violently assaulted by the people, and torn to pieces. In consequence of this outrage an armed galley being sent by the Porte, to enquire into the fact, and to demand the murderers, the whole people assembled themselves upon the shore, openly and unanimously avowed the fact, and declared that they were all equally concerned in the action — all equally guilty, if it were guilt to destroy a tyrant! This unanimity and boldness had the desired effect: the Turks were overawed by it, the galley retired, and the affair was no farther enquired into.

In this island there are sixty-four villages, some of them indeed very small, consisting of no more than seven or eight houses, and the inhabitants are estimated at fifteen thousand. The pasture is good, and the fruit is excellent. The country is well planted, particularly with mulberry trees on account of the silkworms. The island is beautifully diversified with hills and dales. The dress and manners of the inhabitants bespeak their affluence, and content is visible in every countenance; but that which most forcibly strikes the traveller's eye, and particularly that of a young traveller, is the wonderful beauty of the women, to which their dress not a little contributes, which, far differing from that of the other islands, is to the last degree elegant and graceful.... They are sprightly and affable, and peculiarly remarkable for their skill and agility in dancing, a talent which we put to the test in a ball which was given by our Consul, at which all the belles of the island were assembled, and jollily danced with us till midnight, not only Greek dances, but minuets also, the knowledge of which they have probably retained from the instruction of their old masters the Venetians, to whom also they may be possibly indebted for their dress, which somewhat resembles that of the Venetian contadine, who are remarkable even in the well-dressed Italy for the superior elegance of their garb.

The silk trade of this island, its principal branch of commerce, is said to be decreased; and yet the Venetian Consul residing here was candid enough to assure us, that, though he did believe that the Tiniotes paid more taxes to the Turk than they formerly had paid to the Venetians, yet that he was convinced they were now richer than ever they had been under the government of his masters. A certain proof of what is generally supposed that the Venetian manner of governing their dependencies is a very bad one, and that the despotism of a republic is by far the worst of all despotisms.

SYROS

I have little to say of Syra, the ancient Syros, birthplace of Phere-
cydes, the disciple of Pittacus, and master of the Great Pythagoras,
only that it is the most Catholic and dirtiest of all the islands. Those
of the Latin rite predominate here so much that there is but one
Greek church, and not more than five families of that sect in the
whole island. The Capuchins have a convent here under the protection
of the French King, and indeed no country was ever better suited for
the reception of that dirty confraternity, to whose zeal however we
may probably ascribe the ascendancy of the Roman religion in this
island. The capital is liker a pigsty than an habitation for Christians
of any sect. Pigs and Capuchins are indeed in such abundance here
that one can scarcely walk through streets without stumbling over one
or the other of them.

This town is however so whimsically built, and the view of it
from the sea is so singular and so romantic that we thought it worth
our while to make a drawing of it.... It is built round a steep and high
pyramidical rock, every tier of houses forming a sort of step, so as
that the flat roof of the lower house serves as a courtyard to the
upper, only a little incommodated by the chimney. On the summit of
the rock stands the church and convent of the Capuchins, forming as
it were the point of the pyramid. The people here seem hospitable
and good natured, and are said to be industrious. Indeed if a barren
soil be, as is generally remarked, an incitement to industry, no people
ought to be more industrious than the inhabitants of Syra, and a
present made to us of some excellent figs, which even this rocky
island produces in great perfection, and of a large quantity of incomparable honey, was a proof of their hospitality. The dress of the
women, where it is distinguishable through their rags, is whimsical,
and not so ugly as that of many other of the islands, as it keeps up
their breasts, and shows their waists.

Here as usual, bitter complaints are made against the extortion and
tyranny of the Captain Pasha, and indeed if what they say be true,
they have reason to complain. Twenty purses, which is more I should
conceive than the rental of the island, are, as they tell you, upon an
average annually taken from them, and those, who are not able to
pay their contribution, are stripped of their clothes, an article I should

suppose of no great consideration either to them or to their tyrants. We climbed to the top of a very steep hill, which rises immediately from the harbour, and commands a fine prospect of Delos, and the neighbouring isles.

Respecting this hill the inhabitants have the following tradition, which, though not grounded upon any ancient relation that I know of, may possibly be true. They tell you that when the ancients intended a voyage to Delos they always touched at this island, and purified themselves in a very fine fountain, which is still extant here, and that, if the wind did not permit them to pursue their pilgrimage, they ascended this mountain, and from hence beholding the sacred island, performed their devotions. This tradition is in some degree authenticated by the remains of some great building, probably a temple, which still exist on the top of the hill, and by the fountain, the stone work of which is apparently of high antiquity.

This island, however barren and ugly, by no means wants cultivation, and is forced by the toil of the wretched inhabitants to produce good corn, wine, and figs, a great deal of cotton, and some olives. Tournefort, I suppose on account of its Catholicity, is lavish in its praise, but it seems to me to serve only as a contrast to the surrounding islands, and to look like Macartney in a circle of beauties.[1] There is however reason to believe that Syros, notwithstanding its present misery, formerly held no inconsiderable rank among the islands. The many marble fragments, which lie scattered all round the harbour, indicate the magnificence of the ancient capital, which was there situated, and some inscriptions and basso relievos in a good taste of sculpture, serve to evince that this has been a place of consequence. Indeed, if the tradition above mentioned can be depended upon, even from this circumstance alone it must have obtained a great degree of wealth and of consideration, and the island devoutly and necessarily visited by all persons on their pilgrimage to Delos could not fail of being rich, populous, and cultivated.

[Here Charlemont added a long note on Homer's reference to Syros in Odyssey 15, 402, and on the possible Phoenician origin of its name.]

[1] It is uncertain who this Macartney is. He cannot have been the George Macartney (afterwards Lord Macartney) referred to in Charlemont's letters as he was a good-looking man.

PAROS AND ANTIPAROS

Through all these islands we received every mark of civility, kindness and hospitality from the Greek inhabitants, but we never had an opportunity of putting this last virtue to the proof so thoroughly as at Paros, where we found ourselves in a situation so singularly disagreeable that I cannot forbear to mention it, though by so doing I should incur the accusation to which most writers of travels are liable, who foolishly and vainly suppose that their readers will interest themselves in their distresses as much and as ardently as they themselves have done. Finding that it would be very inconvenient and dangerous, if not impossible, to go with our great ship, which was of above two hundred tons burden, into the small creeks that serve as ports to many of the islands, we hired a Greek bark or felucca, in which we might be able to make our tour of the Cyclades with greater ease, convenience, and safety; and leaving our frigate with orders that she should make sail for the bay of Parechia, the capital town of Paros, and wait for us there, we took with us what money we thought might be necessary for the time of our absence, and left our treasure on board. We had now completed our tour, and were landed in the island of Paros, from whence we had only to visit Antiparos, which lies at the distance of an hour's sail. Here [we] viewed with astonishment the famous grotto, which, both in magnificence and difficulty of descent, even exceeded our expectations. This wonderful and magnificent cavern, together with its dangers and difficulties, is so accurately described by Tournefort, as to render any farther account of it unnecessary. One curiosity has however been discovered since his time *viz.* a small chamber in the rock in which are two springs of water, only nine feet distant one from the other. One of these is perfectly fresh, cold, and sweet, while the other not distinguishable by the taste from the saltest sea water.

We [now] began seriously to examine the state of our finances, and upon an exact inspection into each man's purse, were shocked to find that our whole remaining treasure amounted to the sum of three sequins, or one guinea and a half! The wind was, and had for some time been, in such a point, that we clearly perceived it was impossible for our ship to make its destined station, so that, without a favourable change, which our sailors assured us was not soon to be

65

expected, we could not possibly be relieved. A council was now called, in which, after much sad deliberation, it was determined to prevent the immediate discovery of our poverty by gallantly paying what we owed here, and forthwith to return to Paros, where, though we should probably be penniless, we had some reason to expect a good reception, as we had already experienced the good nature and hospitality of the Vaivode of that island, with whose son we had been well acquainted at Micone, and who, upon that account had been extremely kind to us. With aching hearts we paid our bill, and half a sequin, about an English crown, remained among us. This to make the greater show, we changed into paras, the smallest Turkish coin, and distributing them equally, determined to be charitable, as far as our stock would go, to all that should ask us, in order the better to conceal our indigence — and never sure did almsgiving so entirely proceed from ostentation! One circumstance however made sadly against us. Our appearance was as poor as our pockets. Our clothes, which had never been splendid, were dirtied and torn by climbing rocks and creeping into caves. My Hussar jacket, which I usually wore, and which was now my only suit, was all in rags. Burton's long plaid banian,[1] at the best the worst of nightgowns, was torn and greasy. But the most wretched figure of all was Dalton our painter, who, having had the misfortune to spill upon his coat a lampful of stinking oil, was now reduced to a waistcoat of green silk, formerly laced with gold, the back of which was pieced with the canvas remnant of an old picture, while the mutilated figures appeared like a sign hung out to testify the poverty of the miserable inhabitant. Scott and Murphy were the best clad — but alas, bad indeed was the best! In this sad trim we arrived at Parechia, where, notwithstanding, we were received with the utmost cordiality and cheerfulness by our host the Vaivode, who, like the chief magistrates of all the smaller islands, was a Greek. He lodged us in his house, and entertained us nobly during our abode there, which was of eight long days, for the wicked wind during all that time continued so adverse that it was utterly impossible for our ship to approach.

Often, during this tedious and melancholy interval, did I walk ἀκέων παρὰ θῖνα πολυφλοίσβοιο θαλάσσης,[2] endeavouring, and straining my eyes to descry the wished for vessel. But all in vain. The Aeolian deity was deaf to my prayers, nor had I any Deiopea[3] to offer him! The winds continued contrary, and our sitation grew daily more lamentable. How did we curse the importunate females, who, in

---

[1] A loose flannel gown, jacket, or shirt.

[2] 'Grieving by the shore of the boisterous sea' (Homer, *Iliad* 1, 34, and elsewhere).

[3] A nymph offered by Juno as a bride to Aeolus, King of the Winds (Virgil, *Aeneid* 1, 72).

our walks through the town, crowded about us, as wealthy strangers, teasing us to purchase their cotton stockings, the manufacture of the island! how did we blush, with shame and vexation, when the amazing wealth of England, a usual topic, was the subject of discourse! The hospitality of our host however amply made up for all our sufferings, and our dear fat landlady, of whom I still think with gratitude, and whose portrait I yet behold with affection, did everything in her power to render our abode delightful. Mirth and festivity employed our days, and our evenings closed with dancing. Every amusement was provided to divert that anxiety, which was but too visible, and with this view the best company that the island could afford was constantly invited to the hospitable board of our generous landlord. Among many other agreeable connexions which we by this means contracted, we had the good fortune to get acquainted with a very great personage indeed — no less than the Archbishop of Naxia, Exarch or Primate of the Aegean Sea who happening to come hither upon ecclesiastical affairs, principally to collect the revenues of his magnificent diocese, was immediately waited upon by the Vaivode, whom we, most willingly, accompanied in his visit. If his ecclesiastic dignity and wealth were equal to the parade of his titles, he would certainly be the first of prelates. His pompous direction is as follows: τῷ πανιερωτά-τῳ καὶ θεοπροβλήτῳ Μητροπολίτῃ τῆς ἁγιωτάτης Μητροπόλεως Παροναξίας ὑπερτίμῳ καὶ Ἐξάρχῳ παντὸς Αἰγαίου Πελάγους Κυρίῳ Κυρίῳ Ἀνθίμῳ προσκυνητῶς.[1] So that from hence we may perceive that this personage was peculiar Metropolitan of Naxia, and Exarch of the Aegean sea, of which Naxia is the principal diocese. We may also observe, from the repetition of the word κύριος, that the modern style of address by repeating the title obtains here also. Thus the French direct à Monsieur Monsieur.

The company consisted of the Archbishop, with a priest his attendant or chaplain, the Vaivode, our ragged fraternity, and an *aoidos* or bard, a personage who usually attends upon such occasions. The dinner was composed almost wholly of kid, which in these islands is accounted the first of delicacies, and for which Paros is peculiarly famous. The method of nourishing, and fattening these animals is somewhat particular. As soon as the kid is of an age to leave the dam he is put into a narrow pit, or dry well, with which kind of receptacles these countries abound, the necessary effect of former populousness. Here he is constantly confined, and fed with the milk of two cows, remaining in this state of inaction till he is six months old, at which period he is grown to a great size, is fit for eating, and is indeed a most

---

[1] 'To the Most Holy and God-chosen Metropolitan of the most-sacred Metropolis of Paros and Naxos, and most honourable Exarch of all the Aegean Sea, the Lord Anthimos, in humble prostration.'

delicious food. This in particular, on which we feasted, had been carefully attended to, as he was saved out of a number presented by the Vaivode to the Captain Pasha. Several excellent dishes were made out of this animal. A part was roasted, and the remainder was dressed with different kinds of savoury sauce, in the manner of ragouts and fricassees. (It is more than probable that two kids were dressed upon this occasion, as one of these animals, however large, would have been scarcely sufficient to have feasted eight people.)

And here I cannot avoid remarking how very anciently this has been a favourite food in the east. With this meat Jacob deceived his father Isaac, and that it was esteemed a present fit for a king we may perceive by David's presenting a kid to Saul when he was sent for to allay that Prince's frenzy by the sound of his harp (1 Samuel 16, 23). Manoah also (Judges 13, 15) prepared this delicacy for the angel, whom he looked upon as a noble guest, and not as a heavenly being. But to proceed: this dainty then under different appearances all of them excellent, and the most exquisite fruit, principally grapes and figs, composed our dinner. Meanwhile the bottle was not neglected, and the wine was incomparable. The bard arose with a full goblet in his hand, and began a health to the archbishop, which he ushered in by an extemporary stanza, composed and sung in his praise, and while he emptied the goblet, the whole company joined in a loud chorus, beginning and ending with the word χαῖρε — and expressive of their wishes for his Lordship's prosperity, health, and long life. My turn came next, and the bard, with the same ceremony, sung a stanza in my commemoration. The chorus was re-iterated. The goblets were again emptied, and the hall re-echoed with χαῖρε — χαῖρε. Thus were the whole company celebrated man by man every stanza differing from the former, and containing something peculiarly adapted to the person whose health was drunk. I was celebrated for my nobility, and for the extent of my travels, Burton for his extraordinary size, Dalton for his skill in painting, Murphy for his attachment to me, and Scott for being the Patroclus of that Achilles Burton. But the words of the chorus were always the same, and still concluded with the repetition of χαῖρε — χαῖρε! The toasts continued for some hours, and we parted with regret, extremely pleased with our classical entertainment.

Another circumstance happened soon after, which served to divert our melancholy. We were present at a Greek christening in one of the principal churches where the singularity of the ceremony was to us a matter of curiosity, but that which principally amused us was the odd behaviour of the *papa* or priest, who seemed as careless as if he had been employed in the most trifling affair, talking to the bystanders of indifferent matters during the most sacred part of the ceremony, and handling the poor little animal in so rough and awkward a manner that we expected every instant some fatal accident. In these amusements, in viewing the ancient quarries which have rendered Paros so famous, and in travelling through every part of the island, which is very beautiful and well cultivated, we passed away the tedious hours.

And indeed all was but barely sufficient to keep us from despondency. Fears of the most serious kind began to intrude themselves. We knew little of our Captain's character, and what we did know was not of the most comfortable kind. We had a good deal of money on board, and our stores were valuable. The ship was well manned, and in some sort armed. We had heard and read of seamen seizing a favourable opportunity to turn pirates, and though the wind alone might have accounted for the delay, we sometimes persuaded ourselves that there was a possibility of the vessel's having reached her station. The object of our fears was certainly of the most improbable nature, but eight long days had now passed in hourly expectation of relief, and in hourly disappointment. In those sad reflections, to the gloom of which every hour added shade, we were involved, when at length the wind changed, and our ship appeared in view.

I will not attempt to describe our transports. The Argo, freighted with the Golden Fleece, was not more acceptable to the Greeks! A boat was immediately procured, and we rowed on board, where we were received with the firing of guns, and every mark of nautical joy. Our first care was to new clothe ourselves, and our next to ransack our treasures for proper presents to our kind entertainers. Watches, silver, etuyes, pistols, and English cloth were lavished among our friends, who had no reason to repent their hospitable charity. The Vaivode was invited on board, and splendidly entertained, and we waited on him back to Paros, where, at his request, we passed another day, which was scarcely sufficient to express our acknowledgements. This island excels most of the Cyclades in beauty and in cultivation, having more soil and verdure than any other of the smaller islands. It prides itself upon being the birthplace of Archilochus, that first and famous writer of iambics, whose satire was so keen and so effectual as to make its unfortunate subjects hang themselves....

[Here Charlemont adds a long note on Archilochus.]

Alas, why have not we such satirists? How useful would they be to society in the present times!

Its capital Paros, was accounted the most splendid among the cities of the Cyclades, and Parechia, which stands on the same site, clearly exhibits the marks of its ancient magnificence. The houses, the walls, and the numerous little chapels, which surround it, are all built out of the ruins of ancient edifices. Not a cottage but has its doorcase of the finest marble, the remains of ancient architraves and friezes. But the most striking object of all is the old ruined Castle, situated upon a hill near the sea, the walls of which are wholly constructed of the finest marble columns, laid upon their sides, of architraves immense in their proportions, and of cornices most beautifully wrought. The shore beneath the Castle has also apparently been covered with columns, many of which still remain though many have been taken away to be employed in modern buildings, possibly in the construction of the fortress above mentioned. There are among these columns a few which bear evident marks of the greatest antiquity, being squared into polygons after the manner of some which we had before observed at Delos. Many inscriptions are also found here, and in different parts of the island, and in this class of ancient treasure Paros must be allowed a pre-eminence over every other part of the world, as from hence were brought the famous Arundelian marbles, those infallible guides, which lead us through the perplexed mazes of ancient chronology.

From the extent of these vestiges that of the old metropolis may with much probability be ascertained, which apparently extended itself quite round the extremity of the bay, and from hence appears to have been a city equal in size, as well as in magnificence, to the accounts which we have received of it; and the green hills, scattered with fine trees, which surround the present town, and beautifully rise above it, sufficiently evince the loveliness of its situation. The port however is by no means a good one, its navigation being obstructed by several banks of sand, which render it dangerous even for caiques, and almost impracticable to ships of burden, notwithstanding which the corsairs, who are well acquainted with its different channels, frequently come into its smallest creeks, and, in spite of the boasted and dear bought protection of the Captain Pasha, disturb and harass the country. There are however some excellent harbours in the island, which sufficiently account for its ancient maritime power. That of Sancta Maria is accounted the best, but the port of Drio, on the western coast, is chiefly frequented by the Turks, and here, at our first arrival, the Captain Pasha had anchored, this being his fixed station till all the neighbouring rocks have brought in their tribute.

The churches here, which are very numerous, are in general, built in a pretty style of architecture. That of the Madonna, which stands not far from the town, though by no means equal to the others in point of taste, is however a considerable building, and accounted the largest and most magnificent church of the Archipelago. Though it belongs to the Greeks, the Latins have an altar or chapel here. This fact I mention for its singularity, as I never met with any other instance in Greece of the least appearance of friendship or toleration between the Greeks and the Romanists — and their priest informed us that the temple was erected by a scholar of the famous architect who

The cave on Antiparos

built Sancta Sophia at Constantinople. If so, the scholar has even out-done his master in bad taste.

All the eatables on this island are incomparable. The mutton is excellent. The game, particularly partridge, with which it abounds, is beyond compare the best I ever tasted. The fruit is in great abundance, and of a most exquisite flavour. The wine is remarkably pleasant, though very strong. A considerable quantity of cotton, the growth of the island, is here manufactured, which, together with pitch, barley and olives, forms the principal trade. The Turk receives from hence thirty purses annually, which tribute, joined to the ravages committed by the corsairs, struggles against the soil and climate to keep the islanders poor. The people of Paros are accounted the most sensible, and the best conditioned (I'm sure we have reason to think so) of all the islanders, and are supposed, after the Athenians, to speak the purest and most elegant Greek. The women, who even in the time of Aristophanes were famous for their beauty, are still extremely hand-some, but disfigure themselves by a dress still uglier and more whim-sical even than that of their neighbours, for a sample of which I have my dear and never to be forgotten fat landlady's portrait.

But the renown of this island through all antiquity has chiefly been produced by its excellent quarries of white marble, by means of which it is become, as it were, the mother of all statuary, since from its womb has unquestionably issued all the fine sculpture of Greece. The beauty of Parian marble has become proverbial, neither is there, in my opinion, any stone that can be compared to it. The Pentelican or Hymettian seem nearest to it in excellence, but the preference given to the Parian by the ancient sculptors sufficiently evinces its pre-eminence. Some indeed pretend that the marble of Carrara is better fitted for sculpture, as it is easier worked, and more obedient to the chisel, but the Parian, from the peculiarity of its grain, inter-spersed with shining particles infinitely minute, has the great advanta-ge of representing far better the softness of flesh, and indeed the works which have proceeded from it sufficiently prove its superiority beyond all competition. The Carrara marble is besides seldom to be found pure and without spot, while that of Paros is so perfectly im-maculate, so wonderfully pure and spotless, as to be excelled by nothing but the complexion of Glycera — *splendentis Pario marmore purius!*[1]

With infinite delight we visited the ancient quarries, the extensive excavations of which are fully sufficient to account for the numberless gods and heroes that from hence derive their birth. The entrance of the great quarry is dignified and adorned by a basso relievo, cut on the solid rock, which has in this place been hewn perpendicular. It consists

[1] 'Gleaming more purely than Parian marble' (Horace, *Odes*, 1, 19, 6). Charle-mont discusses the line in a long note.

of twenty-nine figures representing Bacchus, and his associates the Bacchanals, and is dedicated to the nymphs of the country with this inscription in capitals:

ΑΔΑΜΑΣ ΟΔΡΥΣΗΣ ΝΥΜΦΑΙΣ[1]

This was undoubtedly the work of some statuary, who, waiting here to load his marble, amused himself with thus exercising his talent. The design is good, though the workmanship is apparently careless, and the heads are left unfinished, but its situation gives a merit to this piece of antiquity far beyond its intrinsic worth. Many vast blocks lie here ready hewn, and fit for exportation, and it would, methinks, be worth while to send a vessel on purpose to carry them away. Another quarry had lately been discovered in the same mountains, which is unquestionably the Marpessus of which Virgil [wrote] : *Quam si dura silex, aut stet Marpesia cautes.*[2] Into this we crept with much difficulty, as the entrance had been but partially cleared. At the bottom of the cavern the surface of the rock was worked by the chisel into parallel lines about half an inch asunder, which led us to believe that the practice of the workmen was to square and smooth the surface of the block, before he cut it out from the quarry. These quarries, says Pliny [36, 14], speaking of some eminent sculptors of Chios, were worked by the light of lamps, and thence the stone came to be called lychnites — from *lychnos* [lamp].... And indeed it is evident that they could be worked by no other means, as the caverns are deep, and admit of no light but by the entrance, which is too narrow, and too distant to give light to the place where the stone is quarried. On the road to these quarries, which is for the greater part over a rock of this white marble, and within about a quarter of a mile of them stands a Greek monastery, which is, it seems, the principal of the island. The building however and its inhabitants are equally miserable. It contains but two Fathers only, whose abject state and mortified appearance fully exemplify the poverty of ancient monks, before the holy brethren retreated from the world to eat and drink at free cost and more at their leisure. The patron of this convent is St. Minas, a holy personage of whom I know nothing. But the Greek saints are little known. These sectaries, not contented with having the great luminary of their Church, a Patriarch or Pope of their own, have also innumerable saints of their own proper manufacture, and perfectly distinct from those of the Latins....

Thus have I endeavoured to give some account of whatever appeared to me worthy of notice in the more remarkable of the Greek islands which we visited in two courses made by us through the

---

[1] 'Adamas the Odrysian to the nymphs.'

[2] 'As firm as hard flint or Marpesian rock' (*Aeneid* 6, 471). Charlemont adds a note.

Aegean Sea, the one in our voyage from Italy to Constantinople, the other on our way from that metropolis to Egypt, towards which astonishing country, whose wonders will probably add a third part to these essays,[1] we set sail from Paros. On our return from thence, bound for Athens, we again traversed the Archipelago, having thus left no part of it unseen, and little of any note through its whole extent unexamined. I shall now proceed to mention such islands as in this our third course we visited, but as little occurred consonant to my principal purpose, the delineation of manners, I shall shorten my relation as much as the licence I have hitherto allowed myself will permit.

[1] Apparently Charlemont never wrote this. Some account of his Egyptian visit is given by Dalton in his *Antiquities* and *Views*. See Appendix.

PASSING CYPRUS

October the 22nd

— We sailed from Alexandria, intending for Cyprus, and in spite of an unfavourable wind, came at length within sight of this isle of Venus. As we approached the land the wind became more and more contrary, and settling at last into a strong gale, obliged us to lie off and on, still hoping for a favourable moment to make good our landing. But our hopes were vain. The Paphian goddess ... angry perhaps that during our abode in the inhospitable and ungallant regions of the Nile, few or no sacrifices had been by us offered to her divinity,[1] forbad our entrance into her sacred isle, and by her well-known interest with Aeolus, and with her uncle Neptune, frustrated our anxious expectations, and defeated all our endeavours. In short, a strong and settled easterly gale now blowing, we were compelled, after much time spent in vain attempts, to content ourselves with a near view of Cyprus from the sea, and unwillingly to change our course, steering directly for Rhodes; unwillingly I say; for though we knew there was little in Cyprus worthy of our inspection, the fame of the island, and our devotion towards its patroness, made us wish greatly to visit it.

[1] Charlemont adds a tantalizing note here: 'This extraordinary fact will be explained when we come to treat of Egypt and her barbarous customs.'

RHODES

Our voyage was tedious and troublesome, and after struggling for seven long days with calms, hard gales, and contrary winds, on the 30th we at length anchored in the harbour of Rhodes. This port, though small, considering the extensive commerce which was anciently transacted in it, is however excellent, being well protected from every wind, and having water sufficient for ships of great burden to anchor close under the Castle, which is built on the edge of the sea. At its entrance are two square towers, one on either side of the channel, upon the walls of which the Cross of the Knights is still to be seen. Upon the rocks, on which these towers are erected, the feet of the famous Colossus are supposed to have been placed, which however I take to be impossible, as the utmost height assigned to this wonder of the world is eighty cubits, one hundred and twenty feet, and the rocks are about two hundred feet asunder; a space impossible for a statue of these dimensions to bestride. A mole indeed, projecting from each of the rocks, might have rendered the stride conceivable, and, though the entrance would have been by this means greatly narrowed, it might still perhaps have been sufficient for the small vessels of the ancients.

But, though by this supposition one difficulty seems to be removed, another still remains of equal force. When overthrown by the earthquake, the ruins of the Colossus, thus situated, must probably have fallen into the sea, and consequently could not have been visible, as they certainly were in the times of Strabo and of Pliny, and even so late as at the conquest of Rhodes by the Saracens in the year of our Lord 672 ; neither could they, without infinite skill, cost, and labour, have been recovered to have laden, as we are assured, nine hundred camels with the brass which composed this monstrous statue. But, as all modern authors, from what authority I know not, seem to be agreed in placing the Colossus at the entrance of the harbour, and as the unvarying tradition of a fact, which must have been universally known so lately as in the year 672, seems to carry with it a great degree of weight, we will, for the present, suffer these difficulties, however great and even insurmountable they may appear, to give way ; and this we are inclined to submit to principally that we may be enabled to indulge ourselves in the pleasure of admiring the stupendous grandeur of the idea, that a statue should be erected between whose legs the greatest vessels then known should conveniently pass and repass and whose stride should be the entrance to one of the most trading harbours of the ancient world, belonging to the capital of that island, which for a long time maintained the empire of the sea! Another cause, I must confess, of my present partiality to this improbable situation is that it has afforded to our immortal Shakespeare that noble image of the despotism of Caesar:

> Why man, he doth bestride the narrow world,
> Like a Colossus ....

The town is small, but well built. Its principal street, which is still named the Street of the Knights, is now nearly uninhabited. The arms of the several nations still remain fresh and unbroken on their different colleges. Among others we observed those of England. These colleges, or auberges, as they are called at Malta, are not unhandsome, considering the early age in which they were erected. St. John's Church, the ancient Cathedral, is now the principal Mosque, and is not without a degree of magnificence. The palace of the Grand Masters is almost a ruin, though some apartments are yet kept in tolerable repair.

In one of these is confined, and closely imprisoned, a brother of the Persian Emperor,[1] of him I believe, who was dispossessed by Couli Kan. This Prince, upon the downfall of his family, fled to the Grand Signor for protection , and was sent hither, where he has been ever since kept a prisoner. In this manner it seems to be the policy of the Ottoman court to treat all such princes as seek refuge under her power. We have already seen at Scio a Tartarian prince nearly in the same situation, but his close alliance to the Ottoman blood has probably rendered his confinement less strict, and his treatment more liberal. There may also be many reasons for the particular severity with which the Persian prince seems to be treated. The Turks and Persians are natural enemies, both on the score of religion, and on that of dominion, and probably also this unfortunate prince is thus strictly guarded, as by his escape would be lost a pretender to the crown of Persia, to be made use of on any convenient occasion. Over the gate of a ruined church we observed the famous inscription, by which the Grand Master d'Aubusson, according to his vow, consecrated this church to the Virgin Victorious over the Turks. This edifice, which does not seem to have been very magnificent, was erected immediately after the glorious defence of Rhodes against the fleet and army of Mahomet the Second, commanded by the Pasha Paleologus, and consisting of one hundred and sixty ships of war, together with

---

[1] Tahmasp II, who took the name of Nadir Shah, and was succeeded by Ali Quli Khan.

at least one hundred thousand fighting men.

We made the tour of those fortifications, which, upon this occasion, were so nobly defended as to baffle all the power of the Ottoman Empire under one of its greatest princes, and found them remarkably strong for the age in which they were constructed. The breaches, which are perfectly repaired, are however still discernible, and raised in our imagination a painful idea of the numbers of human creatures who perished in their attack and defence; neither could we help sighing at the reflection that, after so much blood spilt with so much glory, this fortress should, two and forty years afterwards, have been delivered into the hands of the Turk by the infamy of a Christian traitor. This shameful event happened in the year 1522, under the reign of Soliman the Second, and the traitor's name was d'Amaral, a Portuguese Chancellor of the Order. Through the whole town images of Saints, the arms of the Order, and of the several Grand Masters, are still to be seen, the Turks probably suffering them to remain as trophies of their final victory.

Here our *firman,* which in the anarchical state of Egypt had been well nigh useless to us, came again into credit, being received and read with the utmost respect by the Mazulheim or Deputy Governor, who commanded here during the absence of the Pasha, that great officer, whom we had seen a prisoner at Malta, and whose extraordinary history will hereafter be related, having, about a year since, accompanied the Captain Pasha in his return to Constantinople. We waited upon the Deputy, who received us with the utmost politeness, and in return we were honoured by him with a visit on board our ship, a very great compliment and condescension, as the government of Rhodes is accounted among the Turks an office of very considerable dignity. This visit was, as usual, preceded by a very handsome and acceptable present of sheep, wine, and fruit, which we however, as is always the practice, returned with usury. But all the great men here were not so polite as the Mazulheim. We could by no means obtain leave from the Cadi to examine some ruins situated upon a hill which overhangs the town, and which are called old Rhodes, the obstinate Turk refusing our request, though accompanied and backed by the usual mollifier, a present. But upon enquiry we found that our loss had not been great, as these ruins are no more than the remains of a Christian town or rather a fortress,[1] and the reason of our being refused by the Cadi, under whose immediate command this hill is placed, was that, as it commands the fortifications, it was deemed improper that Christians should be allowed to reconnoitre a situation, the importance of which

[1] If Charlemont is referring to what is now called Monte Smith, the ancient acropolis, there are in fact considerable monuments there now. But possibly they were hardly visible in his time.

78

was obvious.

During our abode in this island, where we remained seven days, we received every sort of politeness from the inhabitants, as well Turks as Greeks. Among other visits we were honoured by one from the Archbishop of Rhodes,[1] a very great dignitary in the Greek Church, with whose manners and conversation we were so much pleased that we took the opportunity of our residence here to see him often, and to contract some degree of intimacy with him. But politeness and affability are by no means confined to the Greeks. The Turks here are by far the most conversible of any we have yet met with. Their manners are gentle and easy, and their natural civility entirely supersedes that air of unbending superiority which usually marks these conquerors and masters of Greece. Indeed it is physically impossible that it should be otherwise. The climate of this delightful region is naturally fitted to inspire its inhabitants with every social virtue, and the fiercest of barbarians would speedily here be softened into humanity!

The influence of this genial air is immediately to be observed in the appearance of the people. The men are handsome far beyond the usual course of nature, and such women as we saw are also remarkably pretty. I say such as we saw; for this being a Turkish town, none but a few Greek females of the lowest rank are to be seen in the streets, and the more beautiful women, Greeks as well as Turks, are, as usual, shut up in the harems. Indeed we have as yet seen no city so perfectly Turkish as this, no Greek whomsoever being permitted to reside within its walls, which prohibition takes its rise, as I suppose, from its being a fortress, and esteemed by the Porte a place of the first importance. Perhaps also, as the Franks were so long in possession of Rhodes, the Porte may apprehend some attempt to regain it, and may dread a collusion, with that intent, between the Knights of Malta and their Christian brethren the Greeks. There are no remains of the ancient city, once so renowned, but the incredible numbers of beautiful altars which are everywhere to be met with in the streets, sufficiently evince its magnificence. Among these we observed one of a singular form, being double — that is to say two cylindrical altars united upon the same base. We met also with the mutilated trunk of an ancient statue, which was not so disfigured but that we could easily perceive the excellence of its workmanship. The famous Laocoön, now at Rome, was the work of Rhodian artists, and sufficiently proves that the well-known fame of this island for its productions in the elegant art of statuary was perfectly well grounded.

This is the only island we have yet seen where the people do not complain of oppression, the number of Turks who dwell here making it, as I suppose, esteemed by the Porte rather as a Turkish than as a

[1] The Archbishop was Jeremias III from Patmos.

Greek island, and the important resources drawn from it, principally in point of marine, rendering it a favoured spot; and indeed the effects of this favourable treatment are visible through the whole country. In several excursions which we made to visit the interior parts of the island, we were so struck with its beauty, both from nature and cultivation, that we doubted whether we had yet seen any island comparable to it. The environs of the city are charming beyond expression. The Greeks, who, as I have before mentioned, are not permitted to live in the town, have built their houses as near as they can adjoining to it, and, as they are very numerous, the whole eastern coast of the island, on both sides of the city, appears like one continued village of neat and well built habitations thickly interspersed in an endless grove of orange, lemon and pomegranate trees, which last beautiful plant grows here in the highest perfection, and to an amazing size. Among other villas we were conducted to one belonging to the Pasha, which is indeed perfectly delightful, the house, the Chiosks [kiosks] or summer houses, and the plantations being by far in the best Turkish taste of any we have yet seen. The taste indeed is rather formal, and somewhat in our old style of gardening; but perfection in any style is beautiful, and the novelty and extreme luxuriancy of the plantations far more than compensate for any deficiency in their arrangement.

With such a climate every vegetable must necessarily flourish! Extreme heat or cold is never felt here. Snow never falls, except upon one very high mountain towards the centre of the island, which serves as a magazine of this delicacy, so precious in all warm regions. It was now November, yet everything here was fresh and verdant. The orange, the lemon, and the citron still perfumed the air with their perpetual flowers, and, joined to the bushy pomegranate, clothed the whole region with green. Summer still seemed to dispute the sovereignty of the year, and to baffle in this her chosen retreat all the efforts of her rude antagonist. But it was a summer mild and temperate, far different from the scorching heats we had lately left behind us in Egypt. Constant sunshine gilded all around us.... In a word the fabled region of the hyperboreans seems here to be realized....

The more distant parts of the island, though not so richly cultivated as this charming coast, are however naturally fertile and beautiful, and by no means deficient in point of cultivation, especially in vineyards, which produce a very great quantity of excellent wine, an article for which Rhodes was always remarkable. There are also in these parts very extensive woods, which afford a great deal of fine timber proper for ship-building, in consequence of which there are many docks in the island, and ships of great burden are built here, many of them ships of war, Rhodes being among the most considerable of those parts of the Empire which are obliged to furnish galleys for the Turkish fleet, maintaining, for her quota, three galleys of the largest size, and concurring with Cyprus in the honourable privilege of carrying the three lanterns, in token of pre-eminence, at all times during the absence of the Captain Pasha. (The Ottoman fleet consists of galleys built at Constantinople at the immediate expense of the Grand Signor, and of others which are furnished by the maritime provinces and cities of the Empire in proportion to their abilities. Of these Rhodes furnishes three, Cyprus as many, Negripont four, Smyrna one, and Candia one, and so on. It may appear singular that the quota of this last mentioned great island should be small, but this only tends to show the comparative strength and abilities of Rhodes.) In the presence also of that commander the Pasha of Rhodes, when on duty, is always, if my information be true, second-in-command. These woods produce also pitch in great abundance, which, together with the wine, and many kinds of naval stores, is the principal commodity for exportation.

[Here Charlemont dilates on the contrast between modern Rhodes and ancient Rhodes in her prime as a naval power, and on the modern history of the island. Later he has a long note on the Colossus.]

CNIDOS

And now as I am about to deviate from my original plan by entering into a detail which will contain little more than a description of ruins, being the venerable remains of two ancient cities of very considerable note, and as I shall also take the liberty of transporting my reader from these islands which are the immediate subject of this part of my essays, to the continent of Asia Minor, I think it necessary to apologise for such transgression, assuring him that his voyage shall be as short as possible, and that my only reason for thus transgressing is my hope of contributing to his amusement by leading him into scenes of historical notoriety, which have not, that I know of, been as yet described, and one of which was now, I believe, for the first time discovered and visited.[1] The city to which I now bend my course is no other than the famous Cnidos, the favoured seat of that universally adored divinity

Quae Cnidon
Fulgentesque tenet Cycladas et Paphon
Junctis visit oloribus.[2]

the Queen of the Loves and Graces, *Regina Cnidi Paphique,* was now at length propitiated. Our sacrifices were accepted, and the goddess, who had angrily forbidden our entrance into Cyprus, kindly now interceded with the winds to conduct us imperceptibly and unknown to ourselves towards another of her favourite dwellings. Here then, in order to give the reader a more accurate idea of our course, I shall take up my Journal, of which the following pages will be little more than a transcript.

Friday, November 7th

— Having been detained by contrary winds somewhat longer than we proposed to stay at Rhodes, we this morning about 10 o'clock joyfully set sail for Athens, the final object of our voyage, and which all

---

[1] In a note here Charlemont says he is not certain whether the ruins of Cnidos had been previously described, adding 'of the other city, Halicarnassus, we are certainly the first discoverers.'

[2] 'Who holds Cnidos and the gleaming Cyclades, and visits Paphos with yoked swans' (Horace, *Odes* 3, 18, 13-15).

the beauties we met with in our way could scarcely prevent us from impatiently longing to see. The wind not being fair, we continued tacking all day between Rhodes and the mountainous rocky coast of Caria, now called by the inhabitants Carimania, this part of which was anciently named Doris. The tops of the mountains, which are extremely high, are covered with snow, and have a most wintry aspect, forming a perfect contrast to the torrid plains of Egypt, the burning sands of the desert, and those scorching heats which fourteen short days have suddenly changed into winter. We are now in sight of the island Chalcis or Chalcia.... On the opposite continent was the city of Venus, Cnidos.

Saturday, November 8th

— All last night, and the greater part of this day, we lay becalmed close under the continent. We are now surrounded with islands, having a near view of Rhodes, Scarpanto, Piscopi, Nisari, and Stanco, whose ancient names probably were Rhodes, Carpathus, Chalcis, Telos, Nesyra, and Cos. There are several others of little note, small and mostly uninhabited, which lie close along the main.

Sunday, November 9th

— Little wind all night. In the morning a breeze springing up, we opened fast the island of Stanco, sailing close to the land along the Carian coast. Being now within about three miles of the point of that promontory of Doris, which forms the southern or south eastern side of the Sinus Ceramicus, now called the gulf of Stanco, we could plainly perceive on the declivity of the mountain, walls of a great extent, and other considerable ruins, which seemed to indicate the remains of a great city. The wind not being fair for our intended course, and the situation of this place agreeing exactly with that of Cnidos, we were tempted to lower our boat, and to row ashore. Though from the ship we could perceive no harbour, as we approached the land it opened to us, and discovered a most excellent port, beautifully romantic, and formed by a peninsula which was joined to the main by a very narrow isthmus.

The first object which struck us upon our landing was a most noble theatre all of white marble, finely situated upon the side of a hill, which rises above the harbour, and commands a prospect at once extensive and beautiful. The breadth in front was 190 feet, and the depth 150. The arena measured 80 feet broad by 60 deep. We counted thirty-six steps or seats, each 13 inches high by 30 broad, all of them perfectly entire, and jointed with the nicest accuracy. One circumstance appeared to us singular, as we had observed it in no ancient theatre we had yet seen. The face of the seats is hollowed in, or worked into a concave form, for the greater convenience of sitting. This theatre has only one landing space or interval, in the centre between the lowest and the highest seats. (Such intervals are termed by Vitruvius [5, 3, 4] *Praecinctiones,* and, in another place *Itinera,* and were not only of use as passages for getting to the several parts of the theatre with more ease and convenience, but also as divisions to mark those particular ranges of seats which were allocated to the different ranks of citizens.) The form of the theatre is as well as I can judge, semicircular, and at the extremities of the curve are two doors of entrance one fronting the other.

Above this theatre, a little higher up the hill, we discovered the beautiful remains of a magnificent temple, richly ornamented, and of the Corinthian Order. Its materials are of the whitest marble, probably Parian from its purity and its grain. Several capitals and cornices finely wrought, but above all a pediment of excellent workmanship and exquisite taste, though somewhat impaired by time, clearly evinced that it had been built in the best age, and in the purest style of architecture. This was perhaps the temple of Cnidian Venus, which Praxiteles enriched with that famous statue of the goddess, universally esteemed by the ancients, his masterpiece, and the noblest effort of the art, which has rendered Cnidos renowned through the world, and brought strangers from all parts to visit it.

[Here Charlemont quotes ancient descriptions of Praxiteles' Cnidian Aphrodite. Cf. Introduction p. 10].

That this was the temple of the tutelary goddess there is some reason to presume, as well from its marked superiority in style and in magnificence to all the other ruins of this city, as from its architecture being of the Corinthian Order, which, with the Ionic, was usually appropriated to the temples of goddesses, as the Doric was to those of the gods and heroes, from which general rule Minerva was however excepted, whose male character well entitled her to the more masculine Order. Pausanias reckons three temples at Cnidos dedicated to Venus, 'the most ancient to the Dorian Venus, the second to the Acraean, and the most modern to her whom most men name the Cnidian Venus, but who is called by the Cnidians the Euploean.'[1] Now as the Corinthian is one of the more modern Greek Orders it is probable that the temple in question is that which he mentions last, in corroboration of which opinion it may be added that we could plainly make out, notwithstanding their ruinous state, several other temples some of which bore evident marks of the highest antiquity, their columns being in that very ancient style which was possibly in use before the invention of the Orders, or at least before the birth of true taste, and which we had before observed in that ruin at Delos, which is supposed to be the Temple of Apollo. Instead of being round

---

[1] '... she who gives fair sailing' (Pausanias, 1, 1, 3).

these columns are many of them polygons, and their capitals are of a singular form, ill profiled, rude in the workmanship, and apparently indicating the infancy of the art. One of these edifices I should suppose to have been that Temple of Dorian Venus, which Pausanias mentions as the most ancient of the three.

Still farther up the hill, and above these very ancient temples, are great and magnificent ruins, which from their appearance seem to be the remains of stately palaces. Many terraces still exist, supported by walls of white marble, strongly built, and of excellent masonry. Door cases also, of the most beautiful, though simple architecture, are yet standing in many places, and several columns of the Doric Order, though for the most part fallen, still remain entire. Here also we observed many subterraneous passages, the use of which it is not easy to ascertain.

We now arrived at the walls of the city, which are nobly built with stones of a vast size, excellently jointed, and in one part of them still remains a square tower tolerably entire, of strong and simple architecture, which was probably accompanied by many others at equal distances, serving as flankers to the line of fortification. Even at the very summit of the mountain great ruins are visible, which appear to be the remains of a fortress or citadel, commanding the town, and from its situation strong, and difficult to be attacked.

Having now traversed every part of the hill, and viewed, with a delight tempered by regret, the remains of this once magnificent city, we descended to the harbour, where we discovered new marks of grandeur. This port has been adorned and fortified all around with walls, excellently built with great blocks of stone, and of an immense thickness. The gate ... leading to the sea, still exists tolerably entire, has its foundations cut in the solid rock, and is a building of great strength and magnificence. We now crossed the narrow neck of land which joins the peninsula to the main, and found on this side also an excellent port, and the remains of a town, though apparently not so splendid as that on the other side. Close to the sea is a round tower of considerable dimensions, elegantly constructed of white marble. On this side also great walls surround the port, which is nearly equal in security and in capacity to that on the other side of the headland.

[Here Charlemont discusses ancient descriptions of Cnidos, and concludes as follows] :

There can, I think, be no doubt that the ruins, which we have now described, are the remains of Cnidos, as their situation in every particular, exactly corresponds with all the geographical accounts which have been left us: Cnidos ... at the extremity of that peninsula which contained the greater part of the district of Caria anciently named Doris. And indeed there was no other city upon this coast, Halicarnassus only excepted, which lay on the other side of the Sinus Ceramicus, whose ancient character could in any degree account for remains so extensive and so magnificent. Neither could there possibly be a more beautiful or more commodious situation for a great city. Its ports, as we have seen, are excellent; and besides those two which are formed by the peninsula, it possessed another, of less capacity but secure and well defended, behind that hill on which the greater part of the city was built, and which was anciently called Promontorium Triopium, now Cape Crio. Its convenience for trade must have been great, as no place could be more commodiously situated to traffic in the commodities of the Continent with all the islands, as well as with every maritime city of the Mediterranean throughout its whole extent; and this situation must also have greatly contributed to the delight, as it certainly did to the wealth, of the inhabitants, who in their parties of pleasure could every day vary their visits to innumerable great and polished nations.

The country, though mountainous, is pleasant and fertile, producing, wherever there is the slightest sprinkling of soil, the finest herbage, thickly intermixed with aromatic plants of a fragrance at once delightful and healthful. Of the climate I need not speak, having already described it at Rhodes, from whence this place is not sufficiently distant to occasion any material difference, neither could Venus have chosen any habitation more worthy of Loves and Graces; and we now returned to our ship, blessing the contrary winds, which have been chiefly instrumental in procuring us the examining such ruins as have afforded us the highest delight both as antiquarians and as lovers of arts.

COS

Monday, November 10th
— This morning, the contrary winds not permitting us to entertain
any sanguine hope of making much progress in our course towards
Athens, we stood in for Stanco, or Stanchio, as it is more usually
pronounced; anciently Cos or Coos. The present name Stanco is apparently derived from the Greek words εἰς ταν Κῶ (τὰν Doric for τὴν)
in like manner as the name by which Constantinople is now usually
called, Stambol, is supposed to be formed from εἰς τὴν πόλιν. About
eight o'clock we cast anchor in the principal harbour of the island,
which is only fit for good weather, being a deep bay entering far into
the land, but having its entrance open and unprotected. At the head of
this bay is situated the capital town, called by the name of the island.
It is small and ill built, having little in it worthy of the traveller's
notice. Its principal curiosity is a great and most beautiful tree,
planted in the midst of a square, which serves as the market place.[1]
This tree is a *platanus,* and its amazing size and beauty brought to
our recollection the wonders related of this favourite plant by the
ancient poets, orators, naturalists, and historians. Notwithstanding the
lateness of the season, and though in our northern regions it is one of
the first to cast its leaves, in this its native clime its foliage was still
unimpaired, being only tinged with an autumnal hue, and casting a
delightful, and, if we may believe the naturalists, a most salubrious
shade over the whole square, which it completely covered with its
spreading branches. The trunk measured twenty seven feet and a half
in girth, that is to say above nine feet in diameter, and the branches
spread above fifty yards, being supported at their extremities by
stone pillars; to prevent them from breaking by their own weight.
There are here but few remains of ancient magnificence, yet that this
has been formerly a place of considerable note is sufficiently evinced
by several basso relievos, which, though ill-treated by time, are of
excellent taste and workmanship, by some pretty altars, and by a
few ancient inscriptions.

[1] Choiseul-Gouffier (see Bibliography) has a fine engraving of the famous plane
tree of Cos which still survives.

I shall say little of the country, lest I should tire my reader by a repetition of florid encomium. In beauty it resembles that of Rhodes, and in point of cultivation perhaps surpasses it. The coast is fertile, highly improved, and richly planted, and the very mountains are cultivated even to the summit. The French carry on a considerable trade here, loading with raisins, which are excellent, and with pitch and timber, brought hither from the coast of Asia. These are the principal exports of the island, together with its wine, which is tolerably good, though not equal to its ancient character....

[Here Charlemont discusses ancient references to Coan wine and cites classical commentators. He quotes classical sources on the Asklepieion, but appears not to have visited it. He shows much interest in the transparent 'Coan garments' mentioned by ancient writers — 'this amorous manufacture as he calls them].

BODRUM AND HALICARNASSOS

Upon our enquiring among the inhabitants of Stanco for old marbles, as was usually our custom, we were informed that, if we crossed over to the continent we should find them in great plenty at a town and castle called Bodroumi, which lay nearly opposite to the island. This intelligence, joined to our knowledge that the situation of the great and ancient city Halicarnassus must be somewhere thereabout, determined us immediately to try the truth of the report, and setting sail about two o'clock we arrived two hours before sunset, at a small port, called Patera, formed and protected by the Cape of that name, which is at the extremity of the promontory that bounds the Sinus Ceramicus, or Gulf of Stanco, on the northern side. This port, though none of the best, we chose in preference to that of Pietromi, which lies farther within the Gulf, and is much safer and more spacious, because from this we could sail with the wind. Our first care was to dispatch our dragoman to Bodroumi, with orders that he should wait in our name on the Governor of the Castle, and lay our *firman* before him; and going ashore ourselves, we passed the evening in rambling about the country, and finished by drinking the King's health, this being his Majesty's birthday.

On the shore we found some fishermen with a singular kind of fish, which they call *tapodi,* and which I take to be the *polypus* described by Lucian in the fourth of his *Marine dialogues* [4,229]. We could readily discover the κοτυλάς or little cups, with which it fastens itself to the rocks, and fishermen told us the same stories of it for which it was anciently famous, such as changing its colour to that of the stone of which it lies, and growing again when cut, the smallest portions sprouting into an entire fish. It has many tails, and no bone in any part, not even in the head. We bought some, and eating of it, found it tolerably good, and as firm when boiled, as it was flabby when alive. They are found in great quantities on this coast, and throughout these seas, and sometimes also, as I am informed on the coast of Italy, where they are called *pulpi,* another proof of their being the polypus.

Tuesday, November 11th

— We were a little alarmed at our servant's not returning last night, but this morning soon after sunrise he arrived with a favourable answer from the Mazulheim or Governor, and with horses sufficient for us and for our attendants, the length of the way having alone occasioned his delay. About eight o'clock we set out and, travelling eastward with the Gulf on our right hand, in little more than an hour we arrived at Pietromi, a town small and ill built, inhabited principally by Turks, though with a mixture of some few Greeks. Our road was through a mountainous country, yet was it easy to perceive that the soil is naturally excellent, for wherever a sprinkling of it is found among the rocks, it produces the finest and most abundant herbage. From Pietromi we continued our journey, still keeping the Gulf in view, and bending a little to the southward, till in about two hours we came within sight of Bodroumi, which, with its Castle built upon a high promontory or peninsula, affords a most pleasing prospect. Near the town we observed several ruins, detached from each other, which upon examination appeared to be the remains of ancient sepulchres. At the distance of about a mile we were met by some servants of the Aga of the place, who complimented us in the name of their master, and mounting us upon his horses, which they had brought for the purpose, conducted us to the town, a polite attention on the part of the Turk, which may hold its place among many others recorded in these essays.

At our arrival our first care was to visit the Mazulheim, who received us most politely, and, upon our desiring his permission to enter and to inspect the Castle, immediately complied with our request, and when we intimated a wish that we should be allowed to make drawings of such antiquities as we might find, assured us that we were at full liberty so to do. We now hastened joyfully to profit of this kind permission; but upon our quitting the apartment we were stopped by the Cadi, or Chief Officer of Justice, who in all Turkish garrisons is placed as a curb, or rather spy, upon the Mazulheim, as this latter is also upon him. The sour magistrate without much ceremony forced us into his chamber, and, with a stern countenance, demanded of us how we durst presume to think of entering the Castle without his permission first obtained! We replied that having shown our *firman* to the Mazulheim, and obtained his leave, we had not supposed it necessary to ask permission of any other. 'The Mazulheim,' rejoined he angrily, 'is an old man, and easily imposed upon. Show me your *firman*, or you shall not proceed a step further.' Here a difficulty occurred. Conceiving the *firman* to be of no farther use we had left it on board; but the Cadi continuing inflexible, and deaf to all our entreaties, we were compelled for the present to defer our visit to the Castle, and to dispatch a messenger for the passport, which was now become absolutely necessary, determining in the meanwhile to pass our time in examining the environs of the town.

After about a quarter of an hour's walking we discovered, upon the rising of a hill which looks towards the sea, the magnificent

90

The Castle at Bodrum and a piece of sculpture

remains of a noble theatre. This spacious edifice is three hundred feet in front; the depth of the arena is sixty-four feet; and the height of the whole is one hundred and fifteen feet. It has thirty-six steps, or seats, of marble, hollowed in for the convenience of sitting, nearly after the same fashion as those of the theatre at Cnidos, and four passages, or *Praecinctiones,* of two feet five inches broad, and at the distance of twenty-five feet from each other. The walls of this structure are singularly built with great blocks of marble, not all of equal size, nor laid in level lines, the upper ashlar being for the most part dovetailed or let into the lower, a manner of building which, though it may be deemed deficient in point of beauty, adds, as I should conceive, greatly to the strength of the edifice, and was probably for this cause preferred. But for this, and for other singular circumstances in the structure of this theatre I must refer my reader to a drawing made upon the spot, which will give a better idea of these singularities than any words can convey.[1]

The view from hence, as from almost all ancient theatres, is extensive and beautiful. Indeed I have seldom seen any to be put in competition with it. The harbour, which is capacious and noble, bends itself into a perfect semicircle, and is bounded by hills romantic in their shape and beautiful from their verdure. From the centre between the extremities of this curve juts out a lofty peninsula on which the Castle is built, itself a noble object; and the mouth of the bay is decorated by many fine islands, at a just distance as well for beauty as for protection. The town also, though neither large nor well built, has its share in the prospect, and adds the idea of population to this romantic scene. The hill above the theatre is cut into several grots or caves, the use of which it is not easy to guess; but which may possibly have served as places of burial; and in a field below we found an altar, large in its dimensions, and enriched with figures in basso relievo in the finest taste, of exquisite workmanship, and apparently of the best age for sculpture. Not far from hence, we discovered the remains of some very considerable building, of which part of a Doric portico is still standing tolerably entire. Here also we found several inscriptions, some of which we copied on account of their singularity. Returning now to the village we found that our *firman* had been inspected, and that our dragoman had agreed with the Cadi to give him four sequins for his permission, a bargain which we immediately ratified, and, once more repaired to this almost impregnable Castle, where having fed the porter also, the gates were at length thrown open, and we entered....

The Castle has formerly belonged to the Knights of Rhodes, as appears from the crosses and coats of arms which are to be seen over

---

[1] See Appendix.

all its gates, as well as from its fortifications which are planned and constructed in a manner superior to the usual skill of Turkish engineers. But we had neither leisure nor inclination to dwell long upon the examination of its works, for our eyes were immediately attracted and fixed by several basso relievos set in the inner walls, which at the first glance we perceived to be both for taste and execution by far the finest we had ever beheld. The story represented in them is a battle with the Amazons, and they have probably been the frieze of some noble temple, though our imagination prompted us immediately to suppose that they had made a part of the renowned Mausoleum, which ennobled the city of Halicarnassus, and was ranked among the Wonders of the World, which pleasing supposition was still farther fortified by a more attentive investigation of their astonishing beauty. Delighted with this discovery we had already begun to make drawings of them, when the Adjutant of the place told us it was time to be gone, and fairly turning us out, shut the gates against us, nor could all our entreaties prevail upon this turbaned Turk to readmit us.

Provoked at this disappointment, which was still more embittered by our having been thus tantalized with a bare glance of these masterpieces of art, and by our eager desire to investigate their beauties, and in some sort to make them our own by exactly copying them, we complained of the treatment we had received of the Cadi's imposition, and of the Adjutant's insolence. The good old Governor returned for answer that the Cadi was a rogue, and the Adjutant an impertinent fellow, and assured us that, if we would stay that night, he would the next morning send his own secretary with our painter, who should sit by him till he had completed his work, advising us however, as the soldiers were all armed, principally on account of the measuring rods we had carried with us, which they foolishly imagined were meant for measuring the works, to leave those behind us, and to enter the Castle only one at a time; and this discourse he concluded by a gentle hint that a little coffee would not be disagreeable to him. Thus our negotiation ended, and we carried our point.

We now returned to our lodgings, where finding upon examination that there was a scarcity of beds, Scott and Murphy repaired to the ship, while Burton, Dalton, and I, who were less delicate in point of accommodation, determined to remain that night in the village. The remnant of the evening we passed in rambling about the environs, still discovering fresh marks of the situation of a great town, such as extensive substructions, great and well built walls, cornices, and other members of architecture, pieces of columns, and many other indications of ancient magnificence....
Wednesday, November 12th
— Early this morning Dalton went to the Castle to work at the basso relievos, while I wandered about the hills tracing the circuit of the

(above and opposite) Parts of the frieze of the Mausoleum of Halicarnassos

ancient walls, which are very extensive. The structure of these walls is fully adequate both in strength and in magnificence to the splendour of the city formerly encompassed by them. They are excellently built with very large blocks of stone, and the manner of their construction is the same with that which we had before observed at the Theatre, a mode of building from its strength peculiarly well adapted to the walls of a city. The country is mountainous and deficient in point of cultivation, yet abundant in the gifts and beauties of nature. Where it is most rocky a plentiful variety of the most fragrant aromatic herbs is produced, and wherever there is any soil it is luxuriantly fertile. Every hill affords a new and delightful prospect. The air is pleasant, dry, and wholesome. Even at this season no disagreeable cold is felt, and the summer heats are moderated by constant breezes from the sea. Immediately behind these hills there are, as we are informed, extensive valleys of the utmost fertility, abounding in all the necessaries and luxuries of life. These circumstances, together with the natural strength of the ground in point of defence, the great convenience of the situation for trade, and the excellence of the harbour, all concur to render this spot a site worthy of a great city, such as Halicarnassus was; and that here it was situated is, in my opinion, uncontrovertible....

[Here Charlemont reviews ancient descriptions of Halicarnassus and adds a note on the ancient Greek predilection for building on peninsulas.]

Cellarius indeed, erroneously in my opinion, places Halicarnassus at the inmost recess of the gulf, but the far more accurate D'Anville assigns to it the very situation of which we are now treating. But this matter is put out of all possibility of dispute by a very curious inscription which I copied in the town of Bodroumi, in which the words

$$\text{Ἁλικαρνησσὸν Ἁλικαρνασσέων,}[1]$$

so spelt, are remarkable, and serve to prove beyond all controversy that here was situated that great and renowned metropolis, the capital of Caria, which had within its walls one of the Seven Wonders of the World, the sepulchre of Mausolus, whence all mausoleums are named, built to the memory of her husband by the faithful Artemisia, whose pious design of eternizing her husband's name has succeeded, though the monument itself has perished, since together with the fame of the edifice the memory of Mausolus is immortalized....

[Here Charlemont quotes classical descriptions of the Mausoleum and gives, in a fuller supplementary note, his own views of the situation, citing Sir Christopher Wren's discussion of it in his Parentalia.*]*

[1] 'Halicarnessos (Ionic form) of the Halicarnassians (Doric form).

From these quotations it appears that, however stupendous this monument might have been in its magnitude, and however excellent in its architecture, it has principally obtained the honour of being ranked among the Seven Wonders from the sculptures with which it was ornamented, and this circumstance I mention with pleasure because, from the inimitable excellence of those basso relievos which we discovered and copied here, but of which our copies convey an idea faint indeed! we have reason to suppose that the world is still in possession of a portion at least of these masterpieces which have been the admiration of all antiquity; and we cannot but flatter ourselves that we have had the glory of being the discoverers of this inestimable treasure. A pride, which even our faint and inadequate copies, to which I refer my reader, will, I doubt not, in some degree justify.

In this town was the infamous fountain Salmacis, which, according to report rendered those who drank of it soft and effeminate, though Strabo [14, 2, 16] judiciously remarks that this effect did not proceed from the quality of the water, but from the wealth and consequent luxury of those who lived near it.

[Here Charlemont quotes 'the first legible words' of 'a curious inscription which he copied at Bodrum:

ὁ Ἁλικαρνασσέων καὶ Σαλμακιτέων

and argues that the second name was taken from the fountain of Salmacis by barbarians, quoting Vitruvius, 2, 8, 12. Later he reviews further classical information about Halicarnassus].

But be this as it may, it was happy for us that the waters of this country are not now indued with any vicious quality, for, as we could procure no wine here, we were obliged to drink water, and should consequently have felt its pernicious effects. There is no wine made in this neighbourhood, though anciently, as we know from Athenaeus [1, 32] the wines of Halicarnassus were remarkable for their salutary effects.... Matters however in this particular are now altered for the worse, and we should have drunk nothing but water if a French captain, whose vessel lay in the harbour, had not sent us a little wine, which, though very bad, was however acceptable. The French send a few ships hither — indeed where do they not send them? — to be laden with timber and pitch.

The town of Bodroumi is small and wretchedly built, and the inhabitants, a mixture of Turks and Greeks, are extremely poor. From the fertility however of the neighbouring country they are well provided with the necessaries of life. Their fruits in particular are excellent, and here, for the first time since I left Constantinople, I met with very well flavoured apples. The people of both denominations seem extremely addicted to jealousy, insomuch that it suffices to look steadfastly at the wife, to put the family into the utmost confusion and even to induce them to quit the house.

Having observed a very long inscription upon a stone, which formed the upright of the door belonging to a small house in the village, I set myself down to copy it, but was presently interrupted by a cobbler, the owner of the hut, who told me peremptorily that I must not sit there, for that his harem was near that door. I could not avoid smiling at the *cobbler's harem*, but the matter was of a nature too serious to admit of joking, and I found myself obliged, after much altercation, to pay a sequin in order to induce the jealous Turk to evacuate his house, which was accordingly done, the wife being brought out muffled and veiled from head to foot, and deposited in the harem of one of the cobbler's friends and neighbours. To this inscription I have already alluded and a very curious one indeed it is, no less than an ancient law of Halicarnassus. The character [lettering] is excellent and, for the most part, tolerably distinct. The language is very obscure, probably from its great antiquity, or rather perhaps from the constant obscurity of all law language. In some places also the inscription is defective, yet still I hope to be able to make out its meaning, so far as to render it one of the principal curiosities we have met with in our voyage.

The inscription, which has been more than once mentioned in this article, appears to me so very curious that I have thought it worth while to insert a copy in these essays which will be found in the next page. As it was taken down by me, who am but an indifferent copyist, and as the first copy, which was written with a lead pencil, has been somewhat obscured by time and rubbing, much latitude may be taken in endeavouring to make out its sense.[1]

Having now viewed everything worthy our examination we began to think of leaving Bodroumi, but first I returned to the Castle to take a last attentive view of those wonderful basso relievos, of which we had now made competent drawings; and quitting them with reluctance, we now set out for our ship, being conducted a nearer way over the mountains by the servants of the friendly Aga, who again accommodated us with his horses. About nine o'clock we got on board, fully satisfied with our curious excursion, which had made us acquainted, as the first discoverers, with the renowned capital of Caria, and had enriched us with drawings of the finest basso relievos, by far the most precious remains of ancient Greek taste and workmanship that our travels have, as yet, afforded us.

[1] Despite Charlemont's modesty this inscription was well copied. It is published in *The Collection of Ancient Greek Inscriptions in the British Museum* 4 1 (1916) pp. 49-54 by G. Hirschfeld, who attributes priority in copying it to Charlemont. It records a local decree about land tenure and may be dated to before 455 B.C. Charlemont offers three copies of it, one rather untidily written and two neatly transcribed, as well as a later translation on a later page.

FROM BODRUM TO CYTHNOS

a dangerous storm

Thursday November 13th
— About five this morning we set sail, and three p.m. saw ahead of us
the islands Calymna, Leros, anciently Leria, Patmos, Nicaria, anciently
Icaria, and Samos. The first of these islands was famous for honey, as
we know from Ovid [*Metamorphoses* 8, 222].

At night we got into the midst of a multitude of small rocks,
which, the weather being thick and squally, rendered this the most
dangerous night we have yet passed.... The wind blew strong and
gusty at south. The lead was constantly in the water. Three men
were placed at the head to watch the rocks, and the steersman was
all night continually repeating from them the alarming words, 'a rock,
a rock, starboard, starboard.'

Friday, November 14th
— The morning at length dispelled our fears, and we now find ourselves
among our old acquaintance, seeing the opposite sides to those we saw
before of the islands, Amorgo, Nio [Ios], Naxia, Paros, Antiparos,
Micone, Delos, and Tino. On the other side of us are Nicaria and
Samos.

Saturday, November 15th
— The wind veering, and blowing fresh against us and the sky threatening tempestuous weather, we were compelled to put into Syra. Two
vessels, alarmed as we were, took shelter also here.

Sunday, November 16th
— The weather not being yet settled we still continue here much
against our inclination. Went ashore and rambled about the island, but
found nothing new.

Monday, November 17th
— The wind growing favourable about nine this morning we set sail.
Already we had made with a fine fair gale ten leagues of our short
course, and were gaining the channel between the islands Zea [Keos]
and Thermia [Cythnos], when on a sudden the sky was overcast.
The horizon was covered with black clouds streaked with a treacher-

99

ous gleamy light. Thunder rolling all around us with its horrid growl and boding voice foretold an approaching tempest, and quick lightnings flashing from every side made the gloom more dreadful. The black waves rising in heaps with their hollow roar seemed to imitate the thunder, and, in their colour, the lowering black of the clouds.... All things conspired to assure us of a most violent and, still worse, of a contrary wind. The Captain roared out his commands. The seamen bustled. Our pilot himelf, though a Greek and well acquainted with these seas, seemed astonished. Every circumstance now concurred to warn us of our approaching danger, and to persuade us to get as soon as possible into the port of Thermia which was to the leeward, and which our Palinurus[1] assured us was perfectly secure, telling us at the same time that a violent *fortuna,* the common name in these parts for a storm, was at hand.

Changing then our course we stood in directly for the port, and with some difficulty were able to make it; but here we soon found that we had gotten from Scylla to Charybdis, for the pilot ignorant of its situation, suffered us to pass by the secure anchorage, and steered us in so close to the land, that we were within less than ten feet of being dashed against the rocks; and, this danger luckily past, we found ourselves in a situation equally perilous, being compelled to lie so near the shore, and so exposed to the sea, that it depended entirely upon the winds changing a few points to break our cables, which were none of the best, in which case we must necessarily either run ashore, or be driven against the rocks. We now endeavoured to recover that safe creek, which we had unfortunately passed, striving against the wind with our utmost efforts. But all was in vain. The gale grew stronger and stronger. A point of land alone defended us, and the slightest change of wind would infallibly deprive us of that protection, and we were compelled to lie all night in this anxious situation, depending for our safety on the constancy of the inconstant wind.

Tuesday, November 18th to Saturday 22nd

— The elements did not threaten in vain, for last night a most violent tempest at n. n.-east arose, and continued for three days without intermission.

Wednesday

— It raged with the utmost fury, the sea being so agitated even in the harbour that the Captain could not venture to lower his boat lest she should be stove to pieces, so that there was no possibility of getting ashore, and we were forced to remain on board in the utmost peril, tantalized by the sight of land within a few yards of us. The waves were driven against the rocks with such a violence that the spray flew more than a hundred feet high. We now dropped our sheet anchor,

---

[1] The pilot of Aeneas's ship in *Aeneid* 5, 833 ff.

100

and thus we lay with all our anchors and cables out, in anxious doubt of our safety, but expecting the worst, dreading every instant to part our cables, and to be dashed to atoms against those rocks upon which we would have given the world to have set our feet, and which we viewed at once with looks of fear and of desire!

Thursday November 20th

— The storm seemed to abate, and the sea being somewhat less turbulent, with much difficulty we got out our boat, and rowed ashore, experiencing a sensation of delight upon our first setting our feet upon firm ground much more easy to be conceived than expressed. As no transition can be more sudden from sickness to health, from terror to confidence, from danger to safety, so is there, I am confident no circumstance of life which affects the mind with equal pleasure to that which is afforded by the first feel of land after a long and perilous storm at sea.

CYTHNOS

This island, anciently called Cythnus, is now named Thermia from Θερμός ... on account of its hot springs, the two principal of which are in a large plain close to the harbour where our vessel lies. The ground near the springs, which is sometimes overflowed by them, is encrusted with a brownish yellow stuff, near two inches thick, and extremely hard, probably the effect of iron mines through which the waters flow and by which their heat is occasioned. They are accounted excellent for many complaints, and the inhabitants use them internally and for bathing. Nothing ancient appears about them except the remains of a brick conduit through which they have apparently flowed, as is evident from the stuff with which the channel is encrusted.

We now set out on foot towards the principal town of the island called also Thermia, and after having mounted by a steep ascent through craggy rocks, and paths scarcely passable by horses, for the space of two miles, we were agreeably surprised to find ourselves in a fine extensive plain, richly cultivated, and producing corn in great abundance. This plain ... extends itself over the greater part of the island, the shore alone being mountainous and rocky, in which circumstance Thermia is peculiar, almost all the other islands having mountains in their centre, between which and the sea the ground is usually level, fertile, and cultivated. The town, or rather village, is small, and prettily situated, but now nearly uninhabited, the plague having a few years since swept away the greater part of its inhabitants. The people are poor, but civilized, and extremely obliging. The Vaivode, whom we visited upon our arrival, received us with great state and ceremony in an unfurnished barn, where he sat on a little sofa, raised at one end of it, with as much pride as a monarch on his throne. Having procured horses we traversed the plain to the opposite coast of the island, which is about three miles distant from the town, in search of a ruined city, which Tournefort calls Hebreocastro and of the magnificence of which he speaks largely. But of all ruins these best deserve the name, consisting of nothing but a few square stones, which seem to have been part of an ancient castle. Near these stones, however, we found a half sarcophagus, which we caused to be uncovered. It is very entire and adorned with basso relievos of tolerable workmanship and is a good style of sculpture. This city from its name must have been built in the time of the Greek Empire, and has been inhabited by Jews.

The Thermians, notwithstanding their present poverty, the effect I suppose of the plague abovementioned, are not without manufactures, having abundance of the best silk, and of cotton, which they work into a sort of yellow gauze, extremely pretty, and used by the women for veils. The island abounds in barley, wine, honey, wax, and wool and partridge are so plenty here that the neighbouring islands are furnished from hence at the cheapest rate with that sort of game. The circuit of Thermia is about forty miles, and its inhabitants are said to amount to four thousand, almost all of them of the Greek Church, there being very few Turks, and scarcely any Latins among them.

The amenity of the country and the goodness of the people rendered our abode here agreeable enough to make us wish to prolong it, but the neighbourhood of Athens, and our anxious longing to visit that renowned metropolis, joined to the circumstance of our being here by compulsion, made us impatient to be gone, and the violent storm, which had raged with the utmost fury for three days, being now over, and the wind tolerably fair, on the 21st we made several attempts to get out to sea, but were prevented by the shifting of the wind, and by the inconvenient narrowness of the entrance into the harbour.

Saturday, November 22nd
— After dinner the wind growing more favourable with much difficulty, and great joy, we at length got out to sea.... The breeze, sporting with our impatience, once more shifted against us, and it was not till after the efforts of several hours that we gained the channel between Zia and Thermia, when, a favourable gale springing up, we scudded before it with amazing velocity, and about ten at night saw close along side of us, by the light of the moon, which shone with unusual splendour, the much longed for Promontorium Sunium, now called Cape Colonni, from the remains of the Temple of Sunian Minerva,[1] with which its summit is crowned.

A little without the Cape an island of considerable length extends itself, called by the Greeks Macronisi, and by the Franks Isola Longa. This island, which some geographers account the first in the Cyclades, reckoning from Attica, was anciently called Macris and Helena, which last name it received because here Paris first enjoyed the dear-bought fruits of his fatal theft. The island is at present desert, and so bare of soil that we can scarcely suppose it even could have been cultivated to any great advantage, which may also be inferred from its ancient name Κρανάη, *aspera* [rough]. Yet Goltzius produces two coins

---

[1] Now attributed to Poseidon.

with the legend ΕΛΕΝΙΤΩΝ. The heads of both are profiles of Venus and the reverse of one is an amphora; of the other a bat in front with its wings stretched out. From hence we may justly infer that in the prosperous days of Greece, her population was so excessive, that no spot, however barren, was left without inhabitants, and every degree of cultivation of which it was capable. This island is about five miles distant from the Attic coast. Within the cape is the small island Patrocle, called also Gaidronisa,[1] and Ebanonisi, from its abounding in ebony wood. It is still uninhabited as it was in the time of Pausanias.... We spent the greater part of the night in contemplating this interesting coast, our minds wholly absorbed in the ideas of its ancient fame and splendour, neither could we help comparing its present shadowy appearance, seen as it now was by the uncertain light of the moon, to its actual state of obscurity, bereft of the daylight of learning and civilization, and of the bright sunshine of liberty!

[1] Gaidouronisi, island of the donkey.

AEGINA AND PIRAEUS

Sunday, November 23rd
— This morning at sunrise we found ourselves opposite to the great island Aegina, now called Eiana, anciently famous for disputing the palm with the Athenians in the glorious victory of Salamis.... This country and kingdom of Aeacus is about thirty miles in circuit, twelve from the Peloponnesian coast, and five and twenty from Piraeus. In times of remote antiquity it was called Oenone, and in the last century it was made famous by the barbarity of the Venetians, who in the year 1654, landed upon it, and carried away into captivity six hundred Christian Greeks, of whom they made galley slaves. This island lies south west of Athens, and gives its name to the gulf, which was formerly called Sinus Saronicus. Close to the Attic shore, and north west of Athens lies the island Colouri, the Ancient Salamis, the famous seat of Ajax, who, according to Homer, brought from hence to the confederated fleet no less than twelve ships of war, but more especially renowned for the ever-memorable victory of Themistocles. This island is said to be about forty miles in circumference, and has two large villages upon it.

We were now at the entrance of the Piraeus, degraded by the modern name Porto Lione, and the wind failing us, were compelled to be towed in. At the entrance the remains of an ancient mole are still visible, and the foundations of a great square tower, which, though now insulated, and almost in the middle of the channel, was once probably connected with the mole, and built at its extremity, either as a fortification, or possibly as a lighthouse. (Upon farther inspection we could plainly discover the remains of a mole on each side of the channel, built in seven fathoms water and leaving the entrance about forty yards wide). On either side are considerable ruins of ancient walls, possibly of those built by Themistocles which extended from the city to the harbour, and which might have been continued all around the port, as a means of fortifying it. Yet the utter demolition of these famous walls would rather induce us to believe that these, though certainly ancient, are of a date somewhat more modern. The excellence of this harbour is fully adequate to our ideas of the city to which it belonged, and of that maritime strength, which ruled the seas, and owned the eastern world. Secure from every wind, it is capable of containing in perfect safety a considerable navy, even as ships of war are now built.

The view from hence I will not pretend to delineate, but will refer my reader to an accurate drawing made upon the spot, which will better represent it than any words of mine.[1] Neither shall I attempt to describe the ideas raised in our minds by the various objects now before us, which, adding veneration to the natural beauty of the prospect, exalted our sensations far beyond the usual effects of admiration. The sun was now past its meridian height, and, shining with unclouded brightness, gilded the truely classic scene. Hymettus, and Pentelicus, and Parnes, appeared in full view, and ... a great and cultivated plain, rich in corn, and thickly planted with olive trees. This plain, from the Piraeus to Athens is five miles in length, by about nine broad. Near the sea it consists of fine sheepwalks intermixed with corn grounds, and, as you approach the city, it is richly planted with olive trees and with vineyards. From the port to the city the foundations of Themistocles' wall are perfectly visible, and with certainty to be traced. [Over the plain] Anchesmus showed itself, and the Acropolis reared its venerable head, crowned with the lofty Parthenon, whose massive columns, even from this distance, were clearly visible by our glasses.

We now rowed ashore, rejoicing to set our feet on Attic ground, and, walking round the harbour, soon discovered the three ports, which have given Piraeus the epithet 'triple'.... The remainder of the evening we passed in farther investigation of this classical spot, still discovering new marks of ancient magnificence, such as the remains of great walls, towers, platforms wharfs etc., till, night coming on, we retired to our ship, where we impatiently waited the return of our dragoman, whom we had dispatched with our *firman* to be laid before the Governor, and of morning when we hoped to visit the renowned City of Minerva.

[In scattered supplementary notes Charlemont discusses the ancient sources of information, as well as Le Roy's observations, about the three ports of Piraeus and about the Themistoclean walls. On these last he remarks: 'In examining the walls which surround the Munychian port and the docks,... we found them to be for the most part composed of stones which had apparently been already used, and had been taken from ancient buildings, and particularly of columns split into two or sawed lengthways, than which nothing could answer more conveniently for the construction of this kind of docks, which were meant to keep ships erect when drawn ashore, and left dry or at least without water sufficient to float them....' He concludes: 'Every lover of antiquity will easily conceive the pleasure we felt from our curious discovery' (of the remains of the ancient walls and buildings so cele-

[1] See Appendix.

Piraeus with a distant view of Athens

brated in antiquity, which he claims to have been the first to make).
He then rhapsodizes on what it must have been like when the citizens
of Athens under Themistocles hastily built their walls: 'We seemed to
behold the busy multitude of Athenian citizens, of every condition,
men, women, and children, hurrying on the momentous work, with all
the alacrity and zeal of freemen who labour for their own advantage,
for their own security. Hastily, vigorously, and cheerfully they exe-
cute the task assigned them, and, sacrificing even their prejudices on
behalf of their patriotism, they seize upon the venerable remains of
sacred edifices, consecrated by the religion of their forefathers, and
demolish the still more venerated sepulchres of their ancestors to pro-
vide materials ready fashioned for the fabric upon which the safety,
and the future grandeur of their state depends.... ']

[Here Charlemont apologises for spending so much time in writing at
length about antiquities — 'a departure from those rules by which I
had bound myself,' adding 'indeed at Athens it is difficult to abstain
from this subject, to the contemplation of which every object invites.
Encompassed as I [was] ... by the venerable ruins of the most il-
lustrious of all cities — the awful antiquity of the Temple of Theseus,
the massive magnificence and towering majesty of the Parthenon, and
the other wonders of the Acropolis, the ornamented purity, and
graceful elegance of the Fane of Erectheus, the rich and elegant singu-
larity of the Choragic Monument, the celebrated and instructive
labour of the Eolian Tower,[1] the mindful vestiges of the Odeum, and
of the Theatre of Bacchus, the vast and stupendous splendour of the
Olympian Jupiter, and of the Pantheon — with such objects in my
view, and with a mind overflowing with the reflection of ages long
since past, and of events through all succeeding generations con-
secrated to fame, — the business of a former world! — how is it pos-
sible that I should refrain? Without farther apology then let me
proceed.... ']

[1] The Tower of the Winds. Charlemont explains his use of the adjective 'instructive' here as 'by determining the Greek names of the eight winds, and by ascertain-
ing the points from whence they blew, it greatly facilitates the understanding of
many passages in the Greek authors....' He also has a note, quoting Wheler, on
the Choragic Monument.

The Tower of the Winds

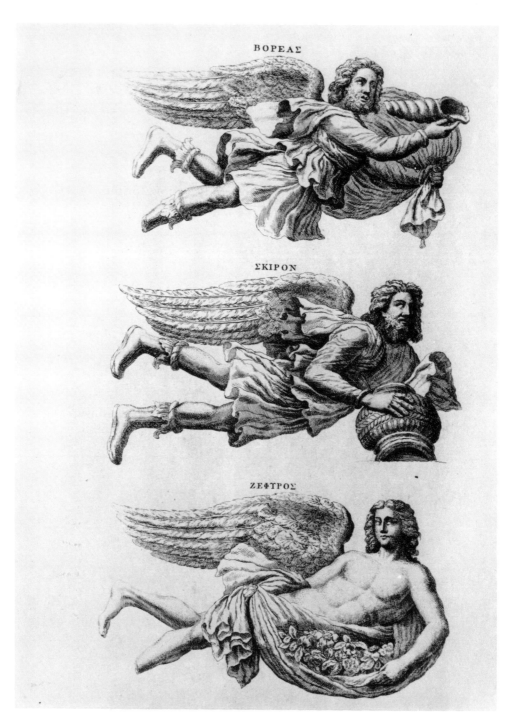

Part of the frieze of the Tower of the Winds

ATHENS

'Circumstances concerning Athens, and the Countries adjacent.'

So much has been lately written concerning the City of Athens that it might be deemed a superfluous trouble both to myself and to my readers should I attempt to give a detail of the various wonders which I have observed in that eminent object of a traveller's curiosity. I shall therefore content myself with throwing together a few remarks, which may possibly have escaped the observation of others. This venerable city,[1] together with the whole region of Attica and the adjacent countries of Eleusis and Megara, have been, as I have elsewhere mentioned, granted by the Grand Signor to his Kislar Aga, as an appanage for the maintenance of his household, and were, when I was there, governed by a slave of the Treasurer, or first slave of this emasculate monster. The city, with its district, pays him annually the sum of fifty purses, and the Treasurer receives from his Lord, as a gratuity, whatever can be made of the government over and above that sum. So that the immediate Governor, or Vaivode as he is styled, who is appointed by the Treasurer out of the number of his slaves, is continually occupied in scraping together whatever he can, in order that his master may be satisfied, and that a competency may remain for himself also. We may easily judge that, where there are so many extortioners to be glutted, the oppression must be great, and such indeed it is, uncircumscribed by law, unmitigated by feeling!

The following instance of tyrannic rapine was given to us by the French Consul,[2] who declared the fact to be true to his own certain knowledge. The year before our arrival, the late Vaivode — the Vaivode is changed every year, a new one entering into office annually in the month of March — having sent information to his master that the Greeks of Attica had lately built some additional churches, received orders from the Porte, through the powerful influence of that wretch the Kislar Aga,[3] whose sordid avarice we have already celebrated,

---

[1] In a supplementary note here Charlemont — with unusual inaccuracy — misquotes and misinterprets the inscription on the Arch of Hadrian.

[2] Etienne Leonzon, according to the *Almanach royal de 1749*.

[3] See Turkish Essay p. 181.

that all these new churches should be shut up till such time as the Greeks should consent to pay for the privilege of using them. The Vaivode accordingly sent for the keys, which could not with safety be refused, and, locking the church doors, would not suffer them to be opened till he had been gratified with a gift of twenty purses. The usual method however of extortion, and that under which the people continually groan, is the tyrannic custom of inflicting arbitrary fines, which are here styled *avanias,* this being the usual mode of punishing, or of compounding for almost every sort of crime. And here it must be allowed that the Athenians themselves are wholly to blame, and can alone accuse their own folly and natural love of litigation, for the evils which they suffer from the rapacity of their masters.

The people of Athens, as is not unusual in the provinces subdued by the Ottoman arms, have been allowed to conduct themselves according to their ancient usages, and to retain the form and the exercise of their municipal government, subject however to the control of the Turkish Vaivode, to whom, as to the last resource, an appeal lies from all inferior tribunals. The principal court of justice among the Athenian Greeks is a tribunal of judges, and, what is very remarkable, these magistrates are still dignified with the illustrious title 'Archontes,' so that it might be possible to deduce a perpetual series of the Archons of Athens from the first creation of that office with very little interruption even to the present day.

(Wheler names these magistrates *Epitropi,* and tells us that the elders of great quality are styled *Geronti* or *Archonti.* But in this he is mistaken. The magistrates are certainly called *Archonti* though perhaps in Wheler's time *Epitropi* may have been another appellation for them. Those in Thebes are styled *Archonti* and *Primati,* while the Elders are named *Geronti,* but not *Archonti.* In Thebes, however, this magistracy ... differs essentially from the Athenian. At Athens the Archonships are all hereditary whereas at Thebes they are but partly so, a few of them only belonging to the ancient families, and the remainder being annually elective by the people; so that the Theban constitution has still a greater air of freedom even than that of Athens. But Thebes also has its Vaivode, and its appeals. When we arrived at Thebes we were respectfully waited upon by a deputation from this tribunal).

The number of these judges is not fixed, but it can never exceed twelve, and the Archonship is hereditary in certain families, any of which being extinct, the remainder of the body has the power of dignifying a new family with that honour. Over these the Archbishop of Athens sits as president, holding in his hands the power of excommunication, the only punishment with which the tribunal is armed, or which it is allowed by the Turk to inflict; neither is the penalty to be deemed a slight one when we consider that it is sometimes carried so

112

far as that no person is permitted even to speak to the excommunicated party under the penalty of equal excommunication. This punishment, as we are told, is not very terrible to the Athenians; and yet it is clear that it can not be without a considerable influence from the following fact. Not long ago the assembly of the Archonti sent a memorial to the Patriarch at Constantinople, praying him to ratify by his supreme ecclesiastical authority a sentence of excommunication issued by them against any Athenian who should for the future give as a fortune with his daughter in marriage more than the sum of 2050 piastres. This sentence was accordingly ratified, and the order has been ever since religiously observed.

All causes whatsoever, civil, or criminal provided the crime be not capital, are heard and decided before this tribunal from whence it would follow that, if the people were wise enough to content themselves with their own national judicature, and to abstain from appeals, all civil power would centre among themselves, and their affairs would be regulated by laws and magistrates of their own. Justice would be properly administered, and the plague of the *avanias*, that most lamented consequence of Turkish bondage, would finally cease. A wisdom however of this sort is scarcely to be expected from any people whatsoever, as we Irishmen have long known to our cost, and consequently appeals are frequent, in the first instance to the Turkish Cadi, or Judge, who, as his reward for deciding and giving judgment, receives one tenth part of the sum in dispute, and finally from him to the Vaivode, by whom both parties are fleeced. Thus we may perceive that the power of the Archontes is, by the folly of the people, extremely limited; yet is this dignity, the highest to which an Athenian can aspire, coveted and sought with the most greedy avidity and, upon a vacancy, every possible means is made use of by the leading men to obtain it for themselves, and for their families.

For this purpose, and for that of procuring Turkish protection, by which they may be screened in their fraudulent dealings, the citizens of Athens are continually occupied; neither is there any city upon earth where faction and intrigue exert their baleful influence more perniciously to the peace of the people than in this wretched town, insomuch that it may with truth be asserted that even in the most flourishing times of the Republic the spirit of party was not more prevalent than it now is in the present deplorable dejection of the State. This similarity between the manners of the modern and ancient Athenians affords me an opportunity of mentioning some other coincidences of a like nature, such indeed as might induce us unreservedly to subscribe to the opinion and fundamental maxim laid down by the great Montesquieu,[1] that 'physical causes never

---

[1] With whom, as noted in the Introduction, Charlemont conversed on his way back from Greece and Italy.

cease to operate, and to produce their effects, notwithstanding the total subversion of every moral cause.'

Having made it my business carefully to enquire into the respecttive characters of the inhabitants of Attica, and of the several districts in its neighbourhood, I found them to be as follows. The Athenians are accounted by far the most ingenious people of Greece, endowed by nature with the most active mind, and the most subtle and penetrating wit, which great qualities, from want of education to give them their proper direction, and from a sad dereliction and perversion, not only of the rights, and consequently the morals of the subject, but of all the duties of government, have degenerated into low cunning and knavery, from whence it follows that the people of Attica are generally addicted to the most refined species of cheating, and the countrymen of Aristides are now perhaps the keenest and the most accomplished rogues upon the face of the earth. They are infinitely more polished than their neighbours, and look down upon the rest of Greece with a sort of contempt. Wheler informs us that the Athenians were in his time the most polished people among the Greeks. They still remain [so]. They are, as I have before mentioned, accounted to the greatest degree factious and intriguing, yet has this spirit its good, as well as its bad effects, being frequently seen to exert itself in defence of the community against the encroachments of tyranny, and the poor Athenians are still able, by their intrigues at the Porte, and by availing themselves of the intervention of their immediate master the Kislar Aga, whose protection they procure by dexterously playing upon his pride and his avarice, often to ruin their rapacious governor, by procuring his recall, and not unfrequently his punishment. Of these effects of their dexterity I have often heard them boast, and that they do not boast without reason appears from the authority of my friend, and immediate successor at Athens, Stewart,[1] who informs us that, during the time of his abode, the Athenians had been able, by their intrigues at Constantinople, to drive away three of their Vaivodes, and to procure their imprisonment.

The people of Attica are allowed by all to speak the purest language, and they pique themselves not a little upon this pre-eminence. The dialect of modern Greek spoken at Athens stands precisely upon the same foot of pre-eminence among the modern Greeks, as the Attic dialect did among the ancient, and a provincial accent or phrase would be as quickly discovered by the Athenian peasants of this day, as the dialect of Theophrastus was by the ancient herb woman. They seem indeed to be, all of them natural orators, and speak not only with the utmost fluency, and precision, but with a grace and manner peculiar

[1] See James Stuart (correct spelling) in Bibliography. Stuart (*DNB*) was in Athens from March 1751 to the end of 1753 see his *Antiquities* 1, vi-vii He states (*ibid.* x) that only two Vaivodes were imprisoned.

to themselves. They consequently are extremely fond of dissertation, and, when assembled at their coffee house, which, as Stewart well remarks, is situated nearly upon the same spot where formerly the Ποικίλη[1] stood, they harangue without end or measure. (Their neighbours the Thebans are reckoned the best conditioned people whatsoever. Goodnatured, honest, undesigning, but heavy and dull, remarkably brave, friendly and sociable, immoderately addicted to drinking, and votaries to Bacchus as devoutly as they could have been when he was worshipped by his countrymen).

[1] The Painted Stoa, north of the Agora. In a supplementary note Charlemont mistakenly follows Le Roy in identifying it with the Olympieion.

REMARKS ON THE PEOPLE OF MANI [1]

The Spartans still possess a great portion of the Peloponnesus, and are now called Maniotes. Their country is divided into two districts, the internal and external Maina, which taken together include the greater part of the ancient Laconia. The internal, so named from its being more distant from the Turkish settlements, and which is that portion which extends itself along the coast has never yet been subjected by the Turks, nor by any other power whatsoever. The country is by nature remarkably strong, consisting chiefly of crags and mountains, so that its hardy inhabitants have at all times been able to baffle every attempt of the invading Turks, who indeed have never thought it worth their while to send any very considerable force against them, conscious that the country, if obtained, would be an acquisition of small consequence, and not ignorant that those nations, who have least to defend, usually make the best and the most obstinate defence, and that conquests seem generally the more difficult to gain in proportion as they are less worth the gaining.

When the Venetians were masters of the Morea, some frigates were sent to demand tribute of this people, and the General of the armament landed a body of troops, which he encamped upon the seashore. The tribute demanded was rather in the nature of an acknowledgement than of tax, being only five *paras,* about four pence, annually for each family. The people desired a day's leisure to consider of the demand, and the next morning coming down in a body, each man holding in one hand his sword, and in the other a flaming torch of pine threatened to set fire to the tents, and obliged their assailants to retire, and to take refuge in their ships. The Venetians some time afterward contrived to inveigle a considerable number of the principal leaders, under the pretence of treating, into their vessels, where they were perfidiously detained, and threatened with death unless their countrymen would consent to the tribute demanded. The people, to save the lives of their friends and chieftains, seemingly acquiesced, but soon after broke through these dishonourable and futile conditions, which

---

[1]   It is not clear why Charlemont put this excursus out of place here. In a supplementary note he says that he learned from d'Anville's map of Greece that he was wrong in spelling 'Maina' as 'Mania,' as he did in his original text, adding: 'It was easy for me to make the mistake as I wrote the word merely from my ear.' The spelling has been corrected in our text. The modern form is, of course, 'Mani.'

had been ignominiously extorted by the blackest treachery.[1]

Indeed the manner of life which these Maniotes are compelled to lead must necessarily render them excellent soldiers, by inuring them to every kind of hardship. They have no towns, and but few houses, dwelling for the most part in caves and such receptacles as nature has afforded them. They are all of them seafaring men and pirates, lurking about the coasts in small vessels and armed barks or feluccas, in which they plunder every ship, of what country soever, which they can attack or board by surprise. Nay, if any vessel should be forced by stress of weather, or from any other cause, to put into their ports, they look upon such vessel as a *deodato*,[2] seize it as a legal prize, and accordingly take possession both of the ship and of her cargo. And yet this same people, though at war with all the world by sea, are perfectly innocuous, and even hospitable, to those who travel into their country by land.

The external, or more northern and inland Maina, which borders upon the Turkish settlements, has also in effect retained its freedom. The people of this district, after having for a long space bravely defended themselves against the Turks, slaughtered a multitude of their invaders, and defeated them in every conflict, wearied with continual war, and desirous of an intercourse of trade with their neighbours, were at length induced to treat with the Turks, and to promise the payment of a certain annual tribute, extremely trifling according to the original stipulation, and which is now become just what they think proper. But the principal and most remarkable article of this treaty is that it is thereby stipulated that no Turk shall ever dwell among them, that the tribute shall not be imposed or allotted by Turkish authority, nor collected by Turkish officers, but that they themselves shall levy the tax according to their own pleasure, and marching out of their country in armed bodies shall deposit the tribute in the hands of the neighbouring Agas. This ceremony they annually perform, and many of the Turks have assured me that it would be much better for them if the Maniotes paid no tribute at all, for these formidable paymasters, in their route through the country, and in their way home, rob and steal to such an amount that they do much more than repay themselves, making no sort of scruple to carry home with them, unpaid for, whatever cattle they can meet with, and whatever else may chance to fall in their way.

All this country of both the Mainas is divided into small districts or principalities, which frequently make war upon each other, keeping

---

[1] Charlemont adds later: 'This account I had from an old Greek who, when a boy, had been on board the Venetian fleet, and was himself a sailor in one of the frigates sent on this expedition.'

[2] 'A gift of God.'

up by this means their military spirit, and so jealous are they of their independence that when necessity obliges them to trade with their neighbours, even this office of peace, for fear of surprise is always transacted sword in hand. They are governed by their own peculiar laws, which appear to be of the true Lycurgian[1] cast, if we may be allowed to judge from one which is in force amongst them. If it is proved of a woman that she is a prostitute, the penalty is that her nose shall be cut off, and one of her ears; and this they exercise with a view, as they say, of encouraging matrimony, which their ancestors also endeavoured to encourage, though somewhat in a milder way.

In the Northern Maina there are a few small villages, yet generally the inhabitants dwell, as in the Southern, in caves and grots. The country is altogether mountainous and unproductive, scarcely affording food in return for the toil of cultivation, which want is in some measure supplied by hunting, a mode of life naturally inducing ferocity of manners; yet are the Maniotes accounted a people of the most amiable disposition, tractable though full of spirit, sensible though uneducated, hospitable (to such, I mean, as come into their country by land), and strict observers of the Greek religion. Such Mahometans as are converted to Christianity take shelter among them, and are safe under their protection. Their number are supposed to consist of about three thousand families. (From this estimate we may in some sort judge of their proportionate numbers relative to the rest of the Morea, since, exclusive of this people, the whole peninsula is supposed to contain not more than six thousand families. But, under every disadvantage, liberty may possibly render this country more populous than its less barren neighbourhood. All the circumstances, related in the text, respecting this people, I have collected from the best authority — from persons who had several times been in both the Mainas, and had long resided among these modern Spartans). [Three thousand families are] few indeed, but from the invincible quality of freedom, able to resist millions of slaves! Nay not only are they anxious for their own liberty, but have endeavoured, as far as in them lay, to defend the privileges even of those who wished to enslave them, when opposed to such as they deemed invaders still more barbarous. Imitating their glorious ancestors they nobly resolved to secure the Morea against the invasion of barbarians, when in the last war between the Venetians and the Turks, they offered, alone and unassisted to defend against the latter the Pass of the Isthmus; a proffer which was rejected by the infatuated Venetians, who in consequence of this refusal, and from a total want of conduct, in nine days time saw the enemy master of their country, having in that short space lost all their strong places, Corinth, Napoli de Romania, [Navplio], and Patras.

[1] Lycurgus, the Spartan lawgiver whose existence is now questioned.

118

ATTICA AND ATHENS (continued)

It would be forestalling my reader's reflection, and affronting his penetration, if I should endeavour more clearly to point out the resemblance between ancient and modern manners in these instances which I have mentioned; but I will venture to assert that, if any person more skilled than I can pretend to be in the manners of the ancient Greeks, and with more opportunity than I have had of cultivating their successors, would take the pains of travelling through Greece with a view to this curious investigation, he would find his trouble well rewarded by the most striking proofs that the modern Greeks, however superficially changed by the sad influence of their present situation, and depressed by ages of misery, still retain the great characteristical marks of that glorious people, who formerly inhabited those renowned regions. Neither can I persuade myself that the people are more changed than the countries which they inhabit, but rather am inclined to believe that the alterations in both are similar and have proceeded in the same gradation, and nearly from the same causes. Poverty, slavery, and a consequent want of cultivation, a total decay of ancient splendour and a miserable decrease of population have without doubt essentially altered the face of these once happy regions.

Yet still the characteristic marks remain, and the several districts might yet be known from ancient description. The soil of Attica is still light and stony, covered with olive trees, which still produce the principal branch of Athenian trade. The plain of Athens alone in a good year produces oil sufficient to load five small vessels, that is to say, ships of between fourscore and a hundred tons. The oil is purchased by the French and is of excellent quality when first made, but by the badness of the casks into which it is put acquires a bad taste, and is, therefore only inferior to that of Lucca.... [Attica is] rich in vineyards and abounding in flocks of sheep. Which last circumstance reminds me to mention how pleasingly we were struck, at our first landing from the Piraeus, at the pastoral elegance of the shepherds and of their sheep. Each flock was preceded by its *vir gregis*[1] with his horns richly gilded and adorned with ribands; and the shepherds were neatly dressed, each having his crook and his pipe. And here I must remark that the soil of Attica was always, even in the earliest times, more adapted to the feeding of sheep than to tillage.... [As in antiquity, too,] Attica still suffers from the want of water, nor does it now possess, any more than it formerly did, either lakes, or copious springs or rivers constantly flowing.... The Eridanus and the Ilissos are dry in

[1] 'Man of the flock,' i.e. the ram that led the flock.

summer, and wells alone supply the inhabitants with water. Pentelicus still possesses its quarries, though its precious marbles are no longer piled into elegant magnificence by the skilful architect, nor animated by the Promethean hand of the sculptor; and the honey of Hymettus still retains its ancient pre-eminence, superior in excellence even to that of Hybla, of a fragrance scarcely to be imagined, produced in amazing quantities, and so much in repute that the imperial Seraglio is from hence only supplied, and the luxurious Monarch of the Eastern World counts it among his choicest dainties.

[Here Charlemont quotes ancient testimonies to the excellence of Hymettan honey and adds: '... whereas I exceedingly dislike that which is produced in our western regions, the taste of the Hymettian appeared to me so very different that I daily eat it with the greatest pleasure, and found it far superior in fragrance even to the Sicilian, which however I could also eat without disgust. The reason of this superior fragrance I suppose to be the quantity and surprising sweetness of the aromatic herbs with which the mountain is covered and perfumed'].

The plains of Eleusis are still as much favoured by Ceres as ever they were, and from this small district a surprising quantity of corn is annually imported into France. Boeotia is still remarkable for the fertility and depth of its soil, producing amazing numbers of black cattle, and the plains of Lebadia are perhaps the most fruitful in the world, those of Lombardy not excepted.

The face of these countries might certainly, by wealth and population, be infinitely adorned, and is now far different from what it was when its natural beauties were heightened by every embellishment of art. Their produce might be increased a hundred fold. Yet still, under their disadvantages, they have not lost the gifts of nature. Why then should not the inhabitants retain their native genius? Want of cultivation in the one, and want of education, with a thousand perverse causes, in the other, will certainly disguise and deform, but cannot obliterate the natural characters of either.

Yet to return to Athens. This for a modern Greek town is by no means inconsiderable, as it contains two thousand houses, to which allowing five persons per house, the number of inhabitants will be ten thousand, which agrees exactly with Wheler's account, and shows that the population has not decreased for these last hundred years, though the people complain that they have been lately more harassed than heretofore by the exactions of their Vaivodes, and that within less than a century the city and its district have been greatly impoverished. But such complaints are usual in the countries circumstanced like this, and the present moment is always depreciated by the unhappy, and too commonly indeed by the happy also.

The Philopappos Monument

Upon walking around the town we judged it to be about three English miles in circumference, but the houses are thinly scattered, and have most of them gardens. There are few Latins in this city, and only one Catholic monastery, belonging to the Capuchins. The inhabitants principally consist of Turks and of Greeks, who, forgetting all animosity, live together like brethren. The Turks have some mosques and the Greeks many churches, and, in and about the city, monasteries without number. This city, formerly a seminary for the whole world, has now but two free schools,[1] founded by an Athenian merchant of Venice, who allows to each of the masters 150 piastres annually; neither are these schools by any means well supplied with students, a defect which may in a great measure proceed from the fault of the masters, who appeared to me profoundly ignorant.

Yet all here are not so. We had the good fortune to get acquainted with a personage of a very different stamp, Father Paeseus, Abbot of St. Cyrianee, [Kaisariani] a monastery upon Mount Hymettus. This person, who is a native of Ithaca, and has received his education at Venice, is a man of considerable erudition, well skilled in Latin learning and a perfect master of the ancient Greek. (The Abbots of this monastery seem at all times to have been remarkable for their learning, for which qualification Wheler celebrates Ezechiel the Abbot of his time). From Father Paeseus we had the pleasure to hear that the country of Ulysses is at this day in a great measure free, though tributary to the Venetians. The people of Ithaca govern themselves by their own laws, having no governor from Venice. They will not suffer the Venetians to fortify the Castle, lest it should be a curb upon their liberty. [As to his knowledge of Latin] this among the Greeks is alone accounted erudition, and the man only knowing in the ancient Greek would by no means, in their opinion, be accounted a learned man no more than we should allow the title of scholar to a person only versed in the language of Chaucer.

Desirous of rendering his talents useful to his country, he has converted his monastery into a sort of college, where several of the youth of Athens are educated in the most proper manner. Happening one day, in conversation with this sage of Ithaca, to mention the veneration in which Homer is held by all the learned in our parts of Europe, he answered, in a sort of rapture, that it was by no means surprising that a poet like Homer should fill with astonishment even those who could barely pick out his meanings, without being sensible of the thousandth part of his beauties. 'For,' added he, 'you must not sup-

---

[1] One was founded by Ioannis Dekas (1680-1762). The other, the Phrontisterion, was older, and one of its benefactors was Stephanos Routis, also a merchant in Venice. Father Paeseus (Paisios) taught there from 1729 to 1740. His original name was Paolos Karavios. Charlemont's name for Kaisariani may be explained by the fact that the Monastery was also known as Syriani.

The Temple then attributed to Theseus (now Hephaistos) from the south

pose that any but a native Greek can possibly understand Homer. The niceties of his language, upon which the transporting beauty of his poetry in a great measure depends, can never be understood by *foreigners*, who of consequence can never enter into his spirit, or feel him as *we* do.'

To this I answered, a little piqued at our not being allowed to understand an author whom we studied with so much pains, that I did believe we entered very thoroughly into the spirit of Homer, and his renown among us, as well as the avidity and pleasure with which he was always read, was a tolerable proof of our understanding and tasting him perfectly. 'Well,' rejoined he, 'let us come to the proof. Hear me read him, and observe the difference between the feelings of a cold scholar who labours through his author in a dead language, and the transported native who enjoys him in his own.' So saying he took a Homer out of his pocket, opened it at random, and read a page or two. But the effect it induced upon him was indeed astonishing. He seemed in ecstasy — totally enraptured. His eyes rolled, his features were changed, and in every particular he appeared like Virgil's Sibyl, full of the God!

[Here Charlemont quotes in Latin Aeneid, 6, 46-51 *in which Virgil describes the Sibyl of Cumae before she begins to prophesy: 'Neither her face nor her complexion stayed the same. Her hair became dishevelled — her breast heaves, her heart swells with frenzy, she seems taller, her utterances are no longer those of a mortal, for now she feels the divine presence of the god coming closer.']*

'And now,' said he shutting the book and endeavouring to compose himself, 'you may judge of the cause by its effects, and if *you feel* in reading Homer *as I do*, you may pretend to perceive his beauties *like me.*'

Whether there might not be some affectation in this transport I will not pretend to determine. I can only say that it appeared perfectly unaffected; and when we consider the very near affinity between the ancient and modern Greek, the one being merely, as it were, a corrupted dialect of the other, (the ancient and the modern Greek are so very like that from a very incompetent knowledge of the former, we could tolerably well, after being a little used to the manner of pronouncing, understand the latter), and at the same time take into our estimate the great advantages which may be derived from local circumstances, we may perhaps be inclined to suppose that our Ithacensian read Homer's Greek not only as a living language, but even as his native tongue, and of consequence with a degree of feeling far different from what we can pretend to. Add to this a delicacy and sensibility of nerve, which our northern climates can never produce, and perhaps my friend's enthusiastic raptures may be allowed real

The Parthenon from the east

and natural. [As to sensibility of nerve] whoever has been present at the first representation of an opera in Italy, and compares the behavior of the audience with that of our connoisseurs at the Haymarket, will easily conceive the difference between southern and northern nerves. The pit in Italy is filled with the lower sort of people, and yet even these cannot contain themselves, but, in spite of their usual veneration for their betters, and even for their Prince if present, burst out into involuntary shouts of applause, and express their ecstasy by the most vehement, and sometimes ridiculous agitations of body. With us, some few seem pleased, and perhaps are so, but the generality, if not kept awake by prattling, appear more inclined to sleep than to transport.

One thing singular I had almost forgotten to mention: the Abbot, like all the learned among the modern Greeks, read Homer's lines entirely by the accent, and yet contrived, I know not how, to make out of them a most enchanting harmony, different indeed from that which we conceive, but fully equal and perhaps superior to it. Indeed I have often since repented that I did not more particularly attend to his manner of reading in this respect, as I might possibly have gathered from it the real nature of those inflections, that were meant to be marked, or noted, by the comparatively modern invention of accents,[1] and which is at this day a difficulty under which the learned seem to labour in vain.

We experienced a very great and sad difference between the islands and the continent of Greece with regard to our intercourse with the ladies, whose conversation had hitherto made a great part of our entertainment and happiness. At Athens in particular, whether from an imitation of the Turks, or, as I am rather inclined to believe, from a more perfect retention of ancient manners, the women are very reserved. Girls are never seen till married, not even at church; and we found sometimes not a little difficulty in getting into private houses in order to copy inscriptions, on account of the women, whose apartment was sacred. They are seldom met in the streets, and go very little abroad. This difference, however, I believe subsisted even from the most ancient ages, and the islanders were, as well as I can recollect, at all times much less reserved than the ladies of the continent.

Yet notwithstanding this reserve, the Athenian ladies are by no means safe either in their persons or reputation, and the particulars just now mentioned remind me of a shocking circumstance which I had forgotten to insert in its proper place. A mode by which government extorts money from the Greeks of Athens, far more odious and cruel than any we have yet enumerated, and particularly worthy the invention and patronage of officers who serve under the Kislar Aga.

[1] In fact they go back to ancient Greece.

126

Parts of the Parthenon frieze

Walking one day, in company with some Athenians, on the Munychian Promontory, a boat happened to pass us, which carried two prostitutes into banishment, to the island of Salamis, a punishment, it seems frequently inflicted on common strumpets. This circumstance gave rise to a conversation in which our companions bitterly inveighed against the Turkish governors for their horrid injustice and cruelty with regard to the maidens of Athens. It has happened not unfrequently, said they, that the Vaivode has privately conveyed some one of his wretched dependents into the house of some wealthy Greek, where there was a daughter of virtue and of beauty, on purpose that this wretch might be caught there by his officers, who were ordered to search the house upon an information lodged by some other of his creatures. In consequence of this detection the girl is supposed to be criminal, and is immediately seized upon, and sent to prison. The maiden in vain protests her innocence. Proofs are strong against her, and the villain, who was suborned to her ruin, confesses his own guilt, which includes hers. She has then no other means left but to claim inspection as a proof of her virginity, compelled thus to the sad necessity of injuring her modesty to secure her fame. Even this fails her, and the shocking, the humiliating, ceremony is gone through in vain. The matrons are bribed to declare her guilty, and the miserable victim is betrayed to ruin and to infamy! Nothing then remains to prevent her from being immediately sold for a slave, the usual sentence against girls of fashion who are proved to be criminal, but the purchase of her pardon by liberal gifts to the magistrate, and families are frequently ruined both in reputation and in fortune by this infamous and tyrannical practice.

Under such circumstances it is not at all strange that the people should be discontented in their present situation, which in itself is a bad one, but must appear wretched indeed if any idea of their former state should ever induce them to make the comparison. And in this respect the Athenians are far more unfortunate than the rest of the Greeks, inasmuch as they retain a stronger idea of their ancient splendour, and of consequence are more apt to repine at their present degradation. Many of them have brought tears into our eyes by asking us in the most pathetic manner whether there were not, in our more powerful and flourishing parts of Europe, some prince or people, who, reflecting on the ancient renown of Athens, and on its present wretched prostration, might be induced to seek by force of arms their deliverance from Turkish bondage. 'Is it fitting,' added they, 'that such a people as we have been, the teachers of mankind in everything that is great, noble, and useful, should be thus debased into a slavery the more abject as our tyrants are barbarians? Are there not in those happy regions from whence you come, and whither you tell us those arts, which once were ours, have repaired, some powerful protectors to be

128

met with, who, remembering what we were, and pitying what we are, will lend a hand to assist us? Indeed they seem by no means to despair of some such event; and, though we could give them but little comfort upon this subject, we thought it would be cruel entirely to destroy their hopes. Traditions of what they have been are strong among them, and their learned men are by no means unacquainted with their ancient history; but, even though such aids were wanting, the wonderful magnificence of the ruins of their city, a magnificence far superior to anything that remains of antiquity, would be fully sufficient to raise and to preserve in their minds a clear idea that they must have been, at some early period, a people of the first eminence.

... Our intercourse with the Turks was at Athens as elsewhere, attended with every circumstance of politeness. Upon our first arrival we waited upon the Vaivode, by whom we were treated with the utmost civility. We presented our *firman*, which the Vaivode received upon the back of his hands, and, bowing down his head, touched it with his forehead. It was then opened and read with the greatest solemnity, and with every mark of the most profound respect. I mention here this reception of our *firman* once for all, as, in the European and Asiatic dominions of the Grand Signor, it is always received in this manner, and with these marks of respect. When we come to Egypt we shall find it less useful, and much less respected. The *firman* is not only a passport, but an order to protect the bearer against every species of insult.

The magistrate then told us that he would cheerfully obey the sublime orders therein contained, and would protect us from all insult, at the same time assuring us that exclusive of his duty in obeying his Master's sacred commands, he should be glad to do us every service that lay in his power. As we proposed staying some time at Athens, we cultivated his acquaintance with more assiduity than we otherwise should have done, and our presents were somewhat more valuable than usual. Our first visit was made acceptable by a chased etuye of silver, some yards of fine English cloth, and a case of pistols. We had many interviews and conversations with him. One in particular in which he desired from us some account of the English Constitution and Government when his surprise at the liberty, which we enjoy, was truly characteristic and ridiculous. (We visited also the Cadi or chief judge, and were very civilly received, and were intimately acquainted with that great and important personage the Archbishop of Athens, who was remarkably kind to us.) Without any replication of presents, we were always not only politely, but kindly treated, and, upon our leaving Athens to visit some other parts of Greece, he gave us, unasked, letters of recommendation to the magistrates of those towns through which we were to pass, a politeness which was of the greatest utility to us.

Neither was his protection at Athens by any means useless, for it must be confessed that we found here come few symptoms of that Turkish spirit of extortion, of which we had heard so much, and hitherto felt so little. Nor shall we be surprised at its showing itself more particularly in this place, when we consider that the governing people receive their offices from our old acquaintance the Kislar Aga, whose currish spirit may be well supposed to descend through all his dependants. The Disdar Aga, or Governor of the Castle, the ancient Acropolis, seemed to be a slave worthy of such a master. As some of the principal ruins, particularly the Temple of Minerva, are within the walls of the Castle, his friendship was absolutely necessary to us, and of consequence we waited upon him with our *firman,* and a considerable present of cloth, pistols and coffee, thus insuring to ourselves a good reception.

Accordingly liberty was given us to enter the Castle when we pleased, to make drawings of the ruins, and to measure them at our leisure unmolested, but my poor friend Murphy who was our principal measurer, and the most minutely accurate that ever carried rule, having unfortunately taken with him too great an apparatus of rods, rules, and lines, we were, upon an information sent to the Disdar of our formidable appearance, fairly turned out notwithstanding all our boasted negotiations, under an idea that we were either engineers, who came to take a plan of the fortifications, or, which was worse and more probable, conjurers, who would make use of these strange instruments to discover hidden treasures, a notion which the Turks are very apt to entertain. In consequence of this misfortune a fresh negotiation was set on foot, more presents were exacted, nor should we at length have been able to carry our point, had it not been for the friendly interference of the Vaivode, who prevailed upon the governor to allow us admittance, limiting our measuring instruments to a ten foot rod, and a foot ruler. Again when, after having finished our designs, and our measurements, we happened to be informed of something in the Castle which we had left unseen, we could not procure our re-admittance otherwise than by a fresh present of an English gun to the greedy Disdar.

[In connexion with the Parthenon] I will relate another circumstance of a nature somewhat curious, and which I the rather mention because the fact was verified by Mr. Wood,[1] an authority respectable indeed, who made the same experiment as I did, and with the same success. In all the buildings remaining at Athens there is nothing more striking than the amazing exactness and contiguity of the joints, which are so wonderfully wrought that the edge of a knife can in no place be passed between the stones. In the Temple of Minerva having ob-

[1] See Introduction p. 3 and Bibliography.

The Parthenon from the east

served a part broken off from the building, consisting of two stones closely jointed, I endeavoured to separate them, in order to discover whether any cement had been used, and of what nature it had been. Not being able by any other means to get them asunder, I endeavoured to break them with a hammer, naturally concluding that they would separate at the joint, when to my astonishment I found that the joint remained perfectly unshaken, the stone having broken beyond it. Whether this adhesion be occasioned by the excellent quality of the cement, which has, in a course of ages, grown harder and stronger than the stone itself, or whether it proceeds from that attraction produced by the exact contiguity of the parts, probably strengthened by an exsudation from the marble, I shall not pretend to determine, though this latter cause appears to me the more probable, as little or no trace of cement was discoverable in the joint.

[As we are on the subject of the Temple of Minerva] I take this opportunity of mentioning a singular circumstance respecting this edifice. Those architects, who had been so amazingly exact in their joints, were not equally so with regard to the intercolumniations, since upon the most accurate measurement we found the columns by no means equidistant. The difference indeed was trifling, never amounting to more than two inches, which inaccuracy in so vast an edifice it was impossible for the nicest eye to distinguish. So true it is that these great masters built for the effect, rather than with that minute exactness on which we pride ourselves. This remark will also serve to show the inutility of those measurements to a hair's breadth upon which Stewart piques himself. This admirable masonry ... was also assisted, particularly in the Minerva, by cramps of copper, with which the ashlars were bound and tied together. (From the use of these cramps a very disagreeable consequence has ensued, as the superficial stones of the building have in many places been broken in order to get at, and to purloin the metal. Had it not been for this circumstance the surface of the Parthenon, where not destroyed by the infernal bomb, would probably to this day have remained perfectly entire).

The great size and massiveness of the blocks of stone used in these buildings, and the nature of the materials, which in almost all the edifices of Athens are of marble from the quarries of Hymettus and of Pentelicus, equal in beauty, whiteness, and splendour to the finest Parian, and probably superior in point of duration ..., together with the excellent quality of the air, and the dryness of the climate and of the soil, are probably the causes why the remains of this City have an appearance peculiar to themselves, possessing a freshness, and an air of newness, which, considering their great antiquity, is perfectly astonishing, every part of them, except where injured or broken by violence, appearing as if newly come from the hands of the workman. And the words of Plutarch, when in the *Life of Pericles*, [13] he is

132

The Erechtheum

speaking of these very buildings, are even at this day perfectly applicable to the state in which they still remain, and in every particular true and descriptive of their present appearance, a circumstance which, by the way, considering the remoteness of the age in which that historian lived, is somewhat extraordinary ... and even at this day the beholder, at the first glance, might with the greatest propriety break out into an exclamation exactly similar, this very circumstance of their apparent freshness being the first idea with which he must naturally be struck in viewing these wonderful edifices!

[Here Charlemont quotes and briefly discusses the famous quotation from Plutarch.]

[With regard to our attempts to survey the Acropolis] I cannot avoid mentioning that our principal enemy on these occasions was a renegado, or Christian turned Turk, who did all he could to prejudice the Disdar against us, and to inflame his avarice. Indeed it is remarkable that the greatest, and I may say the only, enemies Christians find among the Turks are those wretched renegados who with the bigoted zeal of proselytes, heightened and exasperated by their idea of the contempt and hatred in which they suppose themselves held by the sectaries of that religion which they have abandoned, and further inflamed by the base desire of getting favour from their new masters, whom they hope to persuade of the sincerity of their conversion by their inveterate animosity against all who profess the Christian faith, do everything in their power to vex, to counteract, and, as far as their little weight will permit them, to persecute their former brethren.

[Here Charlemont describes at length 'the lamentable history of Athens, from its defeat by Philip of Macedon down to the first withdrawal of the Venetians in 1715. He quotes Giannone's history of Naples on Ruggiero's invasion of Greece about A D. 1140 and corrects Robertson's misquotation of the passage in his history of the Emperor Charles V. (See Bibliography.)]

Such is the lamentable history of the renowned Athens, the favoured seat of the Muses, and, like her own Minerva, the goddess of arts and of arms! Such is the precarious and transitory tenure of sublunary grandeur! Cities, kingdoms, empires, as well as men, though the period of their existence be somewhat longer,... finally perish and fall to decay; and the huge skeleton alone demonstrates the vastness of the once tremendous giant! — What was the British Empire under the administration of William Pitt? Alas, what is it now? Dying dying — dying — and, which is worse, a prey to ignorant quacks, her only physicians, who greedy of fees, study only to make the most of their patient, without ever aiming at her cure! ... Britain! the Greece,

134

Caryatid from the Erechtheum

the Italy of latter Times! The illustrious daughter of the Ocean — the Queen of Commerce! The Patroness of Science — the Mother of Philosophy! Invincible in war — unrivalled in the arts of peace! The Arbitress of Europe! Nay more, the Asylum of Free Men, the Assertor of liberty, and the Scourge of Tyrants! Sad reverse! What is she now! She deserted her maxims. She turned to folly. She became tyrannic. She is fallen! I find in my note book the following fantastical flight on my first contemplating the ruins of Athens, which, with the assistance of a little superstition, might be exalted into *something prophetic,* and therefore only I have copied it: 'Is this the renowned Athens? How melancholy would be the reflection should we suppose, what certainly must come to pass, that in a few ages hence, London, the Carthage, the Memphis, the Athens of the present world, shall be reduced to a state like this, and travellers shall come, *perhaps from America,* to view its ruins.'

ALBANIAN GUARDS

On our journey from Athens to Corinth, Thebes, Negripont, etc., we took with us, as a protection against the robbers, who now, as in the days of Theseus, greatly infest these roads, a janissary and two Albanian guards. These last form the principal military strength of the Grecian continent, and serve in the nature of a militia, for which they are well fitted, being in every respect formed for soldiers, well made, strong and sinewy, light and alert, and accounted men of undaunted bravery. Their dress is peculiar to themselves, shorter than what is usually worn by the Greeks, well adapted to exercise or to war. Upon the side of their head they wear a whimsical kind of small hat, fastened round the hinder part of the head with a strap or riband, wrought with wire, and sometimes plated with brass.[1] The hat is of a hard substance resembling pasteboard, and sufficiently strong to resist the stroke of a backsword, but covers so small a part of the head that it cannot be of any considerable use.

These Albanese are, properly speaking, natives of Epirus, the country now called Albania, which is divided into upper and lower, taking in the whole length of Epirus, old and new, including all the *Illyricae Gentes,* and perhaps a portion of Macedonia, nearly from the confines of the present Dalmatia to the bounds of Livadia, or of Greece properly so called. In the last Venetian war these were the only troops who valiantly and efficaciously resisted the Turks, and, had they been properly encouraged and supported, might have proved still more serviceable, but the infatuated Venetians seemed rather to fear them than to wish to encourage them....

Neither ought we to wonder at the bravery of this hardy race. These were they who, under Pyrrhus,[2] made Rome tremble in the vigour of her commonwealth, and who, in modern times under the

[1] Charlemont refers here to a specimen of such a hat in his possession.

[2] King of Epirus who invaded Italy in 280 B.C.

illustrious Scanderbeg[1] far more deservedly illustrious than his name-sake the great Alexander, considering the principles under which they conquered, defied and withstood the whole power of the Ottoman empire, and that too at a period when it was in its height of strength and glory! Indeed we observed that they by no means regard the Turks with that sort of awe which is remarkable in the other Greeks. A janissary is, generally speaking, feared and honoured like a sort of demi-deity. But the case was far different here, and our two Albanians treated the janissary who accompanied us perfectly as their equal, and without the smallest degree of timid respect, not even fearing, as I have before mentioned, to celebrate in his presence by songs of triumph the victory of their gallant countrymen over those of his party. Such are the Albanese of Greece, and this account of them may be added to the instances already given to show that the inhabitants of the different districts of these renowned regions still retain, in the great outline at least, the characters of their predecessors.

What Mr Chandler, in his account of Athens, can mean by bringing the Grecian Albanian all the way from the coasts of the Caspian, I cannot well conceive. That a country situate on the western coast of the above-mentioned sea, was, so late as in the fourth century, styled Albania is most certain; but that the inhabitants should migrate from thence in order to become peasants or militia in the North of Greece, and even in the neighbourhood of Athens, seems to me somewhat extraordinary, especially when we consider that this Albania has long since lost its name, and is now probably contained in the great province of Chirvan. The truth is that the present Albanians are, for the most part, Epirotes, the ancient Epirus extending to within the distance of not more than forty leagues from the city of Athens, though it be very probable that the denomination may be extended to the natives of some other northern parts of Greece. Neither is the name Albania and Albanese, now given to this country, and to its inhabitants, to be sought for at so great a distance as Mr. Chandler chooses to travel for it. Its derivation may be found nearly upon the spot. Anciently on the borders of Macedonia, in that part of the *Illyricae Gentes,* which is undoubtedly now included in the upper Albania, was a city called Albanopolis, capital of a district, the inhabitants of which were named *Albani.*

[1]   Albanian chieftain and national hero who temporarily liberated Albania from the Turks in 1443.

CORINTH, THE ISTHMUS, AND SICYON

[On our journey from Athens to Corinth] our accommodations were, for the most part, as bad as possible. At Eleusis the only lodging we could procure was an old, waste, uninhabited castle, where we lay upon the ground in a vast room, unfloored, and where of consequence, as it was then winter, we passed the whole night shivering with cold.

To make up for this, the next night, at Megara, we were put in a sort of oven with a chimney in it, where a great fire was made, on either side of which Burton laid his bed, and I my cloak, the only bedding I ever made use of. After I was asleep, Burton, the most chilly of mortals, recollecting the cold he had lately suffered, and determined to enjoy for this night at least, the comfort of warmth, by ill luck for me happened to find a long piece of green wood, which he seized with great joy and laid across the fire, never reflecting that the end of the log came within a few inches of my face. The billet presently took fire and the end next to me began to spit and to flame, scorching my face to such a degree that I bounced up in the greatest terror I ever in my life experienced.

I have said nothing in the text of the many remarkable and classical places which we visited in our Grecian tour, and this principally because I had nothing new to say. This route has already been described by other travellers, and particularly a considerable part of it by Wheler, to whose accuracy I can add little, and to whom I shall refer my reader, contenting myself with mentioning a few circumstances which may have escaped the observation of others, and a few reflections, which occurred to me in my journey, not because they are new, but because they are natural.

The situation of Corinth is well-known, and indeed its beauty is beyond description, neither was there ever perhaps any city so perfectly placed in point of healthfulness, strength, pleasure, and commercial convenience as the *Bimaris Corinthi Moenia*.[1] But this *Lumen*

---

[1] 'The Fortifications of Corinth on its two seas' (Horace, *Odes* 1, 7, 2-3).

Graeciae, as Cicero terms it, this eye of Greece is now darkened! The great and splendid Corinth is now reduced to [several] villages, which are included within the circuit of the ancient walls, and together make up the present town.

Some of them however are very small, consisting only of a few houses. One of the largest is entirely occupied by the Bey, who is a very great personage, commanding more than one hundred villages, if they can be thought to deserve that name, and enjoying a yearly revenue of seventy purses. By this great man, upon his return from hunting, an amusement in which we found him occupied at our first arrival, we were most politely received, and treated with the usual ceremony of coffee, perfumes, etc., obtaining with the greatest ease, his licence not only to visit the Castle, but to travel towards Thebes by a road, which was usually prohibited for reasons already assigned. We were well lodged, and kindly entertained by our Consul, whose name was Paulini, a Greek of a Venetian family.

[The houses] are well and neatly built, detached from each other, and the intermediate space is beautifully planted, and enriched with gardens of orange, lemon, and cypress trees; so that the magnificence of this proud city has now given place to the humble beauty of a lovely landscape, and nothing remains to mark its situation but the ruins of a Doric portico. Nothing can be in a worse style than this portico, which, to show the fragility of beauty, has survived all the beautiful edifices of the splendid Corinth. There are eleven columns yet standing, fluted and shaped in the same manner as those of the Parthenon, but much shorter in their proportions, being, exclusive of the capitals, not more than eighteen feet high, by six feet across at the bottom of the shaft, which gives them an altitude of three diameters only, whereas those of the Minerva are somewhat more than six diameters in height. Their capitals are out of measure clumsy and unprofiled, and the whole of their composition and workmanship would induce me to suppose that they were of very high antiquity, and previous to the birth of true taste. For, though the ancient Corinth was destroyed by Mummius, we know from Pausanias that some of its edifices yet remained in his time, one of which this might have been....[1] These columns are not of marble, but of a hard free-stone, each of them being made out of one stone. Pillars nearly of this sort are to be seen at Syracuse, and at Paestum in Calabria. The Acrocorinthus, a lofty and almost pyramidical rock, which rises abrupt from the plain, seems, as it were, a monument raised by nature to the eternal memory of the metropolis!

This ancient citadel of Corinth has been fortified by the Vene-

---

[1] Lucius Mummius, the Roman Consul, destroyed Corinth in 146 B.C. *Cf.* Pausanias, *Descrption of Greece* 2, 1 2.

tians, by whom it was accounted one of their strongest holds. Nature has made it almost inaccessible. It was the last place [to hold] out for the Venetians, and was taken by Mahomet the Second after a siege of several months. Its walls are very extensive, encompassing all the upper part of the mountain in a circuit of near two miles, and enclosing a small town with several churches and mosques, the inhabitants of the lower city having, many of them, houses here as a security for their persons and effects against the corsairs who frequently infest these parts. [Nature] has farther provided for its security by giving it a fountain of excellent water, which the driest summer has never yet been able to exhaust. This was the famous Pirene, sacred to the Muses, of which I will say no more, its name alone being sufficient to fill the mind with fantastic ideas.

To this spring, which lies deep in the rock, I descended by a very steep and dangerous passage, principally induced by my desire of copying some inscriptions which still remain on the rough stones that compose the wall, and which no traveller had hitherto observed. With much difficulty, by the light of a candle I performed my task, and the fruits of my toil were three short inscriptions which are I doubt unintelligible, but which, if ever deciphered, must, from their situation, be curious. But even though in this particular I should have lost my labour, I was amply repaid by the venerable appearance of the sacred spring, which rises at the bottom of the descent, and is surrounded by ancient walls of excellent masonry, the entrance to the water being ornamented by two Doric pilasters supporting a well-constructed pediment.

The view from the summit of this lofty cliff is wonderfully extensive, and even though it were composed of nameless vales and mountains, would be most beautifully romantic. What must it then be when aided and embellished by all the magic charms of history and of fable? The plain of Corinth, as far as Sicyon, richly cultivated, well watered, and thickly planted, lies immediately under the eye — the Isthmus, with its two seas north-east and north-west — beyond these Cithaeron, Helicon, and Parnassus covered with snow — still farther eastward, Athens, with its mountains and islands, and even the higher points of the Aegean isles — to the southward the endless mountains of the Peloponnesus rise one above the other in a thousand romantic forms. — Argolis to the east — all Achaia to the south-west, and due south the craggy cliffs of the pastoral Arcadia. Such, and much more, was their prospect. Our feelings are easier to be conceived than described!

Yet pleasing as they were how were they dashed with regret when we cast our eyes towards the site of Corinth. How painfully did the ideas of its last and total destruction crowd upon our minds, and how bitterly did we execrate the memory of the worse than gothic Mummius. The mountains which overhang the Isthmus are high, and charmingly romantic in their shape, and the Isthmus itself is so uneven and so rocky that I should conceive the attempt to cut a canal through it little better than chimerical; but that such attempts have been made is beyond all doubt, as we ourselves saw the place where this great work was begun, a part of the cut being still clearly discernible. This inequality of the ground, which often sinks into abrupt and deep gullies, must also have rendered the building of the wall across the Isthmus a work of great labour and difficulty. The vestiges of this wall are still easy to be traced, and a great portion of it is, at this day tolerably entire, which principally proceeds from its having been renewed. We could readily perceive where it had been re-paired in the time of Gallienus, and long afterward by the Palaeologi, or, as some pretend, by the Venetians when in possession of the Morea. These several repairs are plainly to be discovered by the dif-ference of the ancient and modern masonry. The ancient part is built with large blocks of stone elegantly squared and accurately jointed. The modern is ill constructed with stones unequal in size and in shape, for the most part small, and inartificially put together....

[Here Charlemont discusses classical sources on the Isthmian Walls.]

Adjoining to the wall, on the south side, within something more than a mile of the Sinus Saronicus, is an oblong building in a style of great magnificence, of two hundred yards long by one hundred in width. It is elegantly constructed in the true antique manner with great blocks of hewn stone, and has been ornamented with columns, several of which remain tolerably entire, though none of them stand-ing. This I take to have been the great stadium where the Isthmian games were celebrated, and it is probably alluded to by Pausanias, [2, 1, 7] who, in speaking of the Isthmus has these words: ... 'In that place worthy of sight is a theatre, and a stadium of white stone.' Many other buildings still remain on the Isthmus, and on the adjacent hills, but so entirely ruined that they are not worth describing, so, having now mentioned whatever had escaped the notice of former travellers, I shall conclude this imperfect sketch by observing how to-tal the destruction and desolation of Corinth under Mummius must have been, when Pausanias [2, 1, 2] assures us ... that in his time not one of the ancient Corinthians inhabited Corinth, the inhabitants being all of them Roman colonists....

[Charlemont adds a note that Corinth now exports considerable quantities of corn and olives. 'But one of its principal exportations is cheese which is accounted excellent, and is made on mount Parnassus. So that, their old trade failing, the Muses are now become dairy maids

and Apollo a cheesemonger.']

From hence we made an excursion to visit the site of Sicyon, so renowned for its antiquity that some chronologers, principally on the authority of Eusebius, have supposed it to be the most ancient monarchy, not only of Greece, but of the whole world, prior even to those of Assyria and Egypt, and indeed if decay were to be admitted as a proof of age, no place whatsoever can have better pretensions to antiquity. It is now reduced to a small village called Basilica, the name which signifies royal, being I suppose, taken from some imperfect tradition of the high antiquity of its royalty. It lies about six miles north west of Corinth, in a fine plain, richly cultivated, abounding in corn, and planted with olive trees. There is reason however to believe this was not the exact situation of the ancient Sicyon though certainly very near it, as it must have stood in this plain, which is not of great extent.... Perhaps the modern name Basilica, 'royal' may have arisen from the new appellation Demetrias. (Demetrius and his father Antigonus have been, exclusively and peculiarly, styled Kings by the Greeks who were by them restored to the freedom of their ancient constitutions.)

Probably the Acropolis of Corinth

THE ROAD FROM
CORINTH TO THEBES

From Corinth to Thebes, across the mountains, there are two roads, by one of which only, merchandise is allowed to be carried. Because upon this road, which was made by the present Grand Vizir, there is a custom house at a small town called Dervan, where a certain toll is paid to enable the Bey of Corinth to keep a patrol to defend passengers against robbers, and, where, if through the negligence or cowardice of the patrol, or from any other cause whatsoever, any robbery should be committed, the party suffering is reimbursed his loss, be it ever so great. This I mention as an instance, among many others, of the excellence of Turkish police. As we had already travelled a great part of the Vizir's road in our way from Megara to Corinth, we obtained leave from the Bey in going to Thebes to pass by the prohibited road, which, as it crosses a large tract of the Isthmus, that we had not yet seen, was to us the more curious.

... As a great part of this road has probably been untrod by any former traveller I will take up my Journal and present my reader with the following transcript:

On Monday the 8th December we set out at sunrise from Corinth on our way to Thebes, travelling along the road, which, as I have before mentioned, is at present prohibited without special licence from the Bey. This road, after traversing a part of the Isthmus on the eastern side, passing through Hexamillia, and close by the stadium already described, brought us to the coast of the Sinus Saronicus, along which we travelled for some time under the mountains, which are here covered with pines, the sea also being edged with the most beautiful evergreens of various sorts. This verdant scene, joined to the genial warmth of a bright day, made us totally forget that we were now in the midst of winter. We soon discovered, greatly to our satisfaction, that this has been the ancient road, which is evident, as well from the marks of carriages deeply impressed upon the great stones which compose it, as from some inscriptions, which, though illegible, were sufficient to vouch its antiquity. But the matter thus put out of dispute, when being obliged to coast the mountain, which here interrupts the passage, rising steep and almost perpendicular from the sea, we found a way tolerably broad and convenient cut along its rocky side, a work of great labour and enterprise, far above the genius or ability of the modern inhabitants. A solid foundation also is made to prevent the danger of the rocks falling in, by the substruction of a wall of considerable thickness, built up the face of the mountain with great stones well squared and jointed in the true antique style. In some places, where this substruction has given way, the precipice is horrid, and not to be passed without giddiness and terror. In nine hours we arrived again at Megara, from which place we had set out for Corinth, the distance being nearly the same by this road as by that through Dervan, which we had before travelled, and which is the usual route of travellers....

Tuesday the 9th

— Getting on horseback before daybreak, in half an hour we crossed the cultivated plain of Megara, and arrived at the mountain now called Cundora, part of that chain which was anciently famous by the name Cithaeron.... This pass of the mountain, the only one practicable, is wild, rocky, steep, and romantic, but the road is good, and perfectly safe from everything but robbers, with which it is much infested. Here our Albanian guards fired their muskets and raised a song of triumph, which was soon succeeded by a mournful ditty, in commemoration, as they told us, of a bloody action between a party of their countrymen and a part of the Turkish army, which being then on its march to the Morea against the Venetians, was here surprised by an ambuscade of one hundred Albanians, who, lying in ambush at this pass, and suffering the main body of the army to march by them, attacked the rear guard, consisting of a thousand men, and cut them all to pieces. After which exploit, they made a hasty march through passages of the mountain known only to themselves, got before the Turks, and appearing at the gates of Corinth, offered to re-inforce the garrison, where being denied admittance, they turned robbers, and kept the hills for some time, making predatory incursions upon friends and enemies, till at length, after the total expulsion of the Venetians, they were by degrees cut off by the Ottoman troops.

These mountains are not very high, but beautifully romantic, and, even at this season, perfectly verdant, being covered with pines, firs, hollies, and many other kinds of evergreens, among which the arbutus is remarkably conspicuous. After a passage of three hours and a half we arrived at Cundora, an inconsiderable village from whence the mountain takes its name, situated on the declivity over a small plain on all sides surrounded with mountains. The plain however is fruitful, being covered with sheep, excepting only a few spots which are cultivated with corn. Beyond this short interval of flat ground rises another ridge of mountains, much higher than those we have already passed, but the passage through them, though steep, is safe and tolerably easy. In this pass on the right hand we observed a steep round hill, detached from the mountain, the top of which was surrounded with ancient walls, well, strongly, and artificially built with great blocks of hewn stone, after the manner of a fortress meant to command the pass, to which its almost inaccessible situation was well adapted. This, according to the situation assigned to that place by de Lisle, I should take to be Eleutherae, which in early times, and before the Athenians had extended their dominions, divided Attica from Boeotia, and of which Pausanias [1, 38, 8-9] speaks in these words: 'Of Eleutherae, both the walls and some vestiges of the houses yet remain, from whence it is manifest that the city was built a little above the plain near Cithaeron.' But, as the situation here described does not exactly correspond with that of the ruins in question, and as Pausanias tells us that even in his time Ἐρείπια, vestiges, of Eleutherae only remained, I should rather be inclined to suppose this to be the fortress Οἰνόη, Oenoe, which Thucydides [2, 18, 1] mentions as a fort belonging to the Athenians on the borders of Boeotia, which was unsuccessfully attacked by the Lacedaemonians on their march into Attica; and in this latter opinion I am the more confirmed by the similitude of the modern name, these ruins being now called Oenini Castro, the Castle Oenini. A little beyond this fortified hill we crossed a small mountain river now named Caso, but which I do not find marked by any ancient name....

Not far from hence, having now passed the summit of our passage, the mountains open, and disclose a most noble and extensive view of the plains of Boeotia stretching to a great distance, of the lakes Copais and Hylica, of several hills all renowned in story, and of the lofty mountains of Euboea, which bound to the north-east our classical prospect. A little to the westwards, on the declivity of the hill whence the plain begins, is the site of Plataea, famous for the victory of Pausanias and Aristides over the Persians commanded by Mardonius. Having now employed seven hours in passing the mountains, we descended into a most delightful plain, which fulfills all our expectations, and even surpasses the ideas we formed of the celebrated plains of Boeotia. Watered by a thousand rivulets, which descend from the mountains, and covered, excepting only where cornfields and vineyards are beautifully interspersed, with innumerable herds of cattle whose size and condition speak the fertility of the soil, ornamenting the luxuriant verdure by which they are pampered, thick set with villages, and varied with verdant hills and lucid lakes, I know of no country that can dispute with this in the rich gifts of bounteous nature. Neither does its beauty need the striking contrast of the rocky mountains we have now passed. It would appear eminently beautiful even in the midst of Lombardy!

146

THEBES

We now crossed the Asopus, whose waters are by no means equal to its historic fame, and in nine hours and a half from our leaving Megara, arrived at Thebes, which, though built on a hill, is so surrounded by rising ground that it was not visible till we were close upon it. There being no English Consul resident here, we went, as usual, to the house of the French Consul, who being from home, we were politely received, and hospitably entertained by his dragoman to whom, during his absence, he had left the care of his house.

We are now at Thebes, celebrated in history and in fable! Famous for having been the birthplace of two gods, Hercules and Bacchus, but still more justly renowned for having given birth to Pindar and to Epaminondas! Some geographers pretend to doubt whether this be really the site of ancient Thebes, and place its true situation more to the westward in the province now called Livadia, where there are yet to be seen a few inconsiderable ruins. But the following circumstances are, in my opinion, fully sufficient to ascertain to this spot the honour to which it aspires. Its situation with regard to the lakes and to the mountains is exactly that which is described by the ancient geographers, and the eminence on which it is placed appears perfectly fitted for the site of a fortified city. It is just two leagues from the smaller lake, that of Hylica, and somewhat farther from Copais, which lies north-west of the town. The Ismenus is still to be traced in a deep channel close to the walls, though at present it be almost dry, and on the other side of the hill is a small stream which we suppose to be Dirce. The course also of the Asopus, which we crossed in the plain, exactly corresponds to what we read of its situation respecting Thebes. No town can be better supplied with water, rivulets flowing through all the streets, and this water is conveyed through conduits encrusted with cement after the true antique manner, certainly from a great distance, though from whence it is not known, but with a labour far transcending the abilities of the modern inhabitants.

There are however two aqueducts yet to be seen, which I believe to be modern, or at the least not of very high antiquity, but the small quantity of water conveyed by them will be no means account for the ample supply with which this city is furnished, and which can only be derived from the ancient conduits through which rivers of the most excellent water are constantly flowing. The streams that flow through the streets collected together are amply sufficient to work several watermills situated in the neighbourhood of the city.

Part of the walls still remain of a construction which vouches their antiquity, together with two gates, both of them undoubtedly ancient. The one is arched, and considerable in its dimensions. The other is smaller, but of excellent workmanship, in style resembling the more ancient architecture of Delos. The inhabitants also have a tradition current among them that their town has been remarkable for a certain number of gates, which they mistaking for five, call it Pentapyli. Numberless ancient marbles bespeak the site of a magnificent city. Broken columns, capitals, and ancient inscriptions are everywhere to be met with. The impression made by the destruction of Thebes under Alexander is not yet effaced. The inhabitants still traditionally speak of it, telling a silly story of this Prince, who, as they pretend, caused the vanquished Thebans to be collected together in a small village about one hundred yards from the town, and there to be consumed by fire, from which supposed event the village is at this day called Pyra. They show the mounds of earth which were raised by Alexander for the assault, three of which, say they, were raised in one night; and indeed some traces evidently remain of this memorable siege, trenches and other marks of attack being clearly discernible on every side of the town.

Another whimsical tradition is current among the Thebans. They tell you that Alexander, in order that no trace should remain of Thebes, after demolishing that city, caused the stones, with which it had been built, to be transported by his soldiers to the sea. This however could scarcely have been accomplished unless Alexander had had in his army such a harper as Amphion.[1] All ... indications put together seem to amount nearly to a demonstration that this is the situation of Thebes, though now, as in the time of Pausanias, the modern city seems to be confined within the limits of the ancient Cadmea, the hill, on which it is built, being apparently the site of that fortress, while the city of which there are but few remains, extended itself to a considerable distance in the bottom.

The present town is but a poor one, and must have declined since

[Here Charlemont cites Fazio degli Uberti (see Bibliography) to prove that the name of Thebes was Steeve (εἰς Θήβας) in 1360, and adds 'it is not easy by ear exactly to ascertain how the modern Greek names might be written'.]

[1] Legendary king of Thebes who by his magical music caused stones to come together to build the walls.

148

the time of Wheler, who informs us that it is 'close built, better fashioned, and higher than is usual in that country,' and adds that 'it contains between three and four thousand souls.' Its circuit, as in his time, is about three small miles, but within this inclosure not more than half the ground is built upon, and the inhabitants amount to two thousand only, of which about one fourth part are Turks. The Greeks at Thebes, like those at Athens, have their Archonti, whom they also style Primati. This dignity is partly hereditary in the principal families, and partly conferred at the pleasure of the people, who annually elect a certain number of these magistrates. A deputation from this respectable body civilly waited upon us at our arrival, and offered us every service in their power. The city and its districts is however governed by a Turkish Vaivode, by whom, as chief magistrate, all causes are finally decided. The Thebans are accounted the best-conditioned people of Greece, and indeed we found them so. They are sociable and polite, lovers of feasting, and not a little addicted to drunkenness, holding their countryman and tutelar divinity, Bacchus, in as high estimation as ever they did. Indeed he might have afforded them better wine, but such as it is, they drink it plentifully. I doubt not however but that their wine would be excellent, as the climate is fine and the soil incomparable, were it not for the quantity of resin which they put into it, in order, as they say, to make it keep — a custom which prevails at Athens also, and in every part of this continent. Whether from the above-mentioned propensity, or from the influence of the climate, which may be rendered heavy by the nature of their moist and fertile soil, I will not pretend to determine, but the Thebans of this day, as formerly, are accounted by their neighbours, though brave and honest, the least sprightly among the Greeks....

EUBOEA — AND RETURN
TO ATHENS

Quitting now the seven-gated city of Cadmus where our reception and entertainment had been worthy of its ancient character (if not in magnificence, in what is far preferable, in cordial hospitality) at half past twelve on the 11th we set out on our way towards Negripont. For somewhat more than four leagues the plain of Thebes continues, fertile, luxuriant, watered by innumerable rivulets, and covered with numerous herds of large and pampered cattle, interrupted however in some few places by rising grounds, and verdant hills, which, though not equally rich in pasturage with the level ground, serve to diversify the scene, and to take off the dull uniformity of a long continued flat. And here, turning to the left hand we quit the plain, which runs on with little interruption to the sea coast. At this turn we had a most noble and poetic view of Parnassus and Helicon covered with snow. The former appears, from this station, very high and pointed, and the latter, which is also a mountain of considerable height, appears long and ridgy. We now climbed a very high hill from the summit of which the prospect is delightful beyond description. Over a rich and verdant champaign the city of Negripont [Chalcis] appears seated upon the Strait of the Euripus, and commanding the narrow pass of that celebrated canal, which is from hence visible in its whole extent, and which, winding beautifully, like a noble river, between the lofty and romantic mountains of Euboea on the one side, and the flat continent on the other, renders the view inexpressibly picturesque. Beyond this hill the country to the sea is perfectly level, but not so fertile as the Theban plain.

And now, after a pleasant journey of six hours, we arrived at the bridge which crosses the Euripus, where our curiosity tempted us to alight, and to spend some minutes in gazing with astonishment at the amazing rapidity of this so much celebrated current. Here we were met by a train of fine and well-accoutred horses, which had been sent for our use by the French Consul, mounted upon which we made a sort of triumphal entry into the town, all the ships in the harbour saluting us as we passed and the Consul himself receiving us at the gate, with his family and servants in their best attire, and the whole

150

factory of French merchants. By this escort we were splendidly conducted to the Consul's house, where he politely insisted that we should take up our quarters.

The city Negripont, capital of the island now best known by that name, situated upon the same spot where Chalcis anciently stood, which was also the chief town of Euboea, and gave one of its many names to that great island. The word Negripont however is the Italian denomination, the Greeks still continuing to name both the city and the island Egripos, as they did in the time of Wheler. That traveller's derivation of the Italian name seems perfectly reasonable, from εἰς τὸν Ἔγριπον.... The city is built on a small peninsula, or rather promontory, which jutting out from the island, almost meets a corresponding point of land which projects from Boeotia. The channel, that divides the island from the main, is in this place but seventy yards across, and is traversed by two bridges joining each other lengthways, the one of stone consisting of five small arches, and the other, next to the town, a drawbridge, of length barely sufficient for a galley to pass with her oars out. At the extremity of the stone bridge is a strong tower, built by the Venetians when in possession of the island, and still bearing the arms of the Republic. Upon the opposite side, on a high and steep hill, is a fortress, called Cara Bassa [Kara Baba], which, with the tower was meant to command the pass. This latter is now however almost a ruin, the sea having undermined the hill, and upwards of thirty feet of the rampart, together with the Governor's house being fallen in. Such is the extreme carelessness of the Turks, a carelessness the rather to be remarked as Negripont is accounted by them a place of the greatest importance, and one of the Keys of Greece.

The situation of this city is most noble, and highly advantageous as well for the convenience of its port as for its natural strength, improved by art as to render it almost impregnable. It was originally fortified by the Venetians, and the wonderful defence it made against Mahomet the Second sufficiently shows how very strong it must then have been. The victorious Turk repaired the works, which were however suffered to fall into decay, till not long since when the Spaniards had laid siege to Oran, upon an alarm that they meant to invade Greece, an engineer was sent from Constantinople to put this place into a posture of defence, a task which was wretchedly performed, the works being few and weak, and, what I never before saw in any fortification, daubed over with whitewash, which gives them an appearance singularly unwarlike. (We find in the very conceited and partial, though entertaining, memoirs of Baron Tott, instances of this whimsical predilection of the Turks for whitewashing their fortifications.) The suburb of Negripont is much larger, better built and more populous than the city, which is about two miles round, and where none are allowed to dwell but Turks and Jews. All without the walls is inhabited by Greeks, and a few Franks, mostly French, the whole together forming a large and populous town, the population being said to consist of no less than fifteen thousand souls of the three religions. The Turks here are accounted the worst and the proudest of any in Europe, so as that 'a Turk of Negripont' is a proverbial expression to signify the worst of that race. They have an opinion current among them that, if the Mahometan religion were to be lost and extinguished everywhere else, it would be found again here.

The Pasha of Negripont has the title of Vizir, and is a Pasha of Three Tails, his power extending beyond the island over a large district of the continent almost as far as to Thebes. This is one principal station of the Turkish fleet. Some Turkish galleys are usually stationed in one or other of the ports of this island, though more commonly on the opposite coast of Boeotia, where the harbours are excellent, and from whence the pass is immediately commanded. Negripont contributes more to the maritime strength of the Empire than any other of the islands, furnishing four galleys to the Turkish fleet, whereas Rhodes and Cyprus furnish but three each. [Consequently] the Government is accounted an office of high dignity and importance. The name of the Pasha who now presides here is Cuperli,[1] of the first, and indeed it may be said of the only noble family in the Ottoman Empire, for, as nobility among the Turks is only conferred by office, this family is accounted most noble from its having had the singular advantage of producing a surprising number of Grand Vizirs, an honour which no other race in the Empire can boast. The neighbourhood of this town, and indeed the whole island, was formerly much infested by robbers, from which inconvenience it is now however exempted by frequent and arbitrary executions, the policy of the last and present Governors having been to put to death indiscriminately all who were accused of that crime. In the town there are no remains of antiquity, but at three leagues distance to the south-eastward are some inconsiderable ruins, which mark the situation of the ancient Eretria.

The island, which next to Crete is the largest of the Archipelago, is three hundred and sixty miles in circuit. From its northern to its southern extremity it is ninety miles in length, being very long in proportion to its breadth, which however varies considerably from two or three miles to between thirty and forty. From the borders of Thessalia to within a few leagues of the extreme point of Attica it stretches itself along the Grecian continent, from which, at some very distant period, it has probably been torn by an irruption of the sea, the effect in all likelihood of an earthquake.... Its soil is naturally fertile,

---

[1] Turkish Köprülü.

and well adapted to corn, for which it was once renowned. It is now however thinly peopled, and consequently ill cultivated, the flat coast only excepted on either side of the city, which is well improved, richly planted, and thick set with neat villas. This plain, which reaches from the foot of a long chain of very high mountains, that, as in almost all the islands, occupy the central parts, to the seashore, is generally cultivated throughout its whole extent, principally with vineyards and olive groves, and produces all kinds of fruit in great perfection. It also produces considerable quantities of cotton, which, together with oil, is the principal article of exportation.

The Greek inhabitants complain much of oppression, a complaint, which, if the Turks deserve the character given them by common report, may possibly be well founded, though great allowances must always be made for the murmurs of a conquered people, especially where a difference of manners and in religion prevents a coalition between the victors and the vanquished. The only ruins we met with here of any consideration were of aqueducts, and those apparently modern, having probably been constructed under the dominion of the Venetians, but which however from their number and neighbourhood to the city serve to mark its extent, population, and importance, when governed by its first modern masters.

Soon after the year 1204, that period so disgraceful to Christianity, when the princes and potentates of the west, who had leagued themselves under the speciously pious pretence of rescuing the Holy Sepulchre from the hands of the infidels, assaulted, took, and barbarously plundered the first of Christian cities, the Venetians got possession of this island, which, in the shameful partition made of the usurped Empire, fell to their share, together with the greater part of the Aegean isles, the more inconsiderable of which, to avoid the expense of guarding them, they granted to the subordinate dominion and protection of some of their principal nobles, reserving however this, and some other of the more important islands, to themselves, and to their own immediate jurisdiction. Neither, when, in the year 1261, the Greek Emperor had regained his capital by the final expulsion of the Latins, whose shattered remains fled, and saved themselves in this very island, did the Venetians yet resign their usurpation, but kept by force the territory they had gained in spite of the feeble efforts of the decaying Empire. As soon however as the Turks had possessed themselves of the great Metropolis of the East, they seem to have lost no time in endeavouring to reassume this important appendage of their conquest. For, in the year 1470, seventeen years after the taking of Constantinople, Mahomet the Second invaded this island with a mighty force, and laid siege to its capital, 'not a little offended,' says the elegant Knolles, 'with harms done unto him by the Venetians, and perceiving that the Island of Euboea, now called Negriponte, was for

153

the commodious situation and strength thereof, the chief place from whence they wrought him all these wrongs, and whither they afterwards retired again, as unto a most sure place of refuge; determined with himself at once to be even with them for all, and to employ his whole forces both by the sea and land for the gaining of that place.'

To this incomparable historian, whose work is, in my opinion, the test of English historical style and composition, I refer my reader for an exact account of this siege so renowned both in the Venetian and Turkish histories, contenting myself with mentioning, as a proof of the great strength of this place, that it was able, notwithstanding the treachery of part of its garrison, to make a most noble defence against the whole force of the Turkish Empire, Mahomet having invested it with the most numerous army he could possibly draw together, and with a fleet of three hundred galleys; and, though disappointed in the expected relief from the Venetian Admiral, who seems upon this occasion to have been shamefully remiss, yet did the intrepid defenders still sustain the assault, making the victor dearly purchase his conquest by the loss of forty thousand of his best troops, a glorious effort, which, if we may believe the Venetian historians, the savage Mahomet, instead of applauding it, retaliated by the most barbarous acts of cruelty, one among which is so remarkably inhuman, and so sweetly told by Knolles, that I cannot avoid transcribing the passage.[1]

'The Governor's daughter, a maiden of incomparable beauty, was amongst the rest taken prisoner, and for her rare perfection, by them that took her, presented to Mahomet, as the mirror of beauty. The barbarous tyrant, greedy of so fair a prey, sought first by flattering words and fair persuasion to induce her to consent to his desire; but, when he could not so prevail, he fell into another vein, and began to show himself in his own nature, threatening her with death, torture, and force worse than death itself, if she would not otherwise yield unto his appetite. Whereunto the constant virgin — worthy eternal fame! — answered so resolutely, and so contrary to the tyrant's expectations, that he, being therewith enraged, commanded her to be presently slain.'

Others pretend that he slew her with his own hand by smiting off her head with his sabre, which though more horrid is possibly less unnatural, as an immediate impulse of passion, however brutal, is less out of nature than the horror of deliberate barbarity. The name of this virgin martyr was Anna Erizzo. From this period the Turks, notwithstanding some fruitless efforts of the Venetians to regain it, have kept possession of Negripont, which they have ever esteemed one of the most important posts in their Grecian dominions....

[1] *Generall Historie* (1687 edition) 1, 276-7: see Bibliography. This spelling and punctuation have been slightly modernized here.

But the principal curiosity belonging to Euboea is its Euripus, so renowned among philosophers ancient and modern, for the inexplicable irregularity of its tides or currents. Of this however I shall say but little, as to have made proper observations upon it would have required a much longer abode than we made in the island, and as Père Babin's accurate account of it, copied by Wheler, is in the hands of everyone. I shall therefore content myself with mentioning the particulars of its appearance at the time when I saw, and, during some hours, watched its currents.

The day when we observed it was one of its regular days, being the third of the moon. When we first arrived at the bridge it was flowing south-south-westwards or toward the Archipelago, but in about half an hour, it suddenly stopped, and remained for half a minute perfectly motionless, so as that the straws and other light bodies which floated upon its surface did not appear to stir. To this state of tranquillity presently succeeded a current opposite to the former in its direction, and it now began to flow north-north-eastward, almost in the teeth of the wind, which then blew a hard gale at north-north-west. At the beginning its motion was gentle, like the course of a common stream, but, gaining force by degrees, and increasing every moment in its rapidity, in about half an hour's space it began to rush forward with the utmost impetuosity, and with a violence greater than that of the most rapid mill-race. The current continued still apparently increasing for the space of two hours and a half, and then decreased for about the same time, when it again stopped and changed as before. This day it changed but four times, as on all its regular days, which are eighteen or nineteen in the month but on its irregular days, which are eleven in the month, it changes eleven, twelve, thirteen, and sometimes fourteen times in four or five and twenty hours, without any apparent influence from the wind. Nay, if we may credit the officer of the fort on the bridge, whom we questioned concerning his experience of its variations, it is sometimes known to change three, or even four times in an hour. But this, he informed us, seldom happens, and for the most part is accompanied by violent storms.

But, whether this report may be depended upon or not, one thing appears probable, that the variety of its changes have increased since the observations of the ancients, who concur in assuring us that it never changes above seven times in a day, whereas now it certainly varies on some days not less than fourteen times. I shall not pretend to assign any cause for a phenomenon which has puzzled all naturalists ancient and modern, yet may I venture to say that, however this particular current may exceed in the frequency and irregularity of its changes, the appearance in itself is by no means singular. The various and changeable currents in the straights of Messina are certainly of the same nature, and must be accounted for upon the same principle, whatever that may be; and perhaps, if the channel between Sicily and Italy were as narrow as this of which we now treat, the Phare[1] of Messina might possibly be in every respect a perfect Euripus. The current in the Strait of Gibraltar is perhaps still more surprising, where, if we may give credit to the well-supported opinion of Halley,[2] while the upper waters are continually rushing from the Atlantic into the Mediterranean, a current underneath flows constantly with equal force in the opposite direction, thus keeping the waters in exact balance, and preventing the Mediterranean from overflowing, as, in all appearance, it otherwise must.

[Discussion of the ancient references to the Euripus follows here.]

But, to return from this rambling digression, our entertainment at the French Consul's was sumptuous and elegant. In all our excursions we were accompanied by him, and by the principal merchants of the factory, and in every respect he endeavoured to do honour to his country by treating his English guests with the utmost kindness and hospitality.

In all our travels through Greece we met with the greatest civilities from the French Consuls, who are always natives of France, whereas our Consuls, except in some principal trading towns, are usually Greeks, appointed to that office by the Ambassador at Constantinople. Neither is the office to them inconsiderable, as it affords them protection for their persons, and gives them certain immunities in the trade. The politeness however of the French Consul at Negripont, the ancient Euboea, had wellnigh cost me my life. After having entertained us magnificently, he insisted on lending us his horses to carry us to Athens, and, as a proof of his respect, mounted me upon a young stonehorse, beautiful indeed, but vicious and ill broken. For some hours we travelled pretty quietly, till having spent much time in sauntering about the country, every part of which was highly interesting to us, night came on, and we were obliged to keep the beaten road, when, of a sudden, my courser, taking fright, furiously rushed off the road, and in spite of all I could do, ran away with me several miles into the country, which was wild and uninclosed, stopping at length at the edge of a precipice which, through the dusk, I could barely discern; and here he began to kick and to plunge with such violence, that, though I could scarcely sit him, and feared every moment his rushing down the steep, it was impossible for me to alight.

[1] Italian *Faro*, 'a lighthouse,' the local name for the Straits of Messina. See Introduction p. 3.

[2] Edmund Halley, of Halley's comet fame, who also wrote on the tides.

As soon as I was missed by my companions, they rode in search of me, but the first who discovered me was a foot guide, whom the Consul had sent to conduct us, and to bring back the horses. This wise Euboean thought at first to coax the horse by calling him fondly by his name, but, finding that fruitless, he took the much more dangerous measure of throwing stones at him, many of which hit me, and obliged me to entreat him to desist. At length one of our company, riding up to me at no small hazard, put a switch into my hand, for I had no whip, with the help of which I, with much difficulty brought my horse to reason, and recovered the road.

At our departure it was determined, in order to gratify our curiosity by a farther experience of the Euripus, that we should perform part of our journey by boat, the Consul kindly sending his horses round to meet us at our intended landing place, and to convey us from there to Athens, whither we were now returning.

December 13th

— Immediately after dinner we embarked on the Euripus. The weather was delightful, the air perfectly serene and clear, and the sun, which shone bright, gave additional beauty to the numberless beautiful villas, which lie all along the shore to the south of the City, and which, thickly planted with fine evergreens, excluded every disagreeable idea of the present wintry season. To avoid however the rapidity of the current, which was hurrying us too fast from the contemplation of this charming prospect, we kept rowing toward the Boeotian coast, and soon got into a spacious bay, about half a mile below the narrow pass, where the water was still and quiet. This bay, which is formed by a promontory opposite the Negripont, and by another headland which juts out from the continent about a mile below it, is perfectly defended from every wind, and has excellent anchorage all over it. And this is a usual station of the Turkish galleys, which lie here in perfect safety both from winds and currents. But though these are circumstances alone sufficient to recommend it, and though we were much pleased to find ourselves in still water, our pleasure was infinitely heightened, when we began to reflect that we were now in the famous Bay of Aulis, that renowned rendez-vous of the Grecian fleet destined to revenge the rape of Helen, which here remained windbound till the sacrifice of Iphigenia had rendered the gods propitious! We rowed close to the shore, but saw no ruins, nor indeed any mark of habitation, a few inconsiderable huts only excepted. Yet that this is the real situation of Aulis is placed beyond controversy by numberless ancient authorities. *[Which he cites.]*

Having now satisfied our minds with ample meditation on the reverend antiquity of this renowned harbour we set our sail, left the bay, and, having both wind and current in our favour, swiftly glided along the Boeotian coast, and soon reached our destined landing place, which is a small village called Vathy, and seated at the extremity of a capacious and well-defended bay, named by the Greeks *Megalo Vathy*, a name which has remained unaltered from the time of Strabo (9, 8). Near this is another smaller bay, which they name *Micolo [Micro] Vathy*, or little deep. The distance from hence to Negripont is accounted three leagues, and we had performed it in little more than two hours. Here our friend the Consul, who, with two of the French merchants, had kindly accompanied us in our voyage, left us with the most polite and friendly expressions of regret at our separation, and we found his servants and horses waiting to convey us the rest of our journey. The village of Vathy is beautifully situated on the edge of the bay in a fine and fertile plain, which, with a very few hills intervening, extends as far as Thebes, and is a part of the Theban plain, on the beauties of which we have before enlarged. The town is small, but clean, and decently built, and we were able to procure a tolerable lodging, where we got a good supper and slept comfortably.

December 14th

— About ten this morning we set out on the Consul's horses in our way towards Athens, and, keeping along the seaside, soon reached another bay, at the head of which we had reason to suppose, from the appearance of some ancient though inconsiderable ruins, that a city of consequence had formerly been situated. This we take to be the small remains of the ancient Delium, famous for a Temple of Apollo built upon the model of that of Delos....

[A discussion of Strabo's reference to this temple, (9, 2, 7) and of the battle at Delium, follows.]

We now crossed the Asopus not far from its mouth, and soon arrived at the foot of the mountain anciently called Parnes, being once more within the district of ancient Attica. All these borders have been rendered famous by perpetual fights between the Athenians and Boeotians, battles which, however inconsiderable in themselves, have been dignified by the valour of the combatants, and still more by the immortal pen of Thucydides. The road across the mountain is narrow and rough. The hills are steep and rocky, but the vallies are cultivated and extremely pleasant. We dined at a small village called Turchia,[1] I believe of no ancient note, and, after a journey of twelve hours, at ten o'clock arrived at Athens, extremely pleased with our delightful, though wintry excursion.

The next morning we were visited by our Athenian friends, who congratulated us upon our having escaped the perils of a road, which, from the frequency of robberies, is here accounted highly

---

[1] Presumably Koiurka, now called Aphidnai.

dangerous; but against any accident of this kind we had sufficiently defended ourselves by [the] Albanian guard, which we took with us from Athens, and by which we were constantly escorted....

[Here the narrative ends: see Introduction pp. 9-10. On subsequent pages Charlemont discusses at length a reference in Herodotus to the gods of Homer. He incorporated this material in his paper to the Royal Irish Academy in 1790. (See Bibliography.)]

INTRODUCTORY NOTE ON THE
TURKISH ESSAY

A large amount of this manuscript consists of introductions and separate essays written long after Charlemont's visit to Constantinople. These might well interest readers who wish to learn about the attitudes of an Irish nobleman in the eighteenth century towards the Turks and their history, and it is proposed to publish them in full at a later date. But our purpose here is to present the records of Charlemont's actual experiences and encounters during his travels in 1749 and not his personal — and at times highly debatable — opinions. Consequently most of these discursive 'articles,' as he calls them, have not been included here, apart from a few that are based more on what Charlemont saw for himself rather than on what he read about afterwards.

We have followed Charlemont's sequence of episodes as given in his manuscript. As he includes no dates it is not certain that this represents the chronological order. It appears — in contrast with his extensive use of his 'journals' in his Greek Essay — that he wrote few if any day-to-day records of his experiences in Constantinople.

THE TURKISH ESSAY

CONSTANTINOPLE

View of Constantinople from above Scutari

A VISIT TO THE PORTE

Soon after my arrival at Constantople the first and most pressing object of my curiosity was to visit and to examine the *Porte,* that source of Ottoman grandeur and dominion, respected by the Turks as the springhead of all power, of all majesty, from whence all mandates are issued, all dispatches dated, and which gives its name to the Court of the Grand Signor. In this place the Grand Vizir has his palace. Here he holds three times each week, on Wednesday, Friday and Saturday, the ordinary Divan, or High Court of Justice; and here are kept all the public offices of state. In a word the Porte is at Constantinople, in many respects, what Whitehall is in London. To gratify this my ardent curiosity I applied to Pisani, principal dragoman or interpreter to the English nation, and enquired of him by what means I could best visit this interesting place, and with the greatest accuracy, and most at my ease, examine everything which it contains. He advised me, in order to escape observation and consequent trouble, to disguise myself in a Greek dress, and to follow him, as one of his sub-dragomans, or attendants, on the next day when he had business to transact with some of the Ministers, at which time he would take occasion to lead me through all the different apartments, and to show me everything which was worth observing. This advice appeared reasonable. I travestied myself *à la grecque,* and followed my conductor. He first led me into a small chamber, belonging to the office of the Reis Efendi, in which was a window, looking into the great hall where the Grand Vizir was then holding Divan. This being an open court the lower end of the hall was crowded with people, but that part of it where the court sat was kept clear by means of the janissaries and other guards stationed here for that purpose, and everything was conducted with the greatest order, regularity and decency.

The hall is but an ordinary one and has nothing splendid in its appearance. At the upper end of it in a sort of alcove or semi-circular

163

recess raised by three steps above the level of the floor was placed a throne, or chair of state, in which was seated the grand Vizir. Immediately behind him stood an officer holding in his hand a large plume or whisk of feathers which he was incessantly waving about the Vizir's head in order to chase away the flies, which are at this season, the month of June, exceedingly troublesome. On either side of the Vizir stood the Tesheregi Efendi,[1] or Secretaries of the Vizirate whose business it is to receive and read aloud all memorials or petitions which are here presented. Nearly upon a line with the throne at the distance of about four paces from it on each side were placed two benches, at the upper end of which were seated two of the principal judges or magistrates of the Empire: *viz.* the Casiascher of Rumelia to the right, and the Casiascher of Anatolia to the left. These judges sit to hear the causes which are tried at this tribunal, and assist as Council to the Grand Vizir. There are six of them in all differing in their degrees of dignity though all chief judges, two of whom always sit in this court by turns. The titles of the other officers, who compose or attend the Divan will be found in the opposite page, the annexed account of them having been written and given to me by Pisani.[2]

To this high Tribunal, which is a court of appeal, people of all ranks from the highest to the lowest who think themselves aggrieved by former decisions resort for justice; and here they give in their memorials, which consist of an exact detail of their cause and of its progress through the inferior courts, all attested by the proper officers. Both parties attend, and each delivers in his memorial separately to the above-mentioned secretaries, who, having read them aloud, deliver them to the Vizir. The parties are then brought up to the foot of the throne, each between two officers; and, after a little consideration, the Vizir gives his decree, which is signified by tearing to pieces and throwing behind him the petitions which he rejects, or by delivering to one of the secretaries those of which he approves. Thus the cause is terminated, and the parties are instantly led off in the same manner as they were brought forward. If however there should be any great difficulty or nicety in the case he then consults with the judges, who sit there as his assistants, and generally decides according to their opinion. Many poor wretches also present petitions for charity, and, if their claim be approved, which is commonly the case, never go away empty-handed. The Divan sits from early in the morning till

[1] For the correct orthography of Turkish titles and for references to unannotated names see the Index.

[2] A member of a family which provided several interpreters to the British and other Missions. (One of them was involved in obtaining the firman of 1801 which allowed work to be done for Lord Elgin on the Acropolis.) Pisani's autograph memorandum to Charlemont about the officials whom he would see on his visits is preserved with his Turkish Essay.

kimdi or midday. When it is nearly at an end the crier proclaims with a loud voice that all persons should make haste to bring in their memorials as the Divan is going to break up. Soon after this proclamation the Grand Vizir rose, and broke up the court, all the people crying out aloud, in the way of acclamation, 'Long live Sultan Mahmout, and Suleiman his Vizir!'[1]

Such was the so much celebrated Divan, and such the summary method of administering justice, which to an Englishman used to the decent formalities of our courts must appear summary indeed! Here are no pleadings, no oratory, no demurrers, no writs of error. The client has not here the satisfaction of paying to hear his cause ably defended, nor the pleasure of being able to delay from term to term the doubtful sentence. But then on the other hand here also are some advantages, which, however trifling they may appear, may serve in some degree to compensate the want of the above-mentioned privileges. The loser here loses nothing but his cause, and success comes unattended by ruin. The halls in which Divans are held have always windows which look into them from the adjoining apartments, at some one of which windows it may be supposed that the Grand Signor sits unseen and listens to and superintends the trials. This however seldom or never happens, but the idea of it is pleasing to the people.

The chamber, in which I now was, belonging particularly to the secretary of the Reis Efendi, I was here presented to him, and treated with much politeness. He gave me coffee and explained to me, with the help of Pisani, the nature and particularities of the Divan so that I had already acquired an useful Turkish acquaintance.

[1]   The Grand Vizir in 1749 was Essaid Abdullah. He was deposed in January 1750.

VISITS TO TURKISH OFFICIALS

I was now proceeding to visit the other apartments when a message was brought to Pisani which proved to be of the most interesting nature. Whether it was that my new friend the secretary had betrayed me, or that being now for the first time dressed in a Greek habit I wore my clothes awkwardly and was by that means known for a Frank, it was already noised about the Porte that a stranger of rank was there in disguise. This rumour coming to the ears of the several great men then in their respective offices they sent to Pisani desiring that he would forthwith bring the aforesaid stranger to visit them, as they supposed that curiosity had probably led him thither, and that of consequence their persons, offices, and conversation, might be to him as curious as anything he could there observe.

Surprised and delighted at this unparalleled and unexpected politeness I lost no time, but was immediately conducted by Pisani to the apartment of the Reis Efendi,[1] one of the principal officers of state, who unites in his person the high offices of Secretary of State, and Chancellor of the Empire. I found him sitting upon his sofa, and, having been presented, was received with the most cordial, easy, and unaffected politeness. Having first enquired into my name and rank he desired me to sit down by him. He told me that he was happy in the opportunity of seeing me, and much obliged to Pisani for procuring him that pleasure. He then asked me several questions concerning my travels, as: where I had been, whither I intended to proceed, how I had amused myself, whether I liked the abode of Constantinople, etc. He called for coffee, and his servants presented me with a silver vessel, filled with a sort of perfumed marmalade with a large gold or gilt spoon. Of this marmalade, by the direction of Pisani, I put into my mouth a spoonful, which served instead of sugar to the coffee, which was then brought in.

Having drank it, I was going to rise, and to take my leave, but the Reis Efendi desired me to sit still, telling me that he would treat me according to my condition. The servants then served me with iced sherbet, a liquor much used by the Turks and commonly made with liquorice, orange juice, and water, of which when I had tasted, one of

[1] At that time Naili Efendi (1747-52).

them flung out of a silver bottle with a long and very narrow neck rose water upon my hands and habit, with which, having finished to sprinkle me, another servant presented me with a silver urn having its cover pierced full of holes and shaped something like those incense pots which are used in Catholic churches. This, it seems, was full of burning perfumes, but as I did not well know what to make of it, I unluckily laid my hand on its cover, and burned my fingers, at which ridiculous accident the Reis Efendi laughed heartily, and with great good humour told me that he was pleased to see me begin to accommodate myself to their customs, to which he hoped I should not be long a stranger.

Pisani then showed me the method of perfuming myself, by holding the urn between my two hands and putting it into my bosom under my gown or pellice. This manner of presenting with sherbet and perfumes is considered by the Turks as the highest compliment they can pay to a guest of distinction whom they desire to honour. All this time Pisani stood, and acted as interpreter, and the servants or slaves served me sitting upon their heels, a posture, according to the Turkish mode, of the greatest respect and equivalent to our serving upon the knee. I now took my leave, and upon going out of the room was surrounded by the servants, to whom I distributed a few piastres.

I was next conducted to the Chihaia of the Grand Vizir, a Minister of the highest dignity and in effect the second subject in the Empire, being in all affairs of State the Grand Vizir's deputy. To him I was also presented, and was received with equal politeness, and nearly the same ceremonies as had attended my former visit. (The word Chihaia properly means a deputy, nor is there any office at the Porte of more real importance than this. The Chihaia is nominated, not by the Vizir, but by the Grand Signor himself. Through his hands all affairs of State necessarily pass, and the Turks have a saying or proverb which imports that *the Chihaia is for us the Vizir, the Vizir is our Sultan, and the Sultan is no more to us than other Mussulmans.* When the Chihaia is dismissed from office, if not disgraced, he is always promoted to a Pashalik of three tails).

My next visit was paid to the Mektubii Efendi, or Private Secretary to the Grand Vizir, an officer likewise of great importance and dignity. Here also I was most politely received, and entertained, as before, with coffee, sherbet, and perfumes. He asked me several pertinent questions concerning my travels, and particularly desired to know whether I was acquainted with Sir Everard Faulkner,[1] the late Ambassador at the Porte. Upon my answering in the affirmative he enquired in the most friendly manner after his health, and whether anything

[1]   Sir Everard Fawkener (1684-1758, *DNB*) was appointed British Ambassador in 1735. He left Turkey in 1742 though not officially recalled until 1746, when Porter replaced him.

new had befallen him. I informed him that Sir Everard since his departure from Constantinople had been married to a lady, young and beautiful. He charged me not to fail, whenever I should see his old acquaintance, to present his compliments to him and to tell him that he pitied him greatly for having been weak enough to take a young wife in his decline of years.

At all these audiences Pisani, as I have before mentioned, stood, not being considered of a rank to be allowed a seat, and served as interpreter, standing between me and the person with whom I conversed and instantly repeating his words in Italian and my answers in Turkish. This is done with so great facility and quickness that I am confident a conversation thus carried on does not take up one tenth part more time than would be spent in a dialogue between two who spoke the same language.

These three great officers with whom I have now conversed were handsome, well-looking men, of a good mien and presence. The two former were middle aged, the latter elderly and venerable. Their manner was dignified in the highest degree, and yet as pleasing as possible. They seemed to possess, unknown to themselves, an air of superiority which they did not in the least appear to assume and which commanded respect without their seeming to demand it. How different from the petulance of France where every coxcomb assumes a superior air which turns his very civility into rudeness and insult! But that which most struck me and seemed to surpass anything of the kind I had yet seen was their action in speaking, their manner of moving the head and arms. Every gesture was a mixture of ease, grace, and dignity, and, though I could not understand a word of what they said, the very sight of their speaking, if I may be allowed the phrase, was highly pleasing to me.

The Turks in general, and indeed all the Orientals, seem in a peculiar manner to possess a graceful action, which remark may be extended even to the lower classes of the people. Grace indeed, as far as I could observe, seems to be a native of the East and to degenerate as she travels westward. This may perhaps, among other causes, help us to account for the surprising superiority of the Greeks in the art of statuary, since if we critically examine in what peculiar article the Greek statues excel the Roman and those of all other nations we shall, I believe, conclude that this peculiar excellence is grace. I remember once, in visiting one of the mosques at Constaninople to have seen an Imam, or Turkish priest, expounding the Koran to a circle of devout Turks. I was so struck by his action and manner of speaking that I found myself perfectly fascinated by it, and though all he said was unintelligible to me I could scarcely tear myself from him. Indeed so greatly did he please me that I could not help desiring Dalton, our painter to make a sketch of him and of his audience ... where however justice is by no means done to the attitude of the orator.

I now went in with Pisani to visit the Ruus Chifedari Efendi,[1] or Dragoman of the Porte, whose office, though a very important one, is not of equal dignity with the offices of those whom I had before visited. Here my companion was allowed to sit, and treated with some degree of familiarity. This officer is a Christian, and his post is one of the most dangerous that can be imagined. As he is employed on the part of the Porte to negotiate with all foreign Ministers it frequently happens that if the Grand Signor does not choose to abide by the exact terms of the treaties made through his mediation the fault is thrown upon him, and his misinterpreting is supposed to have occasioned a misunderstanding between the negotiating parties. (This however as frequently happens through the fault of our Ministers who endeavour to enlarge the advantages gained by treaties with the Porte by misinterpreting them to the benefit of their respective Courts. However, let it happen as it may, the poor Dragoman is always sacrificed). Upon these occasions he is always the sacrifice, and often pays for the insincerity of the Porte by the loss of his head. Indeed the precariousness of his situation was sufficiently painted in his countenance, than which I have seldom seen any more truly doleful.

All the Ministers who hold their offices at the Porte have, besides their apartments, chambers adjoining, which serve as secretary's offices in which their clerks write. I went into five or six of them and was astonished at the multitude of the clerks, the singular attitude in which they write, and the great expedition and regularity with which business is carried on. We may easily conceive what a number of clerks are necessary, when we consider the amazingly extensive correspondence which is carried on from these offices. Besides all the affairs of the Foreign Department, let us only reflect on the numerous dispatches that must issue from hence to all the various provinces of this wide-stretched Empire. When we thus consider the multiplicity of their affairs, we shall be still the more surprised and edified at the politeness of these great men, who could give up so much of their precious time to the reception and entertainment of a stranger. It seems singular and surprising that public affairs should not suffer considerably from the frequent changes of the persons employed by the Porte in the administration and from the ignorance and inexperience of men suddenly raised to offices of the highest consequence. But this difficulty disappears when we are informed that the under officers such as the head clerks etc., who are in all countries the persons who carry on the general routine of business, are seldom or never changed. Besides this, the Turkish Officers of State are possessed of another very important advantage. The registers of precedents are the

[1] Ioannis Kallimachis was Grand Dragoman of the Porte from 1741 to 1750. The office was always held by a Greek Christian. Charlemont's spelling of the Turkish title is eccentric; he gives the plural form *ruus* for the singular *reis* — chief.

most exactly kept of any in the world, and such is their precision and regularity that any memorial or any fact whatsoever of a hundred years standing may be found in the space of half an hour.

In every chamber there is a director, who has the care and inspection of a certain number of clerks, to whom he assigns their tasks and sees that they are expeditiously and accurately executed. The writers have no desks as with us, but write on their knee, apparently in a most uneasy and inconvenient posture yet nor far differing from that in which Raphael has placed the beautiful figure of the young disciple in the *School of Athens.* All these apartments, even those in which the Ministers sit, are dirty and ill furnished, and the whole of the building is but ordinary. This however is the case of all the public offices I have ever seen, the Bank of England only excepted. We are also to observe that none of the state officers except the Grand Vizir dwell here, but have each of them their separate palaces in the city, and resort hither, as to their respective offices, merely to do business.

I now, for a few piastres, was admitted into the Grand Vizir's private apartments, which are truly magnificent. The rooms are large, lofty, and well proportioned. The ceilings are elegantly carved after the manner which we style arabesque, and richly gilt. The walls of some rooms are covered with large china tiles, which have a very pretty effect. The furniture is, after the Turkish fashion, superb. The sofas are extremely rich, some covered with the finest silk Persian carpeting, others with silks embroidered. The pier glasses, of which there are a great number, are large and fine, most of them I believe from France. But that which seemed to me the most singular piece of magnificence was the number of clocks, all of them English, with which the chambers are crowded. In one large room I counted no less than six standard clocks, such as usually stand in our halls, only rather more elegant. In one of these chambers I saw, from the room adjoining, the Grand Vizir stretched upon a sofa refreshing himself after the fatigue of the Divan. He seemed pensive and melancholy, and was then, possibly, reflecting on the sad precariousness of his situation and on the wretched anxiety which ever attends ministerial power and grandeur.

In order that nothing might be left unseen, Pisani conducted me into the Grand Vizir's kitchen, where however I saw nothing remarkalbe — except the number of the cooks and the novelty of the dishes then preparing may be esteemed so.

We now passed through the Great Hall where the Divan had been held, in which I observed several Turks at their prayers, this place being esteemed consecrated and holy. Nor could I avoid reflecting upon and admiring the striking propriety of this idea and the sound policy of imprinting upon the minds of the people such an opinion, as nothing surely could ever be devised more proper or more likely to procure respect and veneration for the laws than that the Hall of Justice, the supreme seat of judicature, should be venerated and revered as sacred and holy ground.

Having thus completed my examination of the Porte and seen everything there that was worth observation I returned home to the Ambassador's, highly delighted with my morning's work and not a little pleased and surprised at having found such amazing and much more than Christian politeness among a people whom I had been taught to believe little less than barbarous.

AN AUDIENCE WITH THE
GRAND VIZIR

During our abode at Constantinople, luckily for us, the Imperial Minister had an audience of the Grand Vizir, the occasion of which was as follows. The Emperor having lately concluded a treaty of peace with the piratical States of Barbary, with whom he had been at war on account of some depredations made upon the trade of his Tuscan subjects, had, about two months since, signified the same to the Porte by letters from him and from the Empress[1] to the Grand Signor. These letters were, as usual, accompanied with presents and had been graciously received, and other presents of equal value had of course been returned. But the letters remained unanswered till now, when the Grand Vizir gave audience to the imperial Internonce in order to deliver the answer.

We (Burton, Scott, Murphy, Dalton and I) followed the Internonce,[2] Mr Benkler, into a small apartment in the palace of the Captain Pasha, or High Admiral. This palace, which has nothing magnificent in its appearance, is beautifully situated upon the margent or bank of the Basin and commands a noble prospect of the harbour. The chamber, the size or furniture of which was rather mean, was crowded with the attendants of the Grand Vizir, for whom in the corner nearest to the window was fixed a sofa, and opposite to it was placed a stool for the Internonce. After we had waited a few minutes the Grand Vizir (Supreme Vizir), Suleiman Pasha[3] entered. He is handsome, and of a good presence. He is greatly beloved, being of gentle and merciful disposition. But his power is much circumscribed as he is obliged in all affairs of importance in great measure to follow the dictates of the Kislar Aga or Chief of the Black Eunuchs, who possesses the Sultan's ear and favour and indirectly governs the Empire. This subservience of Suleiman has probably been the cause of his remaining so long in his office, which he has now kept for some years, contrary to the established custom, and to the advice of the late Sultan Ahmed,[4] who recommended it to his brother the present

[1] See note 1 on p. 173.

[2] Charlemont adds in a note: 'This title [Internuncio] properly belongs to the Ministers of the Pope and means the agent who is left to transact the affairs of the Court of Rome either during the absence of the Nuncio or before his appointment. The Emperor also gives this title to the person who acts as Minister between the recall of one Ambassador and the sending of another. His dignity is, I believe equal to that of our envoys Extraordinary.'

[3] See note 1 on p. 165.

[4] Achmet III, Sultan 1703-30.

Grand Signor, on his accession to the throne, to change his Vizirs as frequently as possible.

The Vizir was preceded by the Reis Efendi, Secretary of State and High Chancellor of the Empire, on one hand of whom was the Chiaux Bashi, Commander of the Chiaux or Guard of the Gate, and on the other an officer whose post or title I could not discover. At the entrance of the Grand Vizir all the attendants and the people both within and without the chamber, shouted aloud, and cried out 'Long live Sultan Mahmout and Suleiman his Vizir!' which is, it seems, the ordinary form of acclamation. The reason why the Grand Vizir did not make his appearance till after the Internonce had already entered was to avoid the ceremony of rising to receive him, a compliment which the Minister would have expected but of which the Turkish dignity would not admit, the Porte esteeming her Prime Minister too much superior to all Ambassadors to allow of such a condescension.

The Grand Vizir now sat down, and opposite to him the Internonce. When, after some conversation and compliments between the two Ministers, the Vizir among other things telling the Internonce that he had chosen to receive him there rather than at his own palace on account of the airiness and coolness of the place, refreshments were brought in, which consisted of iced sherbet and other cool liquors. Of these they both tasted, and perfumes were served in the manner I have before described at my audience of the Reis Efendi. The Grand Vizir first perfumed his beard, holding the urn or incense pot for a few seconds under his pellice, and then presented the urn to the Internonce who performed the same ceremony. (The Vizir's pellice [i.e. *pelisse*, a long-sleeved cloak] was the finest I had ever seen, being lined with the skin of the black fox, and valued, as I was assured, at 1500 sequins. As the Turks wear no gold or silver the finery of their dress consists entirely in the beauty and expense of their furs).

During this time the Reis Efendi and the two other officers who had accompanied him at his entrance went out of the chamber, and presently returned, the Chiaux Bashi marching first, with a staff, or rather club, in his hand, which is, it seems, his staff of office. With this he violently struck the ground several times, repeating with a loud voice some words to announce the coming of the Grand Signor's letters, upon which all the people shouted as before. Immediately after him proceeded the Reis Efendi, bearing on the palms of his hands three letters, one for the Emperor,[1] another for the Empress, both written by the Grand Signor, and a third from the Grand Vizir to the Imperial Prime Minister, in answer to a letter received from him. The letters were long scrolls of vellum neatly wrapped up in green silk.

---

[1] Francis I (1708-65). Elected Emperor in 1745, formerly Duke of Lorraine. In 1736 he married Maria Theresa of Austria (1717-80) who became Queen of Hungary on the death of her father, the Emperor Charles VI, in 1740.

The Grand Vizir received them from the Reis Efendi in a manner expressive of the highest respect, rising from his seat and with a graceful action bending his head and applying them to his forehead, which having done, holding them in the manner before mentioned, he presented them to the Internonce, who received them also upon the palms of his hands. Immediately after this, *caftans* (habits of ceremony) were distributed to all the attendants and to us among the rest.

The Internonce now having informed the Vizir that he had brought along with him to this audience a nobleman from England whose curiosity had led him to Constantinople, I was desired to come forward and was presented on the part of the Vizir with an embroidered handkerchief, which, though in itself of little value, is esteemed a mark of high distinction and favour. This being done, and the audience now at an end, the Internonce retired, making several low and obsequious reverences which were answered by the Vizir with a slight inclination of the head only, and we of his train immediately followed him. But, not making as much haste as the Turkish attendants desired, with much rudeness they fairly turned us out of the chamber, crying out repeatedly in order to hasten our departure, 'hush, hush, hush.'

Upon this odd ceremony I shall only remark that in almost every circumstance of it, but particularly in that last mentioned, the small estimation in which the Porte affects to hold foreign Ministers is clearly apparent. The Grand Vizir's studiously avoiding the ceremony of rising to receive the Internonce, his making use of the perfumes first, and then presenting them to him, his answering by a careless nod the low reverences of the Minister, were most undoubtedly all intended as slights and done on purpose to show how little the Porte esteems the rank of Minister even from the first of all crowned heads, and of consequence how much she deems herself superior to the potentates, whose majesty these Ministers are intended to represent. And the great rudeness with which we were 'hushed' out of the chamber was plainly meant to answer the same purpose, the Turks being remarkably civil upon all occasions, those only excepted where public Ministers are concerned, in which cases they always behave with studied rudeness.

A fine Arabian horse with magnificent furniture richly embroidered awaited the Internonce at the gate of the Palace, which, together with a *caftan* of the finest sable, with which he had been attired when we received our *caftans*, and several dishes of fruit, sweetmeats, and flowers, formed the Grand Signor's present to him in particular, presents between the Courts having already, as I before mentioned, been mutually interchanged.

174

View of Constantinople from above Galata

A MEETING WITH A
SENSIBLE TURK

There was nothing I more ardently wished for during my short abode at Constantinople — ... only a month, and a great part of that time was necessarily, though foolishly, taken up with ceremonious visits to Ambassadors etc. — than to be made acquainted with some sensible Turk, unprejudiced and well informed, from whose conversation, however circumscribed it should be, I might be able to gather much more information with regard to the real character of this people than I could possibly expect from those Greeks and Franks of whom our society was wholly composed. To procure me this satisfaction I was continually importuning our Ambassador, but his own connexions with Mussulmans were so very limited that for a long time I importuned in vain. At length however he informed me that a Turkish acquaintance of his was just then arrived in town, who would fully answer my purpose. His name was Mustapha Efendi, and he was Turkish Secretary to the English nation. He had in the younger part of his life been a candidate for office at the Seraglio, but, being of a philosophical turn, disgusted and wearied with the anxious business and intrigues of the court he had retired from public affairs and had accepted the aforesaid office of Secretary as a post of little trouble and no anxiety. He was now entirely given up to study and, besides the usual learning of the Turks, of which we shall hereafter treat, he had made no small proficiency in the Latin tongue, a language seldom studied, and little known in Turkey.

(As an instance of this excellent Mussulman's incorruptible honesty, a virtue which the Turks possess in a superior degree, the Ambassador related to me the following fact. Some years ago a difference having arisen between the English and the Russian Courts, the Minister of the latter endeavoured to get at the contents of a certain memorial which had been presented to the Porte by the English Ambassador, and for this purpose he offered any sum of money, that he could possibly desire, to our friend Mustapha who, as *Scrivano Efendi,* or Turkish Secretary, had translated the said memorial into Turkish and had copied and prepared it for delivery. The honest Turk refused the bribe, telling the Minister that he could not be so base as to betray a nation whose bread he had eaten).

At this wished for opportunity I eagerly caught and was accordingly conducted by the Ambassador, accompanied by Doctor Mackenzie,[1] a sensible and learned man, physician to the English factory, and by whom I was received with the greatest and most unreserved politeness. Our conference was, however, but short, and as he again left Constantinople immediately after this visit I never could have the pleasure of renewing it. Such as it was I here set it down, as a small sample of genuine Turkish conversation, from an abstract, (which immediately after leaving him I wrote down) of my questions and of his answers, many of which had, I fear, even then escaped my memory. Neither were my questions in every respect such as I would now wish they had been, turning chiefly upon some particular points of which I then desired to be informed and being greatly circumscribed by the shortness of the interview and by that respectful reserve which always attends a first visit, especially as I then flattered myself that it would not be the last. After the first compliments were over, the conference was thus opened by me:

'My high esteem for the Mussulmans makes me desirous to be authentically informed of every circumstance which may in any way concern them, and, as your opinions must undoubtedly be those of the wisest of your nation, I would wish to trouble you with a few questions, if I might do it without offence.'

Answer.

'You may ask what you please, and take what license you choose in your queries, for, though a good Mussulman, I am not fool enough to be offended at any question you may please to ask.'

Question.

'Do you believe in astrology or the influence of the stars in enabling men to foretell events?'

Answer.

'I do not, but think it a foolish science. For whilst a man pretends to foretell events and to read the heavens he does not know what his own wife is doing.'

Question.

'Can the Grand Signor, according to law, give any Sultana, or woman with whom he has lain, to another?'

Answer.

'He may — to me, if he be so inclined — provided always she hath not brought forth a male child. A female is no hindrance.

[1]   Dr. Mordack Mackenzie, physician in Constantinople 1730-69, who was a great help to Charlemont during his visit there.

Question.

'Can, in that case, he to whom she is given have other women at the same time?'

Answer.

'He can. For example the Pasha of — — —, and for this plain reason: as all his male children by the Sultana are destroyed, without other wives he could have no male issue.'

Question.

'Do you not think this custom of destroying the innocent children a very great sin?'

Answer.

'It certainly is. But convenience has made it a custom.'

Question.

'There are in all religions many things which should be understood metaphorically. Do you believe literally those relations in the Koran, of Mahomet's ascent into heaven, etc., etc.?'

Answer (with a smile).

'Do you believe that Christ came from heaven, and is gone thither again?'

The question repeated.

Answer (by the Turk).

'I am obliged to believe what is written in the Koran. I believe that the world was created, because, when I see smoke, I am sure there must be fire. I have read a translation of the New Testament and believe the miracles of Christ, such as his restoring sight to the blind, his curing the diseased etc. You, Doctor, (Mackenzie) I suppose, do not believe these prodigies. Such miracles would spoil your trade.'

Question.

'You have read the Apocalypse. Do you believe in the truth of the prophecies therein contained?

Answer.

'I do.'

The Ambassador then spoke.

'That is more than I do, for I do not understand them'

Answer to the Ambassador.

'You believe Christ alone, and not his Dragomans, the Apostles Whatever is attested and confirmed to me by a sufficient number of witnesses, that I believe, even though it be contrary to my reason and to the natural and usual course of things.'

Question.

'What is the reason that you, who have had it in your power, have not endeavoured to advance yourself in State offices?'

Answer.

'Because I had a mind to *live more.*'

Question.

'You understand the Latin tongue. What Latin books are you now reading?'

Answer.

'I am studying the philosophical works of Seneca.'

Question.

'What is the greatest number of children, you have known any one man to have?'

Answer.

'Sultan Achmet had eighty.'

Question.

'Do you know whether there be any Greek or Latin manuscripts in any of the Grand Signor's libraries?'[1]

Answer.

'If there be any, they are in the Treasury and impossible to be come at because they are sealed with the Sultan's own seal and are placed near the Harem. But I do not believe there are many, for this reason. The first Caliphs in Egypt found a book in which there was nothing written against the Law but, on the contrary, where many good rules of conduct were to be found. They asked their prophet Omar if they might keep this book (perhaps a copy or even the original manuscript of the Septuagint). But he desired them to burn it, and ordered them to destroy whatever Greek or Latin manuscripts they should for the future meet with.'

[Here Charlemont has a short essay on Turkish attitudes to literature and art. With reference to the destruction of monuments, and works of art he cites similar destructions in the West under Henry VIII and Cromwell in Ireland and Britain, by French and Germans on the Continent, by the Venetians on the Acropolis, and also 'the English outrage against their brethren in America' (which indicates how late this essay was written). As an example of Turkish respect for books he cites the fact that in a 'rebellion' at Smyrna (presumably the riots in 1770) when the houses of all other Consuls were destroyed, the mob spared the British Consul's because it had a library in it. And as an example of Western vandalism he accuses Dr. Anthony Askew (see NDB), who travelled in Turkey in 1747, of erasing inscriptions after he had copied them 'thereby preventing any further traveller from copying (them) and from verifying his transcript or perhaps detecting his errors.' No one else, so far as we know, accused Askew of that. This is discussed by Aristoteles K. Stavropoulos in O Eranistes *17 (Athens 1981) pp. 279-82].*

[1] Charlemont added this note later: This question was asked principally with a view to the discovery of those parts of Tacitus which are wanting, and of the lost decade of Livy, as it has been supposed by many that complete copies of these histories still exist in the Grand Signor's library.'

A VIEW OF THE SULTAN

As while we were at Constantinople there happened no audience of the Grand Signor, the only means by which we could obtain the satisfaction of seeing him was to take the opportunity of his going to the mosque, which he constantly does every Friday. At this time he resided for the summer season at a Seraglio or palace beautifully and pleasantly situated three or four miles above the city, on the bank of the canal or straight which leads to the Black Sea, and called Besigtache, [Beshiktash], from whence he comes on horseback, not to Santa Sophia, the royal mosque which he usually frequents during his residence at Constantinople, but to Zelie Ali Pasha's Giami or church, a mosque situated in that quarter of the town which is called Topchana or the Region of the Arsenal, which church, being built not far from the margent of the Basin, he now frequents for the convenience of returning by water, as is his constant custom.

To this church on the first Friday after our arrival we repaired, and mixing with the mob, which here, as in all other countries, assembles in great numbers upon such occasions, we endeavoured to push ourselves as near as possible to the mosque and to the passage which was left free for the procession. And here I cannot avoid observing upon the great good humour and civility of the populace, who, though we, impelled by our curiosity, pushed forward through them with some degree of violence, never in the least resented our rudeness, but on the contrary seemed willing to make way for us as for strangers to whom the sight was more curious than it could be to them.

The first thing which we remarked was that the lane — lined on each side by janissaries — through which the procession was to pass, was strewed over with fresh earth and water for the greater convenience of riding and to prevent the dust from being offensive. After we had waited a few minutes, which were not ill spent in contemplating the crowd (to us who had never till now seen a Turkish mob, by no means an indifferent object) the procession began by the two Tulbant Agasis or Turban Bearers of the Grand Signor, who preceded him near half an hour, and alighting from their horses placed themselves on each side of the entrance to the mosque. One of them bore in his hands the Turban of State which was of a peculiar size and form and richly set with diamonds, and the other a footstool of rich brocade

180

which he placed near the door of the mosque for the Grand Signor to alight upon.

The Sultan or Padisha now soon arrived, attended by the Chiauxes with their Chiaux Bashi, Guards of the Gate and Messengers in Ordinary, the Capigiler Chiasi and Capigilers or Porters, the Bostangi Bashi and Bostangis or Gardeners, and the Topgi Bashi and Topgis or Gunners, making all together about one hundred and fifty in number.

These were detachments from the several bodies of troops which compose the military force of the Seraglio and form what we may term the Grand Signor's Life Guard. With these forces the Sultans have sometimes been able successfully to oppose the rebellious attempts of the mutinous janissaries, though they failed the unfortunate Osman [1] who perished by placing too much confidence in them. The dress of the Sultan was plain and unornamented, but the trappings of his horse, an animal of the most perfect beauty, were splendid beyond the power of expression and shone with a profusion of various jewels. Immediately about his person marched his Solacks and his Peiks. The former of these have in their caps, which are of a peculiar form and made something like the ancient helmet, large and lofty plumes of ostrich feathers which rise so high and are so numerous as almost to shade him from sight so that his person or face can only be seen by catches. This seems to be done in consequence of that principle generally established in the East that the person of the monarch should be kept invisible to his subjects, an idea which probably has its source in that slavish and impious opinion that kings in all respects are gods on earth and should resemble the divinity as well in his invisibility as in his other attributes. (To the best of my recollection the Solacks carried also in their hands long poles with ostrich feathers fastened at the end of them, which they held about the Sultan's head, and which contributed to hide him from the multitude.) The Peiks wear pointed caps of silver gilt, some bearing in their hands long lances, and others carrying a weapon formed exactly like the Amazonian axe. These last seem to correspond with our Yeomen of the Guard.

Immediately after the Sultan, and close to his person, rode the Kislar Aga,[2] or Chief of the Black Eunuchs, superbly mounted upon a fine horse richly caparisoned and followed by a numerous train of attendants. I could not avoid being sensibly struck, I may almost say with horror, by the extraordinary figure of this personage. If, as it is said with great appearance of probability, deformity be an excel-

---

[1]   Osman II was strangled in 1622.

[2]   Bekir Aga, who succeeded the old Kislar Aga (who bore the same name) in 1746 and was killed in his early thirties in 1752, as described by Porter.

lence in black eunuchs, this monster may undoubtedly claim such a degree of superiority in this whimsical pre-eminence as justly to merit to be their chief. So ugly a human being — if human he can be called, and if ugliness were a term strong enough to express his deformity — my eyes never beheld. Even white men, who have undergone this shameful operation, are generally so impaired by it in their figure as to become objects of detestation. What then must be its effects upon the nastiest, the most deformed of all negroes?

At the door of the mosque the Sultan alighted from his horse, on the footstool before mentioned, and as soon as he had set his foot upon the ground a royal salute was fired from the guns at Topchana or the Arsenal, and all the people, of which several thousands, both men and women,[1] were here gathered together, shouted with such amazing vociferation as almost to deafen us, crying out repeatedly, 'Long live Sultan Mahmout!'

I must here remark that notwithstanding the multitude there had not been during the procession the smallest noise or disturbance, but a respectful silence had been kept and not a whisper was heard through the crowd, which made this sudden burst of acclamation appear the louder and the more striking. The Grand Signor remained in the church, which he had entered attended by the Kislar Aga and other of the principal officers, about an hour, during which time we seized the opportunity of admiring the horses, which the grooms were then leading about, and their trappings or furniture, than which I never beheld anything more magnificent. The horses were most beautiful, all Arabians but of that kind which we seldom import, and which are better fitted for war than for the course, high crested, light shouldered, but broad behind, and the furnitures, which, according to the Turkish fashion, covered a great part of the horse's body, were of a magnificence difficult to describe. Embroidery made the smallest part of their splendour and seemed to serve only as ground upon which jewels of every sort were set in the greatest profusion. That by which I was more particularly struck was the horse on which the Kislar Aga rode. His trappings were of blue velvet embroidered with silver and powdered over with a multitude of pearls. The bosses of the bridle were of gold enriched with precious stones; but the most splendid of all was the breast-plate, set with various jewels of great value, and in its centre or front an emerald of the most enormous size.

The Sultan now came out from the mosque, and, remounting his horse, rode to the waterside which was not above two hundred yards

---

[1] Charlemont adds a note: 'It is a mistake to suppose that women are never seen at Constantinople. Numbers of the poorer sort walk the streets, wrapped up in long cloaks which descend so low as to hide their feet, and their faces so muffled that it is impossible to distinguish a single feature. Indeed that dress is so little tempting that their husbands need be under no apprehension of any attempts on the part of us Franks.'

distant, where a most magnificent barge awaited him, richly gilt and decorated, rowed with twenty-four oars, and steered by the Bostangi Bashi, who claims this honour in right of his office. At the first stroke of the oars another royal salute was fired, and all the people shouted as before.

(Many of the Sultans, predecessors to Mahmout, resided for the summer season at the Seraglio of Scutari, the ancient Chrysopolis, a town beautifully situated on the coast of Asia opposite to Constantinople. As this passage was longer and rather more dangerous than that to Besig-tache, a larger vessel, or yacht, was always made use of, which was steered by the Captain Pasha, who, as we were assured, was obliged at his departure from Constantinople to swear on the Koran that he would bring the Sultan safe back).

A LUDICROUS INCIDENT

And here I cannot avoid taking notice of a circumstance that happened during this solemnity, which, though ludicrous in itself, might have been attended by the most fatal consequences, and I am the rather induced to mention it as it will serve as an instance of the humane good humour and compassionate civility of a Turkish mob.

Frank Burton, the dear and agreeable companion of my travels, who was endowed by nature with every endearing faculty which can render a friend amiable, with every perfection of heart, which constitutes the best and surest foundation for friendship and secures its duration, was also possessed of a quality which was sometimes exceedingly dangerous though never more so than on the present occasion. If, as some philosophers have told us, a principal and peculiar characteristic mark of man which distinguishes him from all other animals be that he is an *animal risibile*, my friend was assuredly in this respect more peculiarly a man than any I ever yet knew. If he happened upon any occasion to be struck by any thing which appeared to him ridiculous it was impossible for him to restrain his laughter, but laugh he must even at the hazard of his life.

Unfortunately for me, during this solemnity he stood close by me and, though the whimsical appearances of many figures in the mob which surrounded us were apt enough to excite laughter, he had hitherto contrived to preserve himself tolerably serious. But when at length the dead silence was all at once broken by the above-mentioned yell of applause, which was accompanied by contortions of countenance, and by attitudes not a little ridiculous, he could possibly contain [himself] no longer but told me with tears in his eyes, half of laughter and half of apprehension, that he must laugh! The consequences immediately occurring to me of his laughing upon such an occasion, when all the bystanders were awed with a degree of veneration which approached near to worship, I besought him to restrain himself, assuring him that our being torn to pieces was the most probable effect which could ensue from his being guilty of such an indecency and putting him in mind of our dangerous situation, encompassed by a savage multitude of barbarians, for such our prejudices then inclined us to deem them. 'Pinch me then,' replied he, 'and hard. Perhaps that may be a prevention.' I obeyed and pinched with all my force. 'Harder still,' said he, 'for that will not do.' Again I pinched.

But, alas, I pinched in vain! The pent up affection burst forth with such surprising violence, with such a thundering explosion, that it almost drowned the noise of acclamation. By the greatest good fortune however the laugh of Burton was totally dissimilar and different from that of either Turk or Christian and had much more resemblance in its sound and effect to an hysteric convulsion than to natural laughter, the effect of which fortunate circumstance I instantly observed in the countenances of those who stood nearest to us. They seemed to pity him, as imagining that he was just falling into a fit, and their compassion was expressed not only in their faces but by their shrinking back from us in order to give him air. This lucky hint I immediately caught and improved and, pretending the deepest concern, (a deceit which my fears made very easy to me), I endeavoured to lead him out of the crowd, which kindly separated itself and made every possible effort to facilitate our escape. Thus at length and by degrees, the fit still continuing with the utmost violence, we freed ourselves from this pressing danger, and Burton finished his convulsions with ease and with convenience.

REMARKS ON THE SULTAN

The present Padisha, or Emperor of the Turks, Sultan Mahmout or Mahmud, is the first of that name, son to Sultan Mustafa, who was brother to Sultan Ahmed, which last, having been deposed by the janissaries and other troops quartered at Constantinople in conjunction with several of the citizens after a rebellion of four days raised on account of the maladministration of Ibrahim Pasha[1] his Grand Vizir, was succeeded by his nephew Mahmud, to whom he resigned the throne, which he had been compelled to abdicate, on the 20th September 1730 (old style).

As well as I could observe, shaded as he was from perfect view, the Sultan appeared to be a man of good countenance and of a graceful person. One circumstance in his figure was so remarkable that it could not escape even our imperfect observation, that, though when on horseback he appeared a tall man, upon his alighting his size seemed to diminish and he appeared at most but of the middle stature, his legs and thighs being very short in proportion to his body. He is greatly beloved by the people, being a prince of a merciful disposition, a character not very common in the Ottoman family, and, though the beginning of his reign had been agitated by domestic disturbances and by insurrections, the natural consequences of a dominion founded upon a revolution, all matters were now apparently so well settled that the happiness of his subjects would probably be without alloy, if it were not for the ascendancy which the Kislar Aga has gained over him. But, as the characters of princes are best judged of by their actions, the surest means by which I can ascertain his character is by relating a few facts for the truth of which I can vouch as they came to me from the most certain and undoubted authority.

Nothing can be a clearer proof of the merciful and pious disposition of Mahmud than his having suffered his deposed predecessor, his uncle Ahmed, to live, contrary to the established policy of the Se-

---

[1] Mustafa II (1664-1703) reigned 1695-1703, dying a few months after his abdication. Achmet III (1673-1739) reigned from 1703 until his deposition in 1730. Damat Ibrahim Pasha was strangled in 1730. Mahmud I (1696-1754) became Sultan in 1730 and reigned until 1754.

raglio, and indeed of all the eastern Courts. This unfortunate Prince has ever since his deposition been kept in confinement, a rigour in this country absolutely indispensable and necessary to the safety of the reigning Sultan. But he has ever been treated with the kindest indulgence and with filial respect and duty. His confinement has been as little strict as possible, and, except his liberty, he has been allowed every convenience and enjoyment of life.

The lenity of this good Prince is also apparent from the manner in which he has hitherto treated his disgraced Vizirs. In almost all the foregoing reigns disgrace and death went hand in hand, and the Vizir who lost his office together with the favour of his master was sure to suffer by the fatal bowstring. But Mahmud has broken through this barbarous custom and has hitherto contented himself with sending the Ministers whom he has displaced into banishment for three or four months only, at the end of which period their exile has been honoured by distant Pashaliks or governments. Not long since his private treasury was robbed of a very considerable sum, and after much search the robbers were at length discovered. When brought to be examined in the presence of the Sultan, it plainly appeared that one of them, and he, too, a ringleader, was not perfectly in his senses. This unfortunate wretch, the merciful Prince, having ordered the other to be executed, freely pardoned declaring that he supposed his crime to be more the effect of madness than of wickedness.

About seven years before our arrival at Constantinople the Grand Signor riding one day through the streets in procession happened to pass by the Palace of the French Ambassador, one of whose servants, intoxicated with liquor, standing at the door with a pistol in his hand, fired it off by way of saluting the Prince. The consequence was that the horse on which the Sultan rode started violently and almost threw his rider to the ground. He however dexterously recovered himself, and stuck firmly in the saddle, but his turban fell off and he remained bareheaded, an attitude, among the Turks (who never take off their turbans) accounted unseemly and disgraceful. The attendants were instantly going to kill the servant but the merciful emperor interposed and forbad them, saying that he was convinced the poor wretch meant no harm. The next day an officer waited on the Ambassador to enquire into the affair, and, being told the whole truth and that the fellow meant no other than to compliment the Prince after the European fashion, went away well satisfied.

The foregoing instances are sufficient to show the merciful temper of this good Prince. But his behaviour to the Queen of Hungary[1] when in the utmost distress, assailed on every side by powerful and inveterate enemies and reduced to the lowest ebb of fortune, proves him

---

[1] See note on p. 173.

to be of a disposition equally generous and noble; and at the same time will serve to show, to the honour of the Porte, which I fear in this instance stands single among all the Courts of Europe, that there has been an example, singular indeed and therefore the most conspicuous, where even in a royal breast policy has given way to justice and generosity!

The House of Austria being, as we may well remember, now reduced to the most extreme state of weakness,[1] the French Court willing to seize this opportunity entirely to oppress and to crush her once powerful rival caused her Ambassador at the Porte[2] to make the most pressing instances to the Grand Signor in order to induce him to attack the Queen in her hereditary Hungarian dominions setting forth, as was really the fact, that a large portion of his own country on that side had been yielded at the last peace and was then actually in her possession, which, as she was now in no sort able to defend it, might with the greatest ease be wrested from her together with whatever portion of Hungary he might think proper to take by way of reprisal and as an indemnification for the great losses he had formerly sustained.[3] The truth of these facts was indisputable. The war also would have been popular, and highly pleasing to the people, as from frequent and bloody depredations on both sides an inveterate animosity ever subsists between the Turks and the Hungarians, and had the Turk at that time seized the occasion, the Queen must have been utterly undone as her Hungarian forces, which by this diversion would necessarily have been detained in defence of their own country, were her last and her only resource. But the noble-minded Sultan rejected the proposal with disdain, and calling before him the Hungarian Minister spoke to him in the following ever memorable terms. 'Formerly your Court betrayed me, and broke the faith of treaties, for which God severely punished you, and gave success to my arms. Should I now betray you, the same God would punish me also. The faith of the Porte has ever been inviolable, nor shall it be violated by me. It is moreover no way suitable to the glory of the Ottoman arms to attack a weak woman in her distress. Write then to your Queen and assure her from me that no advantage shall be capable to induce me to violate these treaties which now subsist between her and me.'

Immediately after this declaration the Sultan wrote a letter to the Queen with his own hand; a compliment which he had never before paid to any prince, the King of France only excepted, desiring her to rest assured of his faith and of his friendship. And, proceeding still

[1] As a result of the War of the Austrian Succession (1741-48).

[2] At that time Michel-Ange Comte de Castellane who was appointed in 1741.

[3] By the Treaty of Passarowitz (1718) Turkey ceded extensive territory to the Austrians. It was regained by the Treaty of Belgrade in 1739.

farther in his humane generosity, he ordered his Vizir to write circular letters to all the belligerent powers offering himself as a mediator to save the effusion of human blood.[1] To which letters, to their shame be it said, no Court, excepting that of France, ever studious to keep well with the Porte, returned an answer in proper time.

It is, I am sure, by no means necessary that I should make any remark upon this noble and more than princely behaviour, only thus much I will say that it will appear still more noble and more extraordinary when we consider that the grand design of the Ottoman Porte has ever been to gain as many Christian conquests as possible, and that there is no means more likely to facilitate the execution of this their darling project than by suffering and exciting the princes of Christendom to weaken each other by their mutual dissentions.

An absolute Prince, graced by such qualities, as these slight sketches of his conduct have now proved the Sultan possessed of, must undoubtedly enjoy in the highest degree the love and veneration of his people, and may therefore be reckoned among the happiest of monarchs; yet is his happiness alloyed by one unfortunate circumstance which embitters all his enjoyments and throws a gloom over his life and his reign. This excellent Prince is yet childless, a misfortune to him the more grievous on account of a traditionary notion which has strongly impressed itself upon the minds of the Turks that the Sultan who remains without children for the space of eight years ought to be deposed, an idea which would undoubtedly long since have operated against him, had he not possessed in so eminent a degree the love of his people. To remedy this evil no means have been left untried. Women of all complexions, of all constitutions, have been brought to him from every region, from every peopled climate. Astrologers have been consulted. All the physicians of the East have given their advice, and nostrums of every kind have been recommended and taken. Even my friend Doctor Mackenzie was lately consulted, whose answer was too sensible and too honest not to be here inserted. 'Does the Sultan eat well?', said he to those who came to take his opinion. 'Does he sleep well? Does he perform all the other functions of nature as he ought? Are his external marks, signs, and exertions of virility like those of other men?' To all this it was answered in the affirmative. 'Then,' continued the honest doctor, 'I can do nothing for him. His case is beyond the reach of art.'

But among all the methods that have been pursued there is one so strikingly whimsical and absurd that I cannot avoid mentioning it. The Sultan was told some years since by his astrologers that upon examining his horoscope and consulting the stars they found it was not in his fate to get a child by land, and that therefore he must try

[1] According to von Hammer the offer of mediation by Turkey in 1745 was initiated by the then Reis Efendi Mustafa.

what could be done upon the water. The physicians also joined in this advice, declaring that the motion of the waves would happily co-operate and greatly contribute to facilitate conception. In consequence of this strange idea a magnificent yacht was built and moored opposite to the Seraglio, in which the Sultan lay with his wives. But, this attempt proving unsuccessful, a kiosk or summer house was erected upon a float fixed by anchors in the very centre of the canal where the motion of the water was most violent, and here also the fruitless experiment was tried. This kiosk, which may well be styled the temple of Venus or Aphrodite, still remains though now uninhabited, and had I not myself seen it I should scarcely have given credit to the relation of so wonderful an absurdity.

EUNUCHS AND THE KIZLARAGA

The difference between the Black and the White Eunuchs is to be met with in every book which treats of Turkish customs. The White, we know, are only castrated, while the Black loose the entire organs of generation. The former are only servants in the Seraglio, and are never upon any account admitted into the Harem. The latter are the guardians of the Sultan's wives, attend on their persons, and are answerable for their conduct. It is a mistake to say, as is generally asserted, that the Black Eunuchs are brought from Ethiopia. They are for the most part Nubians or of those parts of Africa which produce the most frightful negroes. Ugliness is the excellence sought after, which could seldom be found among the Ethiopians who are, generally speaking, their colour only excepted, handsome and well made, with hair and features much resembling those of the Europeans. The Nubians, on the contrary, are flat-nosed, big-lipped, woolly-haired, and in every particular resemble the Guinea negroes. The only tolerable feature they possess is their teeth, which are remarkably white, but in order that their deformity may be complete, they who serve in the Seraglio are chosen from among those who have either lost their teeth, or have them black and decayed. The teeth of the Kislar Aga, such of them as are left, were by much the blacker part about him. The Turks relate a whimsical story with regard to the first introduction of Black Eunuchs, which, as they assert, is not of a very early date. Formerly, say they, the Harem was served by White Eunuchs, or by castrated negroes, but upon an unlucky day a certain Sultan (I think it was Amurath III) walking in a park belonging to one of his country Seraglios, happened to observe a gelding, who vigorously mounted a mare, and seemed in some sort to perform the function of an horse. The Sultan was struck at this novelty, and, immediately reflecting how far analogy might probably extend, bethought himself how very unsafe his ladies were under their present guards. In haste to ensure the chastity of his wives, he instantly returned home, and amputation ensued throughout the whole Seraglio. How far this story may be true I know not, but I relate it as it was told me at Constantinople.

Having in the course of this article mentioned the Kislar Aga (I forget his hated name[1]), I shall here insert such circumstances as came to my knowledge with regard to the character of this odious personage. His figure I have already described as far as I could without turning my reader's stomach. As to his reputation, he is said to possess every bad quality with which a ministerial pandar deprived of manhood can be supposed to be indued. He is said to be rapacious, vindictive, cruel, and treacherous. With regard to the first of these vices an accident put it in my power in some degree to judge of it. Going out one evening from Constantinople with the Ambassador in his carriage towards Belgrade, a beautiful village, within a few miles of the City where the foreign Ministers have their villas we happened to meet the Kislar Aga who with a great train was riding on horseback to take the air. Immediately after he had passed us one of his attendants rode back desiring that the Ambassador would send his master a pinch of snuff. Mr. Porter happened to have about him a very handsome gold box, which he carefully concealed and borrowed from one of us a leathern one such as for convenience we carried in travelling. This he sent to the Eunuch, assuring us that the message was sent with no other intention than to get possession of the gold box which was well-known to the sender and which would never have been restored but have been instantly seized upon and taken as a present, a trick, now stale from use, as it had been frequently played upon other Ministers.

Yet, as it is too often the lot of the best of princes to choose the most unworthy favourites, is this miserable wretch prime favourite to the excellent Mahmud, Vizir over the Grand Vizir and in effect first Minister of this mighty Empire. However, when we consider that such a wretch though in favour has hitherto been able to do but little mischief we cannot but form an high idea of the manly virtue of that Prince who, notwithstanding his unlucky partiality, can so far curb the destructive genius of his minion as to prevent him from ruining the state. Yet is this wretch — with grief and with shame I write it! — Yet is this despicable *thing!* absolute master of Athens and of Attica, which, together with a large tract of the circumjacent country of Greece, has been given to him as an appanage to provide him with pocket money, (no less than fifty purses), and was, when I was there, governed by a slave of his Defterdar or Treasurer, to whom he had allotted as wages the city of Athens, and who had sent one of his slaves to command there as Vaivode or Governor.

Strange and deplorable vicissitude! Athens! renowned and revered through all ages — the boast of Europe! the nurse of demigods! monopolist of learning, of arts, of arms! assertor of the liberty of Greece!

---

[1] Bekir Aga. See note 2 on p. 181.

scourge of eastern tyrants! what are now her wretched inhabitants? Slaves to a slave of the slave of an emasculated negro who is himself a slave! Aristides, Themistocles, Miltiades, Demosthenes! ye heroes, who have not only defended and graced your native soil but honoured human nature by your virtues, how must you now deplore the horrid fate of your miserable country! But no. Your actions in this world must have secured you from suffering such misery in those happy seats you now possess and adorn, nor is it consistent with the divine justice that the rattling of your country's chains should reach your ears! Blest as citizens of the world, your fellow citizens still are free, and Britons are now Athenians!

[Here Charlemont adds a footnote: 'N.B. This was written in the reign of George the Second when England was a free country.'][1]

After this last vexatious and heart-wounding circumstance one would hope and imagine that it was impossible to add anything which could increase our indignation. Yet is there another fact perhaps still more provoking, as it comes yet nearer to the private feelings of every man, of every woman. Though this horrid wretch be loathsome beyond the power of description or even of idea though he be by the help of inhuman art deformed to a degree of nauseous ugliness that nature never knew, though total amputation has bereft him of the possibility even of the most imperfect enjoyment, yet has the mutilated monster a multitude of wives, a harem stored with blooming virgin beauties, doomed to attend the odious call of his impotent lust! Wretched maidens! Degraded, ill-starred women! Condemned to — — — but I will draw a veil over the nauseous scene. Nature starts back with horror at the idea, and the bare recital of such abominations would be a crime against love and manhood!...

[In long footnotes here Charlemont discusses the history of eunuchism from biblical and classical times down to contemporary Italy with its castrati, *citing some contemporary examples.]*

It may however be some little satisfaction and consolation to us to reflect that the life of this miscreant, decorated as it is, though not dignified, by the tinsel of court favour, and medicated, not sweetened, by the enjoyment of power and by the accumulation of riches, is notwithstanding of all others perhaps the most miserable. Not to mention the continual fever and cravings of passions and of desires, which never can be quenched or gratified but which keep him in

---

[1] George II who favoured the Whigs, Charlemont's party, died in 1760. Until then Britain's policies under his Prime Minister William Pitt were generally admired and successful. The efforts of George III to reassert the powers of the Crown resulted in unrest in Britain and Ireland and rebellion in North America.

perpetual torments, equal at least to the fabled pangs of Tantalus, his power, his honours are to the last degree precarious depending upon the will and caprice of an arbitrary master, who can in an instant annihilate him. His accumulated wealth, dear bought by rapine, by extortion, and by the consequent pangs of a guilty conscience, can scarcely be called his own. The slightest change in his master's favour, to which his situation makes him hourly liable, supposing his life were spared, may strip him of all his ill acquired riches; and even though he were suffered to drag on his wretched being to its utmost natural hour, there at once his prospect closes. For he can have no heir, nor can the agonies of being separated from all he holds dear be softened or assuaged by the comfortable hope of transmitting it to a beloved child. Neither can he bequeath it to a friend, even supposing him capable of having any. The Sultan is his sole heir, and all must centre in the royal treasury.

Add to this the anxious miseries attending his employment. Placed in authority over a multitude of restless women, his master's wives, whom, though they fear him, he must always fear, who hate him for his office, and who, secluded from the world and from all wordly amusements, have nothing to employ their minds, nothing to meditate but the devising of means apt and prompt to plague and ruin those they hate. Tormented by perpetual female quarrels, by continual intrigues and never ceasing jealousies, he is perpetually at the crisis of his fate, and liable to be ruined every instant by the complaint of any favoured mistress insinuated to her intoxicated lover in the moment of complaisance. Such is his situation, and if such it be, perhaps the wretch is as miserable as he deserves to be.

And here in some degree to illustrate what I have now advanced concerning the miseries attending the life of this wretched jailer I will take the opportunity of mentioning a fact which happened in the Seraglio during my residence at Constantinople, the only one indeed that ever came to my knowledge well authenticated (told to me by the Ambassador who had it from the best authority), most of the anecdotes reported by travellers being mere forgeries, as the secrets of this prison house seldom or never transpire.

An intimate acquaintance of the Kislar Aga with repeated and pressing entreaties besought his permission that a young slave of the most exquisite beauty should be presented to the Sultan. The eunuch, after much resistance, at length agreed and presented the slave to his master who presently became so enamoured of her charms that the former favourite soon found his visits much less frequent than they had usually been. Enraged at this alteration and inflamed by jealousy, the Sultana immediately sent for the Kislar Aga and with all the fury of a jealous woman ordered him instantly to tell her the cause of this change in the Sultan's affections, informing him at the same time that she was well convinced that he had, without her knowledge, presumed to introduce some new woman into the Harem, an insolence which she would never forgive.

The Kislar Aga not thinking it expedient to deny a fact which must shortly be known publicly pleaded in his defence that he was no other ways instrumental to the introduction of the obnoxious slave than by yielding to the pressing instances of a friend who had recommended to his protection a young woman whose beauty did not appear to him at all dangerous and of whose ascendancy over the Sultan he could not have formed the slightest idea. He offered moreover to undo what had been done and to manage matters so that the slave should be disgraced. The favourite, not content with this excuse, vowed vengeance against the eunuch, a vow seldom broken by the fair sex. She contrived so powerfully to stir up and to inflame the jealousies of all the other women that the Harem was a scene of perpetual confusion; nor was peace restored till the Sultan himself interfered, disgraced the slave, and banished the person who had been the first cause of this fatal introduction, assuring the discontented favourite that he had been put to death.

TURKISH WOMEN AND MARRIAGE

But the love of women among the Turks from the necessary consequences of their domestic economy is far different from that delicious passion which we term love, and from whence, as from their principal source, the most real, because the most natural, joys of our lives are derived. The gratification of sensual appetite seems to be the sole object of their wishes, and even matrimony with them appears to be little more than equivalent to the bought embraces of a venal harlot. Sentiment, delicacy, and all those endearing arts, those nice attentions by which mutual affection is cheaply and deliciously purchased are, we may suppose, scarcely known to them. Enjoyment is all they seek, and this is confined to the body alone, so that the injurious and absurd opinion, that women have no souls — a doctrine, though not general, yet believed by many of the Mahometans — seems, among them, to be founded upon a basis not entirely void of apparent solidity, since, enjoying their bodies alone, they can never be sensible that the lovely partners of their pleasure possess any spiritual part. Neither can it be said of them that this deficiency in the delights of love is in any great degree compensated by their being thereby freed from those torments which usually flow from a too great refinement of passion, since jealousy, that excruciating poison, which too often accompanies the *honey* of love, ... is rather more prevalent in Turkey than in any other country whatsoever....

The reason of this however is sufficiently obvious. Esteem, the only firm foundation of rational affection and the only powerful antidote against the bane of jealousy, can have no place in their hearts. Where there is no possibility of sinning there can be no virtue, or, if there be any, it can have no opportunity of showing itself. Where all women are equally watched, equally guarded, the most virtuously inclined and the most vicious are exactly upon the same footing. No woman can show herself pre-eminent above others excepting only in those qualities which inflame our desires, but in no sort command our regard, and of consequence esteem cannot exist for want of its proper object. Polygamy is also another source of jealousy in the East; and, that it is so, affords a strong argument to prove

196

unreasonableness of this practice, since every man who is jealous of his wives on account of their number tacitly confesses that he is unequal to the task of retaining the affections of many, and consequently that he can have no natural right to more than one. Indeed, if we are to seek for the real source of that degeneracy of manners with regard to the fair sex which is too apparent among the Turks, we may, I believe, find it in polygamy; and wherever this practice has been natural women have been enslaved, and refined love, that only defence of the weaker sex against the brutal encroachments of the stronger, has seldom known a debauchee who has been properly speaking a lover. The necessary causes also from which love arises are not only moral but physical, not only in the mind but in the constitution, and if the latter source be exhausted by that too frequent use, which variety always occasions, few or no effects can be expected to flow from the former.

It must however be confessed that the indelicacy with which we have charged the Turks is not absolutely universal. Instances may be found amongst them of passions more refined, neither have examples been wanting, however rare they may be of men who, possessing variety of women, have attached themselves to one selected from the number, to whom they have devoted the constancy of their lives. Human nature is everywhere one and the same; and, however she may be checked and thwarted by physical and by moral causes by the influence of climate or by the shackles of unnatural manners she will ever be endeavouring to return to herself, and instances of the success of her endeavours will never be wanting. That very jealousy also which I have before mentioned and blamed, though the symptom be a horrid one, serves however to indicate at least a degree of delicacy and refinement and the value the Turks set upon their women, their careful watchfulness over them, and all the consecrated mystery of the harem, would induce us to believe that something more delicate than mere sensuality, or even than the nice point of honour, must be the cause of all this expensive, this jealous, this anxious, care.

The persons of their women are sacred beyond what we can well conceive. They are held to be dishonoured even by being looked upon; and for this reason whenever they are obliged to go abroad, which they never do but for health or change of dwelling, they are carried in close litters[1] with latticed windows, guarded on every side by jealous eunuchs, who forbid all access. Neither is this circumspection confined to the great and rich. The fashion descends even to the lowest of people, who, though their poverty will not allow the expense of attendants or permit them to confine their wives at home,

---

[1]   Charlemont adds a long note here on the use of such litters in ancient Persia and Constantinople.

yet whenever the necessary business of the family compels them to suffer their women to walk the streets are, equally with their betters, careful to hide them from view. Their dress is such as to secure them from being seen almost as effectually as the litters above-mentioned. Their faces are so muffled that not a feature can be distinguished, and their persons are perfectly concealed by a long cloak of thick woollen, made like our watchman's great coat, which covers their very feet; and any attempt to touch, or even to look steadfastly at them, would be a crime which could not escape immediate punishment, as every man would think himself interested to inflict it. But indeed custom has so consecrated the persons of women, and the slightest infringement would be accounted an enormity so sacrilegious, that they are perfectly secure from every species of insult; nor is a crime of this nature ever heard of in Turkey.

When we were in Egypt a janissary attended us whose name was Mahomet, of whom I shall hereafter have occasion to speak, the most faithful and affectionate creature that ever lived. By treating him kindly we had so far won his heart that I am certain there was no danger which he would not willingly have encountered for our sake. One day, in order to try him, I begged of him to let me see his wife, promising at the same time not to speak to her and content to be so hid that she should not see me. His answer, in broken English, which he had learned at our Consul's, to whom he was attendant janissary, was in these words: 'Ah master! Me fight for you. Me die for you — no force. But my wife not show. No good Turkman show his wife.' It must however be confessed that there did not appear any great refinement of love between this couple, for Mahomet's account of his wife was as follows: 'My last wife, no good wife. She not wash my shirt. She not make my broth. I sell her — no force. Buy another. This wife very good wife. She wash my shirt well. She makes broth good. Very good wife!' By the words 'no force,' which was a favourite expression, he generally meant 'willingly, without compulsion,' and sometimes, 'without thinking it a hardship.'

A French physician resident at Cairo informed me that though he had been sometimes sent for to visit Turkish women he had never once been permitted to see his patient, who was always muffled so as to be perfectly concealed from view; and when allowed to feel her pulse he was obliged to content himself with guessing at its movement through a piece of thick muslin. (This French doctor informed me of another circumstance which I mention on account of its oddity. The venereal disorder, that bane to love which has spread itself and scattered its plagues through all the habitable world is very common in Egypt. Our doctor was frequently sent for to women whose husbands had infected them, and, when these innocent creatures gave him an account of their symptoms, they always prefaced their relation by declaring that they had got the disorder by a fright).

Nay, to such a length is this decent prejudice carried among the Turks, that even females are not allowed to see each other undressed; and so nice are they in their notions of decency that two women are never suffered to bathe together — a circumstance which — I am sorry to say it — entirely discredits Lady Mary Wortley Montagu's beautiful and voluptuous description of Turkish bathing.[1]

After what has been said of the delicacy of the Turks it will not appear strange that, among them, to attempt the chastity of another man's wife should be esteemed a crime of the deepest dye, and that adultery should be looked upon with much more horror even than murder. But if their jealousy be so great with regard to their countrymen and brethren, it is carried to a far greater length with respect to us Christians. It would seem indeed as if they thought their women not only debauched but profaned also by Christian communication; and the female who is so far gone in depravity as to suffer herself to be defiled by the touch of a *Giaour* or Infidel is deemed to be no longer fit to live. If a Christian be found in a room with a Turkish woman, even though nothing criminal can be supposed to have passed between them both parties are punished with death.

An instance of this kind happened a few days before my arrival at Constantinople. A Turkish woman of a rank above the vulgar having by some accident seen a young Greek who kept a shop in the City became at once violently enamoured of him, an incident, which, though it may appear unnatural to us, and rather savouring of romance than of reality, is however by no means out of the course of nature among women who are closely confined. As expedients are never wanting where love conducts the intrigue, she contrived, by what means I know not, to escape the vigilance of her guards, and disguised and veiled like one of the lowest class, searched through the streets till at length she found the dwelling of her beloved. In haste she entered the shop, but not finding him there, opened the door of a little counting house in which she discovered him sitting and busied in making up his day's account. She instantly shut and locked the door, but being closely pursued, her guards, even before she could speak to him, broke open the door and seized them both. When brought before the *Cadi* or Judge, upon proof made of their being found together, the man was ordered to instant execution, and was, notwithstanding his plea of innocence, immediately beheaded, and the woman was condemned to be drowned, the usual punishment for women in Turkey.

Her parents however, whose natural affection was strong enough

---

[1] Other travellers attest that she (1689-1772, *DNB*) was correct in saying that Turkish women sometimes bathed together.

to get the better even of their prejudices, desirous to save their daughter's life, by a large sum of money prevailed upon the executioner, who has in Turkey the power of choosing the place of execution, to execute the sentence in that part of the basin, which was near and directly opposite to a Kiosk or Summer House of the Seraglio where the Grand Signor was known at that hour of the day constantly to resort, in hopes that out of his well known mercy he might stop the proceeding and pardon the criminal. As they had supposed, the Prince was at that time in the Kiosk and saw the transaction. But instead of pardoning he made a signal that execution should be no longer delayed, and the woman was accordingly drowned. Nor can there be a stronger proof of the violent antipathy and detestation which the Turks entertain against crimes of this nature than to behold a Prince, whose merciful disposition we have already described and ascertained, refusing his pardon to a wretched woman, who suffered death in his sight. The punishment inflicted on the innocent Greek also, who in a country where the laws are by no means sanguinary was capitally convicted merely for having been the passive object of an unlawful passion, is an extraordinary instance of the power of prejudice, and clearly evinces what I have before mentioned of the unreasonable length to which the Turks carry their prejudiced resentment against any unfortunate Christian, who may be innocently involved in the slightest connexion with their women.

Another affair, nearly of the same nature, happened at Cairo not long before my arrival. A young English gentleman whose name was Lethieulier, nephew to our Consul, had the misfortune to gain the heart or rather to inflame the passion of a Turkish lady, who had accidentally seen him. Whether or not he had in any way encouraged this dangerous passion I cannot say, but one evening as he was loitering in a shop the lady entered suddenly and shut the door after her. The house being immediately invested, our countryman, apprehensive of the consequences, luckily contrived to make his escape by a back door; but the unfortunate lady was seized by her pursuers who hurried her back to the harem from whence she had eloped, where as she never was heard of afterward, in all probability she was privately put to death. Information being given against Lethieulier, and proof made that he had been the object of her passion and that, though but for a minute, they had been shut up together, the strictest search was made and no means left untried to discover his retreat. Had he been then found, his death would have been inevitable; but fortunately for him he was able to keep himself concealed till his uncle, Consul Barton, with the utmost difficulty and for the sum of fifteen hundred sequins accommodated the matter. This accommodation, however, which was difficult at Cairo, where money is omnipotent and where venality is so universal that even prejudices are sold, would probably have been impossible at Constantinople.

The injustice of these proceedings is too striking to need any comment, nor can anything be said in mitigation of it, excepting only that the Turkish law always presumes that it is physically impossible for a woman to be alone with the man whom she loves without criminality, a presumption which perhaps we may not deem absolutely unreasonable when we consider the necessary operation of confinement upon the spirit and upon the passions of women and the sad effects which jealousy and distrust naturally produce even upon the best of female hearts — effects which may perhaps be still worse in proportion as the injured heart is endowed with noble and generous principles.

And here I cannot avoid observing that this very presumption in the law of the Turks clearly, though tacitly, confesses and accuses the unreasonableness and iniquity of their customs. Indeed it must be confessed that the fair sex in Turkey is upon a footing not only disagreeable and disgraceful to them, but shocking and abhorrent to humanity. Degraded from the dignity of their nature, they seem to be considered as little superior to the brute creation, and, like them, are set apart, and assigned to the arbitrary use of a lordly master, for whose pleasure and convenience alone they are supposed to be framed. And, in consequence of this arrogant pretention their education, or rather *training*, has no other tendency than to fit them for those servile, though sensual, offices, to which they are subjected, and for which alone it is presumed that nature has intended them. Immured for life within those detestable repositories, which may well be styled *the mews* for women, dressed and fed and trained for use, one half of the human species, and that too, if not the better, at least the most lovely, is entirely cut off from every enjoyment of society, from every right of nature.

True it is that, even in the act which injures them, they have their revenge. The loss of general intercourse between the sexes is to the men a punishment full as great, and perhaps even worse in its consequences, than the slavish confinement to which they reduce their women. The anxiety by which tyranny is always accompanied far surpasses the vain and unnatural pleasure of despotism, and their tyrants, like political despots, are consequently strangers to the delight of governing subjects who are free and happy, and, as fear is their only engine of government, can never hope to experience the blessings attendant on love. Ignorant of the sincere and spiritual delights which flow from free and unconstrained affection, their best enjoyment is merely corporal, and in proportion as they degrade their women they lower themselves also in their pleasures to the level of brutes. Thus doth nature ever avenge her violated laws, deducing the punishment from the necessary consequences of the act of violation. But what do the wretched women gain by this revenge? They on the contrary are the losers by it, since in proportion as the tyrant is degraded the lot of the slave becomes still more abject!

The women have also their revenge in another particular. The variety in which the Turks indulge themselves forcibly inclines them to transgress the bounds of nature in their sensual pleasures; and this added to their early and premature intercourse with women, is one principal cause that impotency is exceedingly common among them to obviate which misfortune they make use of every kind of inflammatory drugs and of consequence instead of remedying thereby render their inability absolutely incurable. The use of opium also is probably a concurring cause of this misfortune.

But vengeance of love of of nature doth not stop here. There yet remains an odious circumstance, which, though a stain to my paper candour will not suffer me to conceal. There is too much reason to believe that the Turks are greatly addicted to that detestable vice which nature starts at, and which, if there were not too certain proof that such crimes have been perpetrated, no innocent man could suppose possible....

Refinement of manners, however extraordinary and paradoxical it may appear, has generally been productive of unnatural vices. Refinement necessarily produces luxury, one principal of which is an unrestrained intercourse with women, and this naturally brings satiety and a consequent desire and search after novelty. The epicure whose palate has been palled by every exquisite taste which nature affords, seeks novelty even in nastiness, and flavours naturally the most detestable, become delicacies to him, as being alone capable of exciting his depraved and sated appetite. However, as it is certain that a too great refinement of manners cannot be assigned as a cause of the prevalence of this horror among the Turks one would almost be inclined to believe that there was some radical vice in the climate which influences them as it formerly did their predecessors, the Greeks.

Yet let us not accuse nature of those crimes for which our own depravity is accountable. The best gifts of Heaven are by wicked men so perverted as often to produce the worst effects. Thus strength and courage become the means of violence, beauty of wantonness, and power of oppression; and that benign temperature of the air which produces health and vigour, and consequently strong and violent passions, though in itself a blessing, becomes by the wicked and unrestrained indulgence of these passions a source of the most infamous crimes. The unlimited and early use of women among the Turks induces satiety and consequent disgust, and, if the passion still remains after its natural objects are become distasteful, new and unnatural objects are sought afterwards, nature is forced from her proper channel, and the horrors of this vice are substituted for the innocent joys of love. I blush while I recount such instances as have occurred to me in proof of the prevalence of this horror among the Turks, and shall therefore be as brief as possible in order to get rid of an odious subject which I choose to huddle up in a note, that my text at least may remain undefiled.

It has happened to me more than once on board of Turkish men-of-war to have been shown a number of handsome boys attendant on the Captain, who, as I was assured, were kept solely for this infamous purpose. Being becalmed off the coast of Asia Minor, and some of our sailors being sent to cut firewood for the use of the ship, we chose to accompany them for the sake of walking and to see the country. Our sailors, fearless of danger, scattered themselves abroad, while Burton and I walked together with our guns in our hands with which we usually went armed, when suddenly we observed one of our people, a Manx boy of about eighteen years old, running towards us with great symptoms of fear, and presently we perceived two Turks who pursued him. We ran up towards him and presented our arms at the Turks who immediately turned and fled, and the boy informed us that having caught him at a ridiculous and nasty disadvantage they had seized him and offered violence, but that escaping out of their hands and seeing us at a distance, he had ran towards us for protection.

Such are the reflections, which must naturally occur to every feeling heart upon the slightest review of these illiberal customs; and yet — for I would fain afford what comfort I could to my brethren in sensibility — perhaps that delicacy of feeling towards the fair sex to which we are fortunately inclined by the gallantry of our manners may prompt us to push these reflections rather too far and to imagine the situation of Turkish women still more miserable even than it really is. We are apt to measure their sufferings by what we conceive our women would suffer under similar circumstances. But in this we err. Custom has the power not only to render such hardships tolerable but even to make the acting contrary to its despotic institutions, (how irrational soever they may be), unpalatable to ingenuous minds. Our Consuless at Cairo — for I am obliged to bring together all the little knowledge I have been able to collect upon this mysterious subject — was known to many Turkish women, and often visited them. She informed me that when in the course of conversation she told them of Christian liberty, of the unconfined intercourse of the sexes, and of the freedom indulged to women in our countries, they seemed rather to look upon such customs with disgust and horror than with any degree of envy or desire. They exclaimed against our ladies as unnaturally licentious, and treated those liberties which we account innocent as criminal to the last degree. In a word they cried out against our customs as our women would do at the naked simplicity of the Indians, or at the liberality of love which the discovery of

Otaheite[1] has lately disclosed to us. But in matters which are not in themselves really and essentially criminal, custom alone influences; and, if a matron of Queen Elizabeth's time were, in the other world, to be informed of the innocent and laudable institution of the female club, she would rashly conclude that modesty and virtue were absolutely annihilated in Britain....

[Here Charlemont reflects on the end effects of polygamy and of its equivalent in the West, extra-marital 'Christian intrigue.' He continues as follows]:

It may not however be superfluous here to observe that polygamy, the groundwork of female misery in the east, is by no means so universal among the Turks as is commonly imagined. The expense of a well stocked harem is too considerable to come within the faculty of the poorer sort, and the law positively forbids the keeping more wives than can be well and decently maintained, so that men of the lower class are generally obliged to content themselves with one. But as fashion is everywhere established by the great and the rich, and from them descends to the vulgar, every man, even to the lowest of the people, has his woman's apartment, the sanctity of which is as punctiliously observed as in the Harem of the Grand Signor. At Bodromi,[2] a town on the coast of Asia Minor, the seat of Halicarnassus, happening to meet with an inscription of value upon a stone, which served as doorpost to a very small and mean house belonging to a cobbler and being desirous to copy it, I offered money to the landlord for leave to sit at the inside of the door, but was answered that it could not be permitted, as that was the entrance to his harem. However, as I persisted in increasing my offer I at length prevailed but not till the lady had been previously transported by a back door into a neighbour's apartment.

At Constantinople, though all communication with Mahometan women be so strictly forbidden, the most perfect freedom is allowed to Christians with regard to women of every other religion, and we are at liberty to frequent houses of the sort mentioned in the text without being liable to the least molestation or even to scandal, and perhaps with more safety than in any of our own great cities. Gallantry also of a more liberal kind is not unusual, and the mode of living at Constantinople is to a young man as pleasant as in any great city whatsoever. That quarter of the town, which is called Pera and

---

[1] Tahiti. The first European to visit the island was Samuel Wallis in 1767 and the second Bougainville in 1768 but Charlemont's knowledge of island customs probably derives from Cook's visit in 1769, his account of which was published in 1773.

[2] See Greek Essay pp. 88-89.

which forms itself a large city, is entirely peopled with Franks and Greeks who live together in the most sociable manner and, with the public Ministers, form a society as pleasing as possible. The pleasures of the table are well understood and frequent, and scarce an evening passes without balls, concerts or assemblies at all which the intercourse between the sexes is as easy as can be wished. The women are exceedingly handsome and well-dressed, and their manners are remarkably pleasing, a probable indication that they are no foes of love. As a proof of the agreeableness of this place I will only mention that Mr. Falkner, a young gentleman ... [see next page], having while I was at Constantinople received from his uncle a letter which recalled him to England was as deeply affected and as much afflicted at the necessity he found himself under of leaving this city as if his returning home had been to him a real banishment. Such is the freedom indulged to Christians by the Constantinopolitan Turks. But, when we come to treat of Egypt, we shall find in that country the case strangely different. The strictness, or to speak more properly, the ferocity of Egyptian manners is so great, their hatred and contempt of those whom they please to term infidels is so established, so rooted in their minds, that no intercourse, at least of an amorous kind, is allowed to Christians with women of any denomination whatsoever, their wives only excepted; and an affair of gallantry, even between Franks, would be highly dangerous, and, though not punishable with death, would subject the offender to the worst treatment, or at least to the most exorbitant fine. Indeed these barbarians seem to think that they alone have a right to monopolise the joys of love, pleasures, which they esteem too great, too precious, to be indulged by a Christian.

I purposely omit mentioning many circumstances with respect to the subject of this article, which may be met with in every printed account of the Turks. Their marriage laws are too well known to need repetition, and no one is ignorant that every Mussulman is allowed four wives, provided he can decently maintain them, and as many concubines as he chooses upon the same reasonable condition. One thing however may be worth observing, that notwithstanding all this latitude with regard to women, which is still farther increased by the facility of divorce, and though their marriages are so early as sometimes even to precede the age of puberty, the young men among them, whose passions one would imagine might be fully contented in a legal way, do not abstain from frequenting public brothels, many of which are to be found at Constantinople. So true it is that no extent of latitude can satisfy the overheated imagination or set bounds to its wanderings; that the widest extension of legal enjoyment is no prevention against disgust, since it is as difficult to be constant to many as to one; and that in the midst of lawful abundances forbidden pleasure will always be sought after....

It may seem unnecessary to observe that in these houses Turkish women are never met with. The ladies here to be obtained are Greeks, Jewesses, and Armenian Christians, many of whom are extremely beautiful and well skilled in all the necessary arts and allurements of their calling. As it is the duty of travellers to leave nothing unseen, our curiosity, and perhaps something more, has sometimes enticed Burton and me to these hospitable receptacles. The first visit of the kind we paid was in company with Mr. Falkner, a young English merchant, nephew to Sir Everard,[1] who was upon this occasion our kind conductor. We were received in a large chamber set round with convenient sofas by the matron of the house, an elderly Greek gentlewoman who, being whispered by our friend, retired to give the necessary directions. And presently we were surrounded by eight or ten goddesses, in their form and in their situation exactly resembling those who disputed the prize of beauty upon Mount Ida and disclosed the full blaze of their heavenly charms to the dazzled eyes of the Trojan shepherd,[2] a liberality which was more pleasing to us, as it so perfectly contrasted the cloud-envelopped apparitions to the contemplation of which we had been hitherto confined.

With regard to the beauty of the Turkish women I am able to say but little, having never had the good fortune, or perhaps the misfortune, distinctly to behold one. But as the Greeks are generally very handsome, and as the harems are filled with the choice of all the East which is annually brought to Constantinople as to the principal and most profitable market, we must conclude them to be beautiful. And since beauty alone, like lustre to the diamond, constitutes their value (since their personal charms are the only treasure they possess) the only means by which, in the contracted sphere of their confinement, they can become considerable and in some sort reverse their slavish destiny by enslaving the hearts of their imperious masters, the only weapons by which they can subdue their rivals, and procure to themselves that triumph of superiority, which comprehends the whole of their happiness we need not doubt but that every possible care is taken, every method pursued, to preserve these precious charms, and to increase their splendour. For this purpose Nature is ransacked for all her cosmetic secrets — such, I mean, as are innocent in their effects, for I do not find that among the Turkish ladies those wicked and destructive arts are in use, now too common among us, which, like fire to a torch, consume while they brighten. Baths medicated with the most costly drugs, washes impregnated with the most precious balsams of Arabia, all the richest and most odoriferous per-

[1] See note on p. 167.

[2] Paris, Prince of Troy, who judged between Hera, Athena, and Aphrodite, for the prize of beauty, and caused the Trojan War by choosing Aphrodite.

fumes of the East are constantly employed.

But of all powerful cosmetic that which by experience they have found the most efficacious, is an unguent made of the balsam of Mecca, a precious turpentine brought from the neighbourhood of that City which they possess the art of preparing so as to reduce it to an ointment. When I was at Cairo I endeavoured to procure a quantity of this valuable drug, which is the most sovereign remedy I have ever met with in all consumptive coughs, as well as many other dangerous disorders. But it was with the utmost difficulty that by the interest of our Consul I could obtain a single quart of it genuine and unaultered, almost the whole product being annually bought up for the use of the Seraglio, where it is only employed in the manner, and for the purpose above mentioned.

But if the Turkish ladies be so anxiously careful of their beauty we may be very sure they are not wanting in their best endeavours to heighten and to exalt that beauty by the aid of dress and of every adventitious ornament.[1] Of this too a stranger may form a tolerable judgment, as the Greek ladies are fond of finery and exactly imitate the Turks in their manner of dressing. Nothing can be more noble or more graceful than the whole disposition of their garment, to the easy flow of which the awkward stiffness of our gothic habiliments appears gothic indeed. But that in which they most excel is in their various methods of ornamenting the head, all of which are graceful and beautiful beyond expression. Their expense, too, in the article of dress far exceeds our utmost magnificence, and a single pellice, or fur lining, of one of their gowns is often more costly than the whole attire of our ladies. Of jewels also they are extremely fond, and, though we excel them in the art of polishing and setting, in profusion they far surpass us.

It will, I doubt not, appear singular and even absurd to our fine ladies, who however magnificent abroad, are sometimes apt to indulge themselves in the dear privilege of being slovenly at home, that such expense should be lavished, so much pains taken, to ornament a person which is only to be seen by one man and that too a husband. Yet perhaps this apparent absurdity may vanish when it is considered that this one man, this husband, is to the Turkish lady all mankind, and that she is for ever surrounded by a multitude of rivals. Neither ought it to surprise us that the Turkish men are profusely lavish in this article of expense, though the motive of vanity be entirely removed.

---

[1] Charlemont has a note here: 'Fat among the Turks is esteemed a beauty even when it exceeds the embonpoint, and leanness a deformity. There is nothing more certain than that women in the harems are fed with the most fattening food and are in effect crammed for use as we cram pullets. Our Consuless at Cairo, who was remarkably lean, informed me that she was the constant object of ridicule among her female Turkish acquaintance on account of her leanness.'

Love, such as we have described it, is the ruling passion among the Turks. Women, however whimsically they may be treated, are still the adored objects of this their ruling passion, and beauty is the single attribute sought after in these idols of their adoration, the only idols of which that religion admits, whose foundation is sensual love. Is it then surprising that no expense should be spared to exalt that beauty, or to deck and to ornament these only visible objects of their passionate worship.

Having now mentioned everything I could collect upon this difficult subject, I shall here conclude the article, which, considering the small information I fear it affords, has alrpady been too tenuous and (as not quite foreign to the purpose), I shall close my account of Turkish love by a literal translation of three short Turkish love-songs. From such popular ballads the genius of a people may in some degree be inferred. These translations, which I procured at Constantinople, may perhaps serve to give my reader some slight idea of that passion among the Turks, which I have found so difficult to investigate.

TURKISH LOVE-SONGS

Buy me, my lord. Take me, if you think me capable to please you, or if you doubt that I am false or counterfeit money, send me to be proved by the Sheraph.[1]

When I attend on my mistress my posture is that of the humblest slave. But upon the least favourable glance I become in the instant greater than the Sultan!

Ah my love! All my pleasure is to embrace thee! Lying in thine arms I wish that night might be prolonged to all eternity!

[1] A Sarraf was a money-changer.

TURKISH POLICE

There is not, I believe, in Europe any city where the police is so well regulated as at Constantinople. House-breaking and street-robbery, crimes so unfortunately common in our great towns as to render the dwelling in them unpleasant and unsafe, never happen in the Turkish metropolis, and a man may walk its streets at all hours of the night, or even sleep in them with his pocket full of money, without the smallest fear or danger of molestation. No murders, no assaults, no riots ever happen here, nor are those brutal acts of violence by which our impetuous and ill-educated young men are so fond of signalizing themselves ever so much as heard of. Formerly indeed the Turkish sailors, especially those who belong to the ships of war, and whom they term *levantis,* used sometimes to infest the streets, raising riots and insulting passengers, but these enormities have been long since put an end to by the salutary rigour of frequent executions. That sobriety which the law against the use of wine[1] has introduced among the Turks is undoubtedly one principal cause of this civil

[1]   Charlemont comments on this: 'There is no positive law in the Koran against the use of wine but only an exhortation of the Prophet to abstain from that liquor. The Turks give the following account of the origin of this exhortation. Mahomet, say they, travelling in Arabia, passed through a certain village on a festival day, and finding the inhabitants extremely joyous he asked the cause and was told that their gaiety proceeded from their having drunk wine; upon which he blessed the vine for having been the occasion of so much joy. Some days after, passing the same way he found the village almost depopulated, and upon enquiring into the reason of this sad reverse he was informed that the people, having drunk too much, had grown mad, quarrelled, and slaughtered each other. Upon this he cursed wine, and exhorted his disciples to abstain from the use of it.
His exhortation is in general well-complied with, and in consequence thereof the Turks are the soberest people upon earth, yet some of them are too apt to consider the words of the Prophet in the most literal sense, and imagine that if they abstain from the juice of the grape they may drink any other spirituous liquor. Of this we have seen frequent instances. Many Turks, who have come on board our ship, though they have absolutely refused wine, have drunk drams very freely, and even begged bottles of them to carry home. But above all things they seemed to delight in punch, which however the more scrupulous among them would not drink, till we assured them that it was English sherbet, in which confidence they have frequently got drunk with it in the most Christian manner.'

tranquillity. But the source from whence the security of the streets, as well from insult as from robbery, chiefly derives is the sensible, active and vigorous management of the night patrol or city watch.

In order to give my reader some idea of the manner in which this important part of civil economy is directed and carried on, I will relate a whimsical incident which happened to me, and occasioned one of those momentary terrors which, however serious and real at the time, become ridiculous when we find that they have been groundless, and in consequence of which we laugh in the same proportion as we have been previously frightened.

We had not been many days arrived at Constantinople when Frank Burton, whose activity and curiosity with regard to some certain points of natural knowledge were as great as a traveller ever possessed, proposed to Falkner (the young English merchant whom I have formerly mentioned) and to me, a nightly excursion through the streets in search of one of those modern Temples of Venus which are found in every metropolis whatever be the religion of the country, where men of all sects, of all opinions, laying aside their animosities conform to one general mode of worship and join in paying their adorations to the ancient and universal goddess.

The party was cheerfully accepted, and after supper, about twelve o'clock, we set out from the Ambassador's, accompanied only by a Greek conductor who, though born in Greece, probably derived his descent from the illustrious Pandarus of Troy.[1] The idea of a nocturnal ramble through unknown streets in a city of whose inhabitants our prejudices had taught us to form the most terrible notions, our consciousness that the purpose we were going upon was rather of a licentious and, for ought that we knew, of an illegal kind, joined to the pitchy darkness of the night, here unallayed even by the twinkling of a single lamp, and the dead silence which now reigned through this populous and lately busy town, could not fail of preparing our minds to be easily alarmed and startled at any sudden appearance of danger; when all at once the pitchy darkness gave place to the gleam of a multitude of lanterns by which we were surrounded and which glared upon us from every quarter, and the dead silence was broken by the clamour of a large party of men, who encompassed us on every side, armed with monstrous clubs which they violently struck against the ground, accompanying this menacing action by words which we could not understand but which appeared to us threats of immediate destruction.

The surprise of this sudden appearance, which (as we had not heard the smallest previous noise), was utterly unaccountable to us,

---

[1]   In the *Iliad* the chief of the Lycian allies of the Trojans who broke a truce by wounding Menelaos and was afterwards killed by Diomedes. In the later tradition he was portrayed as acting as a 'pandar' between the Trojan Troilus and the Greek Cressida.

210

the blaze of light, which shone in our eyes and dazzled us like a nightly flash of lighning, the number, noise, arms, and threatening action of those whom we deemed our assailants — all these alarming circumstances, aggravated by our ideas of Turkish barbarity, are fully sufficient to account for that terror with which we strangers were for a moment seized. But a moment put an end to our fears. Falkner laughed, and our conductor desired us to be under no apprehension, and going up to the Captain or Constable of the Watch, for such it seems they were, acquainted him that we were English strangers who were walking for our recreation and to enjoy the cool air. The civil Captain wished us good night and a pleasant walk. The lanterns were instantly turned; the patrol marched off as silently as it had advanced; and we were again left in darkness and security.

We now had leisure to inquire into the cause of this alarming apparition, and were informed that several parties of this sort distributed through the different districts were constantly employed all night in patrolling the streets; that each man carries a dark lantern, which is kept covered that their approach may be unforeseen, for which reason also they always march in the most profound silence. By this means such persons as are walking at undue hours are taken unawares and surrounded by surprise. They are, as we before mentioned, armed with clubs, in the use of which they are well instructed, and particularly in the art of throwing them with so great dexterity that, if any person should attempt to escape by running, he is presently stopped by the club, which they throw so dexterously that it gets between his legs and tumbles him.

Such is the Watch of Constantinople, by means of which and of the strict and vigorous execution of the laws against any offenders whom they may apprehend, the streets of this vast and populous metropolis are kept in profound tranquillity; and perhaps this method of concealing the approach of justice, and by that means of encompassing and seizing malefactors by surprise, might be with utility adopted by us. When our watchmen have gone their rounds, which are marked not only by the hour but by the noise they make, night walkers may seize the interval and perpetrate their mischiefs without fear. But at Constantinople, as it cannot be known in what quarter the watch may be at any certain time, the evil-inclined are kept in perpetual check, in constant apprehension, as they cannot divine how near their assailants may be or at what instant they may be surrounded. Without however attempting to decide I shall only say that the effects seem to favour the Turkish manoeuvre, and that the terror which we felt at the approach of these formidable guards is to us a plain proof of the superior utility of this method.

But it is not only the city which feels the excellence of Turkish police. It extends its influence over that vast tract of country, which lies between Constantinople and the Austrian dominions. Not only the roads about the metropolis are perfectly free from robbers but a child may travel unmolested even to the frontiers provided he does not deviate from the great roads. Through the whole extent of this long route, which crosses countries wild, inhospitable, and apparently most dangerous and fitted for rapine, such admirable care is taken, and justice is so well administered, that no such thing as robbery is ever heard of.

TURKISH JUSTICE

And now, without venturing to enter into any minute discussion of Turkish jurisprudence, a task of the most difficult nature and for which the small information which I could procure is but ill suited, I shall under this article briefly mention such circumstances as have come to my knowledge with regard to this important part of national manners; and this I shall do without attempting any order or arrangement, but shall content myself with setting down facts as they occur in my notes.

I do not find that tortures, or cruel punishments of any kind, are common among the Turks. Impalement, that shocking cruelty which we are taught to believe is daily practised, I never so much as heard of, and though perhaps in the more barbarous ages of the Empire this horrible punishment may have been sometimes employed it is now totally disused.[1] The practice however still, as I am told, continues in the piratical States of Barbary, and its frequency there may have misled us to suppose that it is common in Turkey. The usual punishment for capital offences is beheading, as hanging is with us, and this is performed in the easiest and least cruel manner. The criminal is made to kneel down blindfolded, and the executioner, well versed and exercised in his trade, never fails with one stroke of a heavy sabre to sever the head from the body, which is hung up upon a gibbet. In cases of murder execution is performed on the spot where the fact was committed, for there is not at Constantinople, as with us, any particular place of execution. But with regard to the gibbetting, the executioner is in possession of a whimsical privilege from the exertion of which he derives a considerable yearly income. The place of gibbetting is left to his choice, in consequence of which he carries the body from house to house, threatening to hang it up at the door of such as will not make him a certain present. Most people in order to avoid the disagreeable circumstance of having a body dangling at their door for three days, (for so the law directs), pay the necessary tribute,

---

[1]   In fact it was used later by the Turks during the Greek War of Independence (1821-30).

which amounts but to a few paras. At length however he meets with some sturdy fellow, who will not pay, and at his door the body hangs. Hanging also, as with us, is sometimes practised, and in this case the hangman possesses the same troublesome privilege. The most usual punishment for women is drowning. (The punishments mentioned ... are only as are practised in public executions and inflicted on persons of low rank. The great men, and the officers of the Seraglio are never publicly executed. The usual punishment for such is strangling with a bowstring, and sometimes with a silken cord. Often also they are poignarded).

During the whole month which I passed at Constantinople I heard of but one execution, and that was of a Greek who was to be beheaded for murder. However as my residence was in Pera, one of the extremities of the City, others might have happened unknown to me in the distant quarters of this vast metropolis. No constitution whatsoever is, I believe, less fitted than mine to relish scenes of this nature, yet upon the present occasion my curiosity got the better of my weakness, and I joined the procession which was conveying the criminal to the place of execution about a mile from Pera where the murder had been committed. He was guarded, as with us, by the officers of justice unassisted, to the best of my recollection, by any of the military; and, as in all countries, such sights are pleasing to the vulgar, a considerable mob accompanied him, but with great decency and without the smallest riot or disturbance. And here my account of him must end, for after having walked about half a mile my weakness in its turn prevailed over my curiosity, and I grew so exceedingly sick with the idea of the catastrophe that I was obliged to relinquish all thoughts of seeing the execution and to return home.

That murder is uncommon among the Turks seems to result rather from the goodness of their disposition than from the efficacy of their laws which are certainly ill calculated to prevent the frequent perpetration of this horrid crime. If the nearest relation of the person murdered, who is always the prosecutor, consents to pardon the criminal, which he seldom fails to do for a sum of money, the judge, who too often receives his share of the fine, is authorized to remit the punishment. For, says the law, if the person to whom the party properly belonged be content, why should not justice also remain satisfied? How much more liberal and more consonant to reason and to sound policy is the spirit of our law, which considering murder is a crime against the King, who has been forcibly deprived of his subject, views it in the light of treason and makes the Sovereign the principal prosecutor!

[Here Charlemont notes that this custom of compounding for murder gets back to the Koran and is paralleled in Iliad *5, 628.]*

While we were at Constantinople a case of the nature above-mentioned happened in our neighbourhood. A Greek of Pera being accused of murdering another Greek was, as usual, prosecuted by the nearest relation of the deceased, and upon trial was clearly convicted. But upon paying the sum of 4000 piastres, which, as it was generally believed, was divided between the prosecutor and the judge, the murderer was discharged, and without any farther punishment was suffered to remain quietly in the City.

Indeed the accounts which we have received of the shocking corruption and prostitution which prevails among the Turkish judges, have been so frequent and so uniform that it is difficult not to give credit to them; and, if I may be allowed to depend upon the joint testimony of the English residing at Constantinople, most of whom I have consulted upon this subject, bribery is so openly practised among them as scarcely to be disavowed even by themselves. The principal source from which I suppose this infamous practice to proceed is from the iniquitous custom of setting judicial offices to sale, all of which are publicly sold, and the purchase money paid into the treasury or, more probably, embezzled by the Ministers who are entrusted with the power of selling these places. The judge who has paid dearly for his office thinks himself at liberty to make as much as he can of that which he has purchased, and justice thus becomes a mere traffic. Neither shall we have any difficulty to conceive the probability of this effect, when we consider the usual consequence of the sale of parliamentary seats among us.

This destructive custom is not however peculiar to the Turks. The same abomination has long since been established among our polished neighbours the French; and even with us, though the place of judge is always supposed to be gratuitously given to merit, yet sometimes, I fear, though not absolutely bought with money it is still more dearly and more infamously purchased by the sacrifice and by the barter of reason and of conscience in parliamentary proceedings. With us however the admirable institution of juries renders any defect in the integrity of the judge far less hurtful; and, though I know but little of the administration of justice in France, I can easily suppose that the manners of the people, and more especially that point of honour which is established amongst them and which in some degree supplies the place of virtue, may in a great measure obviate and prevent the ill effects, which might otherwise proceed from this abominable practice.

A whimsical instance of bribery was related to us, which happened not long before our arrival. A Turk sold to another a horse for 200 piastres. The horse was by no means dear, but the purchaser, not finding him exactly answer his purpose, and recollecting that he had expended more money than he could well afford, wished to break through the agreements and to oblige the seller to take him back. With this intent he goes to a judge and presents as a bribe half the price of the horse, 100 piastres. The seller, who was aware of his design and resolved to defeat it, had been already beforehand with him and had also bribed the judge with half the sum agreed on to induce him to compel the other to stand to his bargain. The judge received both bribes, and, when the matter came to a hearing, calmly said to the parties, 'gentlemen, it is my duty to prevent differences between Mussulmans. I wish to settle this affair amicably, and without farther litigation — I like the horse. Here is his price. Divide it between you, and I will take him myself.'

And now that I have given an instance of the venality of Turkish judges, it is but just that I should mention one, which may serve to exemplify their quickness and ingenuity in deciding causes of difficulty. While we were at Constantinople, the following remarkable trial happened at Galata, one of the suburbs of this city. A Minorcan vessel being in imminent danger from the violence of a sudden storm the captain with the consent of the passengers, some of whom were proprietors, threw overboard a quantity of rice, which, having been stowed upon deck, must infallibly have occasioned the loss of the ship. Upon his arrival at Constantinople he was sued by one of the proprietors who resided there for 200 dollars, being the value of his share in the rice. When the cause came to a hearing, and evidence had been given in proof of the facts above-mentioned, the judge, after having expatiated on the ill consequences which would ensue from giving judgment against the captain, told the plaintiff, that having consulted his books upon the subject he had found beyond all controversy that he, the plaintiff, had an absolute right to the value of his rice — but then that it was only to its value at the instant of time before it was thrown overboard, when the imminent danger of the vessel which could only be saved by being lightened, made it worth just nothing. Pisani, our English dragoman, was present at this excellent decision, which was related to me by the Ambassador and afterwards confirmed by Pisani himself.

The law's delay, one of those miseries which, according to the excellent Shakespeare,[1] make life burdensome, (and that too, none of the lightest in his catalogue), is certainly less felt among the Turks than by any other people whatsoever. Lawsuits here are generally determined at a hearing. The judge patiently listens to all that can be urged by both parties, examines the witnesses, and then decrees according to the established law. The parties plead for themselves, and produce their evidence, advocates not being allowed them as the judge is supposed to be so fully instructed in the law as to need no

---

[1] *Hamlet*, 3, 1, 72, in the famous 'To be or not to be' soliloquy.

information from counsel, and with regard to the mere relation of facts the parties are esteemed fully competent. Whether this custom be good or bad I shall not venture to determine, but certain it is that delay and expense are both prevented by it. Neither do I conceive that the loss of the community will be esteemed very great, though by this means we do not find at Constantinople those numerous bands of lawyers, which swarm in all other European capitals. If there should be an appeal I have already shown in my account of the Divan how very speedily appeals are determined. (In causes before the Divan it is certain that no advocate is ever admitted, but I am not quite sure whether in civil cases and in the lower courts, the parties may not have a right to be heard by counsel. To the best of my recollection however they have not, though I do not find the point positively ascertained in my notes).

There is a law in force at Constantinople, which must appear to us unjust and cruel. In case of a fire happening in the city it is positively enacted that the man in whose house the fire first breaks out shall die. This severe law is however, I suppose, mitigated according to the circumstances of the case, and as the Emperor has it always in his power to remit the penalty no great injustice can probably arise from it in the city where he resides. It has no doubt taken its rise from the fatal frequency of fires in this metropolis, and from the horrid devastations occasioned by them in a town, the buildings of which are mostly of wood.

The Turkish law with regard to blasphemy is singular, sensible, and far more demonstrative of veneration for the Supreme Being than any penal statutes which could be enacted against this horrid crime. Blasphemy against Mahomet is punished with immediate death, and to call him cheat, impostor, or false prophet, is a crime which never yet was pardoned. But no punishment whatsoever is provided for blasphemy against God; and the reason alleged, in the body of the law, for this omission is that no man in his senses can possibly be supposed to blaspheme the supreme Lord of All Things, his Creator, his Preserver, that a folly of so glaring a nature must undoubtedly be the effect of a distempered brain, and that no consequence of madness can be an object of punishment.

All thefts are not in Turkey, as with us, punished alike but according to their nature and degree. A highwayman, or one who breaks a lock in order to steal, is punished capitally. But a pickpocket, or a person who steals out of an open room can only be condemned to lose his hand, but is more commonly sentenced to the *bastinado*, the usual punishment for petty crimes, which consists of ninety-nine strokes with a stick on the bare soles of the feet.

Civil offices among the Turks are esteemed more honourable than military posts, and the Gown takes place of the Sword. But, as it must ever happen in all despotic governments, power resides with the military, and more than compensates any deficiency in rank. According to law no Pasha can punish the meanest criminal without previously consulting the Cadi or Mullah, i.e. the Judge of the District, and receiving his sentence. Yet the usual practice is directly contrary to this excellent institution. The Pasha frequently invades the province of the Judge, and without any previous consultation inflicts what punishments he pleases; while the Cadi, awed by his power and fearful of offending him, dares not so much as complain. This however can only happen in the provinces. At Constantinople justice is administered with the greatest regularity and decorum.

Sudden passion is not allowed by the Turkish law to be any extenuation of the guilt of murder, nor indeed of any other personal offence, the law rather esteeming it a pretence for the commission of crimes of this nature.

[Here and later Charlemont has a long digression on the Koran and on the religion of Islam in general. He contrasts its strict monotheism with the cult of the Virgin Mary and the Saints in the Roman Catholic Church. He also considers some absurdities in popular Mohammedanism, and adds remarks on alleged Turkish toleration of other religions].

CEREMONIES OF THE DERVISHES

[Charlemont first discusses the origin of the 'order' of Dervishes among the Moslems.]

When at Constantinople we got admission into the monastery of an order of monks called *Mevlevis,* from Mevleva their founder, though they are, I believe, more universally known by the appellation *Dervishes,* this general name of all monks being particularly applied to them as the principal order among Mahometans. On the Tuesday and Friday of every week they perform their functions in public, and this was one of those days. We were conducted into a spacious hall, where a number of people were assembled, like us, to behold the ceremony, though with a more religious view. The crowd pressed toward the extremities of the chamber, and a considerable space was left in the centre which was occupied by the monks dressed, as usual, in a gown of coarse whitish cloth, close before and behind, and fastened about the waist with a leather strap. Over this they wear a sort of jacket, so that their dress appears something like a woman's jacket and petticoat. To the best of my recollection the space where the monks danced was railed in. Women, who are excluded from other religious ceremonies, are allowed to be present at this, a privilege which they never fail to make use of, but so dressed and so closely muffled, that it is impossible to distinguish their shape or to see a feature of their face.

[Charlemont refers here to a drawing of the Dervishes by Dalton. See illustrations].

On their heads they wore caps of the same colour, usually made of camel's hair, and, stiffened into the form of a sugar-loaf.

The rites began with a sermon, to us unintelligible. It was preceded by a short hymn, and its purport was, as we were told, a recommendation to charity and to good works. The Superior of the convent then prayed without book, the people saying Amen to every petition. After prayer the long hymn of which I [shall give a] translation,

(above and opposite) Scenes from the ceremonies of the Dervishes

was chanted by one of the singers accompanied as in the text, and then ensued the dancing. The whole ceremony lasted about two hours, and began at a quarter after two in the afternoon. To the best of my recollection they left off, and began anew several times at a signal given by their Superior, who was present, but did not dance, sitting, as commanding officer, to give the word of command. It was succeeded by a long hymn, performed with great vociferation, and, to our prejudiced ears, with little music, and accompanied by a sort of flute or hautbois and by a large tabor like a small kettle-drum. As soon as the hymn was ended, the instruments changed their tune into something of a quicker movement, and the monks began to turn themselves round with a velocity not to be described or easily conceived. Our most fixed attention could scarcely count the numbers of their revolutions, but, according to our best reckoning, they must have exceeded sixty in one minute. This painful exercise was continued for a considerable time, till at length the music ceased, and they stopped seemingly undisturbed by giddiness, and thus the ceremony ended.

Upon enquiring into the reason of this strange operation, we were told that it was done as a penance for their sins, neither is it improbable that this may be their object, since the idea that crimes may be cancelled by voluntary tortures, however whimsical, seems to have obtained pretty universally among mankind. The torments, which the Indians of the East inflict upon themselves, are well-known, and the Catholics have their flagellations. I find however in a French account of this order another reason alleged [for the dance], which whether it be the true one I shall not pretend to determine. This exercise, says the author, to which they are accustomed from their youth, is performed in memory of their founder Mevleva who turned, say they, in this manner during fifteen whole days without taking any nourishment, while his friend Haraza played upon the flute, in consequence of which turning and fasting, he fell into an ecstasy, had wonderful revelations, and received from Heaven the rule of his order. Pope, without perhaps having this particular order in his contemplation, seems to have assigned another reason for this peculiar ceremony, where he says:

So eastern Priests in giddy Circles run
And turn their Heads to imitate the Sun.[1]

From whence he has taken this idea I cannot at present discover, but

[1] The celebrated English poet Alexander Pope (1688-1744, *DNB*) was interested in eastern affairs and corresponded with Lady Mary Wortley Montagu. His tranlations of the *Iliad* and *Odyssey*, quoted occasionally by Charlemont elsewhere, are masterpieces in their own style. The Mevlevi dervishes do in fact claim to be imitating the sun and the planets in their dances.

it certainly is ingenious. Neither is it impossible that the custom may have been imitated from some more eastern religion, or perhaps retained from the Arabians, who, before the time of Mahomet, professed the Sabean superstition and worshipped the sun.

I shall conclude my account of those monks with a literal translation of their hymn, which I procured from a French gentleman, extremely well-versed in the Turkish language. In order to avoid re-translating I shall give it in the words of the first translator.

EXPLICATION DE L'HYMNE QUE
LES DERVISCHES ONT CHANTÉ

1

Ha! Combien de louange merite, et combien est grand ce Seigneur dont tous les esclaves sont autant des rois!

2

Quiconque frottera ses yeux de la poudre de ses pieds, verra quelque chose qui lui donnera tant d'admiration qu'il en tombera en extace!

3

Celui qui boira une goutte de son breuvage aura le sein comme un ocean rempli de pierreries et de liqueurs precieuses!

4

Je te le dis! ne lasche point dans ce monde la bride à tes passions; quiconque les reprimera sera un vrai Solomon dans la foi!

5

Ne t'amuse point à adorer les richesses, ni à bâtir des kiosks et des palais. La fin de ce que tu auras bâti, n'est que ruine!

6

Ne nourris point ton corps avec tant de delicatesses et de friandises. Celui qui trouve le bonheur n'est autre que celui qui trouve Dieu!

Shortly after our visit to the *Mevlevis*, having gotten admission into a convent of monks whom the Franks name *Hough Houghs* from the kind of noise they make, but whose Turkish name I do not remember, we were witnesses to another ceremony of a much more extravagant kind. These monks have little peculiar in their dress, which, excepting some peculiarity in the turban and that their feet and legs are bare, is like that of other Turks. One essential difference however there is, that whereas the Turks are in general clean and decent in their habits, the clothes of these are ragged and dirty, their beards uncombed and nasty, and their whole person has a squalid and nauseous appearance. The function began with prayers and a long hymn, which they roared out all together as loud as they could bawl, with a wildness of enthusiasm that had something shocking in it and seemed to promise the scene which followed.

As soon as the hymn was ended, they, all of them, the Superior only excepted, who sat apart, and continued to sing with amazing vociferation, began to dance in a circle as close together as they could stand, holding each other by the hands, making the most hideous howling, and distorting their features so as to appear scarcely human. Their manner of dancing was nothing more than an uninterrupted jumping as high as their strength and agility could raise them and the noise they made appeared to our ears a continual re-iteration of the words *Hough Hough*. Thus they danced with the utmost impetuosity round and round till some of them, overcome by the violence of the exercise, giddy with turning, and mad with enthusiasm fell into ecstasies, and crowding together into the inside of the circle howled and barked, shook their heads and distorted their faces and their bodies like men in violent epileptic fits, while the rest continued to dance round them with increased fury, still yelling out their frantic ejaculation, and jumping with their bare feet upon the hard pavement. The frenzy increases — the dance grows more and more furious — they entwine themselves one within another so as each prevents the other from falling — they are now so intertwisted as to appear one great body, a furious monster with many heads, with many legs, jumping with all its feet, yelling with all its mouths — the Superior gives the signal by ceasing to sing — they stop all at once, and a dead silence ensues, which is presently interrupted by another burst of madness — again they stop and again the frenzy recommences, till at length they are quite demoniac, quite possessed! — And leaving entirely the appearance of human creatures, become objects more frightful than imagination can form. Thus the ceremony ended, for they were now so overcome with enthusiasm, so spent with toil, that they lay gasping on the floor, where we left them to enjoy the fruit of their labours in heavenly visions and ecstatic dreams.

I should have mentioned that they had among them several young children, whom they seemed to be initiating into their mysteries. These however did not enter into the fury of the others but only danced round them. The sounds they uttered which to our ears appeared almost inarticulate, are, as I am informed, produced by a perpetual repetition of the words *Allah hoil*,[1] which signifies *God*

---

[1] Perhaps this should be *Allah kâin*, 'God is great.' Charlemont's description of the ceremonies of the Dervishes differs on several points from the modern account in *The Darvishes* by J.P. Brown (edited by H.A. Rose, Oxford, 1927).

is great, and which by their rapid pronunciation is abbreviated into *Houlah Houlah.*[1] These poor enthusiasts are accounted by the Turks a much honester set of men than our former acquaintance the *Mevlevis,* who are generally supposed to be in a high degree debauched and profligate, and of whom the same sort of stories are related as the Catholics tell of their monks , while the sanctity of the Hough Houghs is so greatly esteemed that men of fashion among the Turks frequently as we were assured, enter into their community, frequent their meetings, and take a part in their ceremonies. But, be they ever so fashionable, certain it is that we found ourselves very happy in getting safely out of their convent, as we were by no means assured that in the fury of their zeal, the presence of a Christian might have been pleasing to them.

I was once in a situation not very different from this at Naples, where I was present at the famous miracle of the liquefaction of St. Januarius' blood.[2] The concourse of people in the church was immense, and the Neapolitans are a much more dangerously ill-looking people than the Turks. The priest, for what reason I know not, chose to delay the operation, and the vessel of congealed blood was several times approached to the skull of the Saint without any sensible effect. This delay set the people, who are taught to believe that if the miracle should fail some dreadful catastrophe is to be dreaded, almost mad they groaned, they howled, they beat their breasts with the most frantic action, and seemed just starting into actual frenzy! I had been told that it was not unusual for the priest to protract the operation during the presence of a heretic in order to spread the idea that such unhallowed company counteracted the miracle, and I had heard that this trick was once practised upon

---

[1] Charlemont adds in a note: 'I find another and a much better explanation of the sounds uttered by these enthusiasts in that excellent book the *Bibliothèque Orientale* (on *Hu* p. 460) where Herbelot tells us that the Arabic *Hu,* which is pronounced *Hou,* is sometimes used as the pronoun of the third person, and sometimes as the substantive verb signifying *He is* Hence, says he, this word has become one of the names of God, because it marks his simple and absolute essence answering to the name which God gives himself, *I am He who is.* The religious among the Mussulmans, continues he, often pronounce this word in their prayers and in their raptures, and some of them repeat it so frequently and with such vehemence, crying without any intermission, *Hou, Hou, Hou,* that at length they stupify themselves, and often fall into fits, which they call ecstasies. The Mahometans generally affix this sacred word to the beginning of all their writings and it is usually found at the head of all rescripts, passports and patents. From this discovery may be inferred how very little a traveller can depend upon the information of his countrymen inhabitants of Turkey in points of any nicety. Upon the strictest enquiry among them and other Franks the meaning given in the text was the only one that I could hear of, and yet nothing is more clear than that the interpretation mentioned in this note is the only true one.'

[2] The blood of St. Januarius (Gennaro), a martyr under Diocletian, is kept in a phial in the Cathedral of Naples and is reputed to liquefy on his feast day, 19 September, and on other occasions.

Admiral Byng,[1] who was obliged, not without some danger to his person, to quit the church before the blood could be liquefied. This idea, joined to the horrible appearance of the congregation whose furious looks seemed to my imagination to be fixed on me, terrified me, I confess, not a little, till I was at length eased of my fears by the consummation of the miracle. The joy of the assistants was then as great, as wild, and as savage, as their despair had before been, and I never was in my life better pleased than when I found myself safely out of the church.

Almost every religion has had its enthusiasts of this kind. The ancients had their Corybantes and their Bacchanals. The Indians have their self-tormenting saints. The Italians have their flogging processions and congregations. The processions at Rome on Good Friday, where, though such public discipline is contrary to the ordinance of the Pope, the self-tormenting penitents march in horrid masquerade and mark the way with blood are too well-known to be here mentioned. But as the congregations alluded to are not of so great notoriety I shall here give some account of one of them at which I was present and shall exhibit it as a Catholic parallel to the scene of the Hough Houghs.

On a Friday evening in Lent my curiosity tempted me to venture myself into a church belonging to an Order of flagellant Friars. The church was large and magnificent, thronged with people and illuminated with the utmost splendour. A long sermon was preached recommending mortification and above all things self-discipline as the sure means of washing away every trace of sin. To this edifying discourse an excellent concert of music succeeded, and during the performance several servitors of the Order went round the congreggation with large silver plates filled with scourges made of whipcord twisted and knotted, exactly resembling what we call cats-o'-nine-tails. These were presented to, and most devoutly received by every person present. As soon as we were thus provided with implements fit for the pious operation, the music ceased. Every light was at once extinguished, and we were involved in sudden and total darkness, while at the same instant all the doors were clapped and secured with a noise like thunder.

What followed can only be compared to our idea of the infernal regions — the sound of whips, the clank of chains (for many not contented with the cords had brought with them scourges of iron), shrieks and groans proceeding from a mixture of pain and contrition. Such was the horrid concert which, added to the total darkness, would

---

[1] Probably the second British Admiral of that name, John (1704-57, *DNB*) son of George (1663-1733). He was defeated by the French at Port Mahon in 1756 and subsequently court-martialled and shot — *pour encourager les autres*, as Voltaire remarked.

have been sufficient to dismay the firmest mind, and would certainly have terrified me had not the idea of ridicule come to my aid and, rendering the ceremony as ridiculous as it was shocking, kept me in a balance between horror and laughter. After about half an hour passed in this manner a signal was made for everyone to reclothe himself, and when a convenient time had been allowed for that purpose the church was re-illuminated almost as suddenly as it had been darkened, the music again began, and the ceremony ended by a benediction from the priest. I shall not pretend to comment upon this function, or to compare it in madness and in horror to that described in the text. One circumstance however is common to them both, that sinners of fashion are known to frequent this congregation, as well as to mix in the processions of Good Friday.

An adventure not long ago happened at one of these flogging matches the drollery of which may possibly render it worth relating. An arch wag of Rome had a spite towards a goldsmith of that city whom he knew to be a constant frequenter of this church. He took care to be there the time of the function, and, as soon as the lights were extinguished he rose in his place, and, personating the goldsmith, began to harangue the congregation. After naming himself by the goldsmith's name, he told them that his sins were so enormous that flagellation alone could never expiate them and that a public confession was absolutely necessary, as he had been guilty of fraud, extortion, incest, murder. Here the goldsmith in a great passion interrupted him, swearing that he was an impostor, and that he himself was an honest man, and, though a sinner, incapable of any such horrid crimes. 'Satan avoid!' exclaimed the other, 'wilt though strive to prevent my confession? No, brethren, I am the man, I am the sinful wretch!' The goldsmith now endeavoured to approach, to buckle with his antagonist while some lent their aid and others opposed him. In short the tumult grew so violent that the monks were obliged to interfere and to stop the function. The church was re-illuminated, and in the crowd the impostor remained undiscovered. Half of the congregation went away full persuaded that the goldsmith himself had spoken, who found it no easy matter to re-establish his reputation, which was greatly injured by the consequence of this wicked and whimsical trick.

The French, even in the enlightened age of Louis the XIVth, had their *Convulsionaires,* and we have had our Prophets, and various other frantic sects. Neither are we always to attribute the origin of these fancies to design or knavery. In persons of weak minds and irritable nerves religion will often degenerate into superstition, or rise into enthusiasm. Nay, the strongest minds are not always proof against intense contemplation. It would seem as if the idea of the divinity was so much too vast for the human understanding that our faculties lose themselves in the abyss! And that our intellects can no more bear strictly to contemplate the divine nature than our eyes can fixedly gaze upon the sun, but are both equally impaired if not destroyed by a contemplation to which they are equally inadequate!

There is yet another set of monks among the Mahometans, who are usually termed *Santons*,[1] but whether this be their true Turkish denomination I cannot tell. (The *Hough Houghs* are also called *Santons,* a denomination which seems to me to be given indiscriminately to all poorer orders of monks, particularly to those who extort alms by enthusiasm or pretended madness.) These wretches generally counterfeit madness, it being a received opinion with the Turkish populace that frenzy has something supernatural in it, and that madmen are often saints and endowed with the gift of prophecy.

They are absolute beggars and vagabonds, and, as such, are not suffered, by the excellent police of Constantinople to play their tricks in that metropolis. So at least I suppose, as I never met with any of them there. But in other parts of the Empire they abound, and particularly at Cairo where every sort of disorder is tolerated. I remember seeing one of these pretended saints in that city, whose sanctity consisted in running about the streets stark naked, while the women, muffled as usual, followed him in crowds in order to be cured of barrenness, and happy was she who could contrive to kiss that part of him which was likeliest, if properly applied, to perfect her cure. It may seem singular that in a country where the conduct of women is so strictly attended to they should be suffered to follow this beastly saint for a purpose so beastly. But such is the force of custom, such is the prevalency of superstition, which can prevail over every other consideration whatsoever, and can force us to act in contradiction to our natural feelings, even when exalted by physical causes, and fortified by inveterate habit! Another of these I saw in the same city, who went dressed like other Turks, his head only, which was bald, being totally uncovered. His claim to holiness consisted entirely in the hardness of his skull, which was indeed almost miraculous. Whenever he approached a stone pillar he retired back like a ram and ran tilt against it with such impetuosity and force as must have broken any reasonable skull into pieces, and when from the violence and report of the blow, we expected to see his brains dashed out we perceived him perfectly unhurt and unconcerned.

But the time when we had an opportunity of seeing the greatest number and variety of these Santons was at the procession made through the streets of Cairo at the departure of the caravan for Mecca which, fortunately for us, left that city during our abode there. Here their numbers were indeed surprising and their figures so various and

---

[1] 'Santons' was a general term in the West for Moslem monks or hermits (also called Marabouts). The word is derived from the Italian *santo*, 'holy man, saint.'

so whimsical as to be with difficulty described. Though they did not properly belong to the procession, they accompanied it in crowds, following and closing the march of each particular class, and giving an air of savage wildness to the solemn grandeur of the ceremony. Some were naked, others dressed in the most fantastical manner, and many, who indeed appeared to us most singular, twined about, and I may almost say clothed, with monstrous serpents. The wretches, having the art of extracting the venom out of these dangerous animals, suffer or rather teach them to twine themselves about their naked bodies, and in this hideous garb, the horror of which is heightened by their counterfeited madness, mix themselves with the crowd and accompany the procession. I was however informed that the pilgrims are sufficiently upon their guard against such of these as persevere in following the caravan, keeping them carefully at a distance from their tents, from whence they seldom miss any opportunity of purloining whatever they can lay their hands upon.

VISIT TO A TURKISH BATH

... At Constantinople and in all the great Turkish cities every Turk who can afford it has private baths in his own house, and there are, besides, in every quarter of the City public *bagnios* where they who have not the convenience of private bathing constantly resort. Though it be not absolutely pertinent to the purport of this article, yet, as it seems in some degree to coincide with it, I shall here take the liberty to give some account of one of these public *bagnios* and of the manner in which we were there treated.

Being desirous to partake of this Turkish pleasure pure and unmixed with any foreign refinement, Burton and I directed our janissary to conduct us to a genuine Constantinopolitan bagnio, and in consequence of these orders we were conducted to one of them in the centre of Constantinople at least two miles distant from the quarter of the Franks. Our janissary having signified our intentions to the master of the house, we were led through several rooms, perfectly neat and convenient, all heated by flues and by the vapour of hot water, and each in progression hotter than the former. In the last room but one, which was indeed extremely hot, our attendants assisted us to strip, and when we were naked gave to each of us a short apron which being tied about our middle answered the purpose of Adam's figleaf. We were now shown into the last room, the heat of which was indeed intense. It was neatly paved with marble, lighted from the top by small cupolas closely glazed, and in the middle was a large marble basin, sunk into the pavement and filled with warm water. The door was shut upon us and we sat ourselves down upon mats which were laid on the floor for that purpose.

In a few minutes we began to sweat most copiously and very soon to wish the ceremony at an end. But our bathers did not choose to indulge us in this singularity. There was, it seems, a stated time for us to sit here, and our frequent calls for relief were fruitless. Our pressing petitions were not understood, and, if they had, would probably not have been heeded. We now began to grow very faint and to fear that we should pay dearly for our curiosity, when at length two gigantic Turks entered the chamber, naked all except their short aprons and each of them carrying a tub full of soap suds. They now extended us upon our mats and presently covered us all over with 'this unsavoury lather, not even sparing our eyes and mouths which, though kept shut as close as possible, could not however fail of getting their share. Each Turk now drew on a sort of glove without fingers made of haircloth, and with this they fell to rubbing us with such activity and violence as to make us tremble for our skin. I however, knowing that all outcries were vain, continued passive and silent. But Burton, not so patient, roared like a bull, while his executioner heard him unmoved, without either pity or laughter, but continued his operation with a dignified gravity that had something perfectly ridiculous in it.

As soon as this ceremony was ended another succeeded, equally painful and whimsical. With much force and dexterity they pulled and drew all our limbs so as to make the joints crack; and laying our arms over our breasts they sat down upon them, nor even ceased from pressing them till the same effect was produced from the joints of our shoulders. The disagreeable part of the ceremony was now over, and, to our great satisfaction, we were presently soused into the basin of water where we cleansed ourselves from the suds and lay for some minutes to rest from our fatigue. From hence however we were soon taken and conducted into the adjacent room, and by degrees into others still less hot till, gradually cooling, we were led into a chamber perfectly temperate in which were convenient beds. Two of these being prepared for us, we were laid in them and refreshed with excellent coffee, than which I never found anything more agreeable or more refreshing. Here we lay for about half an hour, when, being told that we might get up, we rose, dressed, and, to our great surprise, found ourselves as well as if nothing had happened and able with more strength and alacrity than we had ever before experienced to walk to the Ambassador's Palace, where however we met with an indifferent reception, being severely chid by Sir James Porter for having ventured ourselves into a public bath, which, as the plague is at all times lurking about some quarter or other of Constantinople, can never be perfectly free from the danger of infection.

[The manuscript continues with a discourse on the religion of the Turks, a description of the pilgrimage to Mecca (illustrated in Dalton's Antiquities), and a revised version of his Introduction. His last words are characteristic: 'In nations as well as among individuals, perfect depravity is as seldom to be found as perfect virtue.']

APPENDIX

RICHARD DALTON, CHARLEMONT'S DRAUGHTSMAN

Born in or about 1715 in England or Ireland,[1] Dalton joined Charlemont's party in Malta, as described in our Introduction. He left it, presumably in Italy, in 1750, and returned to London separately. It seems that he and Charlemont had a quarrel, to judge from a letter from Charlemont's father-in-law in January 1755. A contemporary of Dalton's, Mrs. Delaney, described Dalton in 1773 as 'the most impertinent, troublesome, prating man in the world,' and Sir Robert Strange had trouble with him in 1763.[2] But Charlemont himself was not an easy man for artists to get on with, if his epic quarrel with Piranesi in Rome was characteristic.[3]

After Dalton had returned to London he published a collection of forty prints advertised as *Musaeum Graecum et Aegyptiacum or Antiquities of Greece and Egypt, illustrated by Prints, engraved from Drawings taken on the Spot by Mr. Richard Dalton, in a late Voyage to the Levant, in the Company of the Right Honourable Lord Viscount Charlemont, and Francis Pierpoint Burton, Esq., Ann. Dom. 1749, and 1750* (London 1751). This was followed by a series of other collections in 1752, 1781 and 1790, culminating in a full edition of seventy-nine prints and etchings entitled *Antiquities and Views in Greece and Egypt with Manners and Customs of the Inhabitants from Drawings made on the Spot, A.D. 1749* (London 1791). There is no evidence that Charlemont approved of any of these publications.

While the artistic qualities and the accuracy of these pictures are not of as high a standard as those of Stuart and Revett, it must be remembered that they were the first drawings of many Greek monu-

[1] See *DNB* Supplement volume (1901) pp. 533-34 and Craig p. 55 n. 3.

[2] For the letter to Charlemont see Stanford (1980) p. 82; for Mrs. Delaney, see A.P. Oppé, *English Drawings, Stuart and Georgian Periods ... at Windsor Castle* (London, 1950) p. 10; for Strange see his *Inquiry into the Rise and Establishment of the Royal Academy of Arts* (London 1775) p. 19.

[3] See Craig pp. 85-97.

ments and artefacts to be published in England, and his drawings of sculptures in Cnidos were, so far as we can ascertain, the first to be made in the modern era. (Dalton's sculptural sketches were competently etched for publication by himself: the others were engraved by various English engravers.)

Dalton's *Antiquities* of 1791 does not contain all the drawings he made with Charlemont on their travels in Greece and Turkey. The Royal Library in Windsor Castle has eight others including three which correspond to plates 10, 13, and 14[1] in *Antiquities* (with slight variations). Besides these there is the etching of a Greek woman in island dress reproduced here on page 31 (from the Korais Library and the Philip Argenti Museum of Chian Folklore, Chios). In the Department of Greek and Roman Antiquities at the British Museum there are seven sheets containing sixteen original drawings of the frieze of the Mausoleum at Halicarnassos and of the Parthenon, engravings of which have been published. Further, Charlemont refers several times in his Greek Essay to other pictures of women in Greek costume, some of which he says were in his possession. We have not succeeded in tracing any of these unless our illustrations from the Windsor collection were among them.

Illustrations taken from Dalton's *Antiquities* are specified in the List of Illustrations on pp. x and xi.

[1] See Oppé, *op. cit.*, p. 39. A special study of Dalton and his work is in preparation by Mrs. Cynthia O'Connor of Dublin.

BIBLIOGRAPHY OF WORKS CITED

(Books listed in the sales catalogue of the Charlemont library in 1865, discussed in Stanford (1980) pp. 85-7, are marked with an asterisk.)

ABU'L FEDA, see Gagnier

ANVILLE, J.B.B. d', *[Atlas général]* 1727-1780

ANVILLE, J.B.B. d', *Géographie ancienne abrégée.* Paris, 1769

CELLARIUS, CHRISTOPHORUS, *Notitia orbis antiqui.* 2 vols. Leipzig, 1731

CHANDLER, RICHARD, **Travels in Asia Minor.* Oxford and Dublin, 1775

CHANDLER, RICHARD, *Travels in Greece.* Oxford and Dublin, 1776

CHANDLER, RICHARD, with WILLIAM PARS AND NICHOLAS REVETT, *Ionian Antiquities.* 5 vols. London, 1769-1915

CHARLEMONT, Lord, 'Account of a singular Custom at Metelin with some Conjectures on the Antiquity of its Origin.' *Transactions of the Royal Irish Academy* 3 (1790) Antiquities Section pp. 3-20

CHARLEMONT, Lord, 'Some considerations on a Controverted passage of Herodotus.' *Transactions of the Royal Irish Academy* 5 (1794) Antiquities Section pp. 3-51

CHOISEUL - GOUFFIER, M.G.A.F., de, *Voyage pittoresque de la Grèce.* 2 vols. in 3 parts. Paris 1782, 1809 and 1822

CRAIG, MAURICE JAMES, *The Volunteer Earl: being the Life and Times of James Caulfeild, first Earl of Charlemont.* London, 1948

FROISSART, JEAN, **Cronycles.* Translated by Lord Berners. 2 vols. London, 1525

GAGNIER, JEAN, Arabic text and Latin translation of the *Life of Mohammed* by Isma'il Ibn 'Ali (Isma'il Abu'l-Feda). Oxford, 1723

GIANNONE, PIETRO, *Dell' istoria civile del regno di Napoli.* 4 vols. Naples, 1723

GOLTZIUS, Hubertus, **De re nummaria antiqua.* 5 vols. Antwerp, 1708

GUYS, PIERRE AUGUSTIN, *A Sentimental voyage through Greece,* translated from his *Voyage littéraire.* 3 vols. London, 1771

HAMMER - PURGSTALL, JOSEPH von, *Geschichte des Osmanischen Reiches etc.* 10 vols. Pest, 1827-35

HARDY, FRANCIS, *Memoirs of the Political and Private Life of James Caulfield* (sic) *Earl of Charlemont.* London, 1810. 2nd edn. 2 vols 1812

HERBELOT de MOLAINVILLE, BARTHELEMY d', **Bibliothèque*

Orientale. Paris, 1697

KNOLLES, RICHARD, *Generall Historie of the Turkes*. London, 1603. Six further editions, London, 1610-1701

LARPENT, Sir GEORGE, *Turkey: its History and Progress ... with a Memoir of Sir J. Porter.*London, 1854

LE ROY, JULIEN DAVID, *Ruines des plus beaux monuments de la Grèce*. Paris, 1758

MONTAGU, Lady MARY WORTLEY, *Letters*. London and Dublin, 1763

POCOCKE, RICHARD, **A Description of the East and Some Other Countries*. 2 vols. London, 1743-45

PORTER, Sir JAMES, *Observations on the Religion, Law, Government and Manners of the Turks*. London, 1768. 2nd edn. 1771

ROBERTSON, WILLIAM, *The History of the Reign of Charles V*. 3 vols. London, 1769

SPON, JACOB, *Voyage d'Italie, de Dalmatie, de Grèce et du Levant*. Lyons, 1678

STANFORD, W.B., 'The Manuscripts of Lord Charlemont's Eastern Travels. *Proceedings of the Royal Irish Academy* 80 C 5 (1980) pp. 69-90

STANFORD, W.B. *Ireland and the Classical Tradition*. Dublin, 1976

STUART, JAMES and REVETT, NICHOLAS, **The Antiquities of Athens*. 4 vols. London 1762-1816

THEVENOT, JEAN de, *Relation d'un voyage fait au Levant*. 2 vols. 1664-74. Translated by A. Lovell, London, 1687. Charlemont's library contained two later editions of this translation.

TOTT, Baron FRANCOIS de, **Memoirs sur les Turcs et les Tartares*. 4 parts. Amsterdam, 1784. English translation by 'an English Gentleman.' 2 vols. London and Dublin, 1785

TOURNEFORT, JOSEPH PITTON de, **Relation d'un voyage de Levant*. 2 vols. Paris, 1717. English translation by J. Ozell, 2 vols. London, 1718

UBERTI, FAZIO degli, **Ditta* (or *Dita*) *Mundi*. Vicenza, 1474

WHELER, Sir GEORGE, **A Journey into Greece*. London, 1682. Charlemont owned two copies of this, one annotated by E. Chishull, author of *Travels in Turkey* (1747).

WOOD, ROBERT, **An Essay on the Original Genius of Homer with a comparative View of the antient and present State of the Troade*. London, 1775

WREN, Sir CHRISTOPHER, **Parentalia*. Edited by Stephen Wren. London, 1750

INDEX

236

William **Bedell** **Stanford** is Chancellor of Dublin University and an Emeritus Fellow of Trinity College Dublin. He is also a member (and was formerly a Vice-President) of the Royal Irish Academy which Lord Charlemont founded in 1785. Previously he was Regius Professor of Greek and Pro-Chancellor of Dublin University, Senator of the Irish Republic, Member of the Council of Europe and Chairman of the Council of the Dublin Institute for Advanced Studies. The President of Greece made him a Higher Commander of the Order of the Phoenix in 1980. He has lectured widely, has appeared on television in Europe and North America and is the author of thirteen books on classical literature. These include *The Ulysses Theme, Ireland and the Classical Tradition, Enemies of Poetry, Greek Tragedy and the Emotions,* and an edition of Homer's *Odyssey.*

Eustathios J. Finopoulos has made an extensive study of the literature of travel in Greece and has contributed to several notable publications in that field.

ADDENDA ET CORRIGENDA

p. 43 n. 2
for 'Deputy of the Captain Pasha' read *Deputy Governor.*
p. 47 l. 34
for 'fight' read *flight.*
p. 52 n.
delete last sentence beginning with *Tournefort.*
p. 64 n.
according to recent information from Miss Sonia Anderson some portraits of George Macartney present him as an unattractive man.
p. 122 n.
for 'Paolos Karavios' read *Pavlos Karavias.* Last line: for 'was also known as Syriani' read *was known as Syriani.*
p. 130 l. 2
for 'come' read *some.*
p. 139 n.
for 'Descrption' read *Description.*
p. 146 l. 8
add note after de l'Isle: *It seems likely that Charlemont was referring to Guillaume de l'Isle's well-known map of Greek lands (1707).*
p. 154 n.
for 'Generall Historie etc.' read *The Turkish History....*(1687) The title in the Bibliography is that of the first edition. The quotation has been slightly modernised.
p. 158 n.
for 'Koiourka' read *Kiourka.*
p. 159 l. 7
for '1790' read *1794.*
p. 179 l. 36
for 'NDB' read *DNB.*

244